The Life and Times of Rudolf Steiner

Volume 2

Origin and Growth of his Insight

Emil Bock

The Life and Times of Rudolf Steiner

Volume 2

Origin and Growth of his Insight

Floris Books

Translated by Lynda Hepburn
unless otherwise noted under sources, page 231.

First published in German in 1961 under the title
Rudolf Steiner, Studien zu seinem Lebensgang und Lebenswerk
by Verlag Freies Geistesleben
Volume 1 first published in English in 2008 by Floris Books
Volume 2 first published in English in 2009 by Floris Books

Third edition © 1990 Verlag Freies Geistesleben, Stuttgart
This translation © 2008, 2009 Floris Books, Edinburgh

All rights reserved. No part of this publication may
be reproduced without the prior permission of
Floris Books, 15 Harrison Gardens, Edinburgh.
www.florisbooks.co.uk

The publisher acknowledges the generous help of
Cotswold Chine School which has made translation
and publication of this book possible.

British Library CIP Data available

ISBN 978-086315-684-7

Printed in Great Britain
by Athenaeum Press, Gateshead

Contents

9. Rudolf Steiner and the Theosophical Society — 9
10. The Christmas Festivals — 23
11. The Fifth Gospel — 43
12. The Structure of the Karma Lectures — 65
13. Resurrection of the Word — Logos and the Word of Man — 85
14. From Theosophy to Anthroposophy — 105
15. The Preparation for Esoteric Circles 1904–6 — 125
16. The Creation of Mantric Verse — 145
17. The Dispute about the Holy Spirit — 165
18. Figures in Rome and Byzantium — 185
19. Ephesus and the Castle of the Grail — 207

Sources — 231
Index — 233

Volume 1 of this book describes the first part of Rudolf Steiner's life, that is, up to the point he told in his autobiography. This had a preparatory character as it were, like the exposition for a great dramatic action which was yet to come. Because it was only at the end of this phase of his life, between 1900 and 1902, that he began his real life's work in the service of anthroposophy. The years prior to this are what Emil Bock deals with in the first part of his book, to which he gave the title 'biographical' — in the narrow sense of the word — for in this section he kept by and large to the chronological course of events. But he did not simply retell the things which Rudolf Steiner had already related himself. He portrayed the spiritual and social atmosphere of the cities in which Rudolf Steiner lived before and during the turn of the century — Vienna, Weimar, Berlin — with bold but gentle brushstrokes.

In this second section (Chapters 9–16) Bock gives cross-sections through Rudolf Steiner's entire works. He follows a single theme throughout these two and a half decades in an almost one-sided way at times, then does the same with another theme, and so on. In this way he approaches the 'design' of this biography from different starting points and by different routes, by comparing things which often lie far apart. The background to this is the German and European culture of the first quarter of the twentieth century.

In the third section, Chapters 17–19, Emil Bock opens up the historical perspective dramatically. He focuses on the ninth century and the most important moments in the history of western thought which it contained.

Rudolf Steiner and the Theosophical Society

Between October 18 and 21, 1902, the foundation meeting of the German Section of the Theosophical Society took place in Berlin in the presence of Annie Besant. Rudolf Steiner was appointed as General Secretary. The half century which lies between those October days and the time of writing, encompasses terrible events: catastrophes akin to the end of the world. But it also contains heavenly revelations of inexhaustible abundance as though to equip humankind for its difficult journey: that is, that part of Rudolf Steiner's life's work which was devoted to spiritual research in a very specific sense. Today we can clearly recognize decisive cross-roads in spiritual development that was represented by the inconspicuous event in a small circle in Berlin at that time.

On Saturday, October 18, preliminary talks took place in which only a few people were involved. The next day, Sunday, the members who had come to Berlin as representatives of the small German group which was in the process of formation gathered at noon in the Theosophical Library (at 54a Kaiser-Friedrich-Strasse, close to the Charlottenburg station). Steiner opened the meeting with an address. His words were summarized in the report at the time as follows:

> Anyone who understands the signs of the times cannot fail to see that we are on the verge of a new spiritual epoch, that a new turning point is approaching which is just as important and significant as the one at the time of Augustine or the sixteenth century for example, a turning point in which Germany in particular is called to something of great importance. The most important task devolves on German science in relation to

materialism. We will only be able to be effective if we follow the scientific path.

Within a circle of people who had given themselves the task of cultivating the 'old wisdom' which originated in the East, these words were a rousing signal for developing a western occultism and thus a 'new wisdom' to be gained through the power of the human self in harmony with genuine natural science. Amongst the listeners little more than a preliminary inkling can have arisen of the radically new approach which was heralded.

The discussions closed at 6 pm and 25 people — half of the participants — went off to Friedrichstrasse Station in order to fetch Annie Besant who arrived at 7 pm.

On Monday October 20, the actual founding of the section took place. On behalf of the president, Henry S Olcott, Mrs Besant ceremonially presented Rudolf Steiner with the engagement certificate for the newly founded section consisting of ten lodges (Berlin, Charlottenburg, Düsseldorf, Hamburg, Hanover, Kassel, Leipzig, Lugano, Munich and Stuttgart). A social gathering followed, at which fifty to sixty people were guests of Marie von Sivers. Annie Besant gave a speech. The day ended with a lecture by Rudolf Steiner on 'practical karma exercises' in a vegetarian restaurant across from the Central Hotel.

On the Tuesday (October 21) Frau von Holten, who had been elected as treasurer of the section, entertained the participants in Charlottenburg. This included a lengthy session of questions and answers from Annie Besant. In the evening, Mrs Besant held a public lecture in English for an audience of around four hundred in the Prince Albrecht Hotel on the topic, 'Theosophy, its meaning and objects.' The whole of Berlin was resplendently decorated with flags and garlands which, however, was not for the quiet foundation meeting, but for the birthday of the German Empress on the following day. At the end, Steiner summarized the lecture in German. In the introduction with which he opened the evening, the same beacon of a new spiritual epoch was ignited as at the opening of the internal conference, but this time in front of the general public. The report in the *Vahan* ran as follows:

> Steiner said that many people may have been surprised when he had come out in support of Theosophy in the Giordano

Rudolf Steiner and Annie Besant

Bruno League about fourteen days previously. But just as, based on Kepler's discoveries, Giordano Bruno had demanded the recognition of a new world view at that time, so Theosophy today should bring a new world view, and today as then we are at a turning point in world history. Today the German Section has been founded and the most prominent representative of the Theosophical movement has come here to give the first public address.

Two days later, on Thursday October 23, another important event quietly took place for the inner aspect of the work: Mrs Besant admitted Rudolf Steiner and Marie von Sivers into the Esoteric School (ES). This very strictly ordered association was founded by H.P. Blavatsky. At the time it was not Olcott, the president of the Theosophical Society, who was in charge but Annie Besant who, until then, had held the undisputed spiritual leadership of the Theosophical movement. Rudolf Steiner's membership of the ES arose from his role as Secretary General. Two years later, Rudolf Steiner took on an independent active leading role within the ES with the agreement of Mrs Besant. A year after that, on October 24, 1905, he held the first of the ES lessons in Berlin which, until July 1914, quietly formed a strong current of totally independent new creative spirituality.

*

In fact it must have been surprising and completely incomprehensible at first for all who knew Rudolf Steiner's previous literary efforts to find him as a leading personality within the Theosophical movement. Had he not always stood out as a totally uncompromising free spirit, averse to everything that was traditional and nebulously emotional, be it in his philosophical writings, his literature, theatre and social criticism, or be it in his work as editor of Goethe's scientific writings? What strange change of heart had made him into a Theosophist and official of a society which was totally orientated towards India?

Whatever rumours might have been spread by malicious tongues at the time to the effect that Rudolf Steiner was trying a completely different avenue because his efforts had been without success so far, were proved wrong by the facts. Never had the number of lectures and courses which he was asked to give from the most diverse quarters been larger than at the beginning of the new century, that is, at the

31, St. James' Place.
London, S.W.
7/6/07

Dear Dr. Hübbe-Schleiden,

Dr. Steiner's occult training is very different from ours. He does not know the eastern way, so cannot, of course, teach it. He teaches the Xtian & Rosicrucian way, & this is very helpful to some, but is different from ours. He has his own School, on his own responsibility. I regard him as a very fine teacher on his own lines, & as a man of real knowledge. He & I work in thorough friendship & harmony, but along different lines.

Yours ever sincerely
Annie Besant

point where, also in answer to an invitation, he began his support for Theosophy. Each day of the week was busy.

There were usually three courses running simultaneously at the Berlin Workers' School which had been founded by the social democrat revolutionary, Wilhelm Liebknecht, and was attended by young workers. The main course ran on Tuesdays, always on important historical topics. Up until the summer of 1902 the topic covered was 'the history of literature from Luther to the present.' A new course started on October 7: 'the development of the universe and the social life of animals.' The other two courses had more the character of educational exercises: 'exercises in public speaking and written composition' (Fridays) and 'advanced public speaking' (Sundays).

In the *Freie Hochschule* (independent college) founded by the Friedrichshagen circle around Wilhelm Bölsche and Bruno Wille, a course of ten sessions on 'German history from the Germanic migrations to the twelfth century' started on October 15, 1902, which was held on Wednesdays.

Rudolf Steiner had also been involved now and again from 1900 onwards in the *Giordano Bruno Bund für einheitliche Weltanschauung* (Giordano Bruno League for a Unified World-View), which had arisen from the same circle. However, in 1902, the incisive forward-looking ideas which he had presented in these particular surroundings led to him being asked to give a whole series of lectures. He had publicly professed his support for Theosophy there on October 8 for the first time, something he mentioned in the introduction to Besant's lecture on October 21. The topic was 'Monism and Theosophy.' Eight days later, on October 15, a heated debate took place about this lecture.

A circle of artists, intellectuals and writers who called themselves the Kommenden had specially dedicated themselves to the future out of a sense of the dawning of a new era. This group had been founded and was led by the poet, Ludwig Jacobowski. After the premature death of this friend of Steiner's, Steiner took on the abandoned task with particular devotion. On May 9, 1901 he spoke at Jacobowski's funeral service. Soon afterwards he started a course which took place on Thursdays and by Easter 1902 amounted to 24 lectures. It was amongst the Kommenden that he let his listeners look most clearly into the sphere of knowledge which, since 1899, had opened up to him in a new way. The topic of the first major lecture series was therefore

9. RUDOLF STEINER AND THE THEOSOPHICAL SOCIETY

From Buddha to Christ. Single lectures on Goethe's *Fairy Tale* and 'the nature of the mysteries' were added in the winter of 1901/2. On October 6 a new lecture cycle began on Mondays and by April 1903 amounted to 27 lectures. It had a double title, but with the main emphasis on the second part: 'From Zarathustra to Nietzsche: the history of human development on the basis of world philosophies from earliest oriental times up to the present, or Anthroposophy.' We will return later to the Monday when this course overlapped with the foundation of the German Section.

There was only one point in 1901/2 when Rudolf Steiner's lecturing had reached Theosophical Society circles. Count and Countess Brockdorff held open lecture evenings every week at their house to which they invited speakers from all cultural walks of life. They were members of the Theosophical Society and had given the Theosophical Library a home in their apartment at 54a Kaiser-Friedrich-Strasse. In September 1900 they invited Rudolf Steiner, whom they could never have imagined being a Theosophist. He spoke about 'Nietzsche' and 'Goethe's Secret Revelation' in the Theosophical Library on two consecutive Saturdays. The Nietzsche lecture was in memory of the brilliant thinker who finally died on August 25. The lecture about Goethe's *Fairy Tale* was given for the 150th anniversary of Goethe's birth on August 28, 1899. Contact was thus suddenly established in a surprising way, so that Steiner was asked to begin an ongoing course on the very next Saturday. The 27 lectures (from October 6, 1900 to April 27, 1901) gave rise to the content of the book *Mysticism at the Dawn of the Modern Age* and a further 25 evenings (from October 5, 1901 to March 22, 1902) made up the book *Christianity as Mystical Fact*. It was at the venue for these courses that the foundation meeting took place where Rudolf Steiner accepted leadership of the German Section of the Theosophical Society. A new cycle began immediately on the Saturday evening after the foundation conference (October 25) on the entire area of Theosophy.

*

The fact that Rudolf Steiner remained completely independent and did not move an inch from his own spiritual path when he took on the role of Secretary General in the Theosophical Society, in other words, that he did not cultivate eastern Theosophical traditions never mind having had a 'change of heart,' can also be seen in the fact that the threads of his previous lecturing and teaching activity continued through those foundation days in October. He only cancelled one lesson, that being the one in the cosmology course which was held in the workers' school, because it would have collided with the public lecture by Annie Besant. He continued giving the 'public speaking exercises' in the Liebknecht school and the history course at the *Freie Hochschule* during the days of the foundation conference (Sunday and Wednesday). Above all, he insisted on carrying on with the course for the Kommenden on 'From Zarathustra to Nietzsche' which also had the title 'Anthroposophy,' although this fell on the day when the ceremonial constitution of the German Section and his appointment as Secretary General took place. After the charter had been handed over, while the party was at Marie von Sivers' house listening to the speech by Annie Besant, Steiner stole away from the *Theosophical* circle to talk to the Kommenden about *anthroposophy*. He only returned in the evening. But the topic that he then chose to speak about, 'practical karma exercises,' expressed his desire to continue in an intensified form with what he had portrayed 'outside' in the afternoon. He did not speak about what was radical and new — the spiritual element for the future which first had to be brought down from heaven — only in the form of a thesis or system as he had done on the Sunday for the opening of the Theosophical conference and as he would again do on the Tuesday as an introduction to the Besant lecture: with single-minded determination he undertook to incorporate what was new directly into the actual present.

Rudolf Steiner often mentioned how, in the timetable for October 20, 1902, destiny itself created the clearest runes for his spiritual path and task, above all for his involvement with Theosophy and anthroposophy. Two excerpts are quoted here. In his autobiography he says:

> No one was left in uncertainty of the fact that I would bring forward in the Theosophical Society only the results of my own research through perception … When, in the presence of Annie Besant, the German Section of the Theosophical Society was founded in Berlin and I was chosen as its Secretary General, I had to leave the foundation sessions because I had to give before a non-Theosophical audience one of the lectures in which I dealt with the spiritual evolution of humanity, and

to the title of which I expressly united the word 'anthroposophy.' Annie Besant also knew that I was then giving lectures under this title on what I had to say about the spiritual world.

From the lecture *Awakening to Community* (Stuttgart, February 6, 1923):

> I myself did not seek out the Theosophical Society. People who belonged to it thought that what I was saying in my lectures [*Mysticism* ...], purely in pursuit of my own path of knowledge, was something they too would like to hear. I saw that the Theosophists wanted to listen to what was being presented, and my attitude about it was that I would always address any audience interested in hearing me ... I saw no reason to refuse its invitation to lay before it material that had been given me for presentation by the spiritual world. That I presented it as anthroposophy is clear from the fact that at the very moment when the German Section of the Theosophical Society was being founded, I was independently holding a lecture not only about anthroposophy but with the name anthroposophy included in the title. The founding of the German Section of the Theosophical Society and my lecture cycle on anthroposophy took place simultaneously. The aim, right from the beginning, was to present pure anthroposophy ... During this first phase, the Anthroposophical Society led an embryonic existence within the Theosophical Society ... In this first phase it had a special mission, *that of counterposing the spirituality of western civilization, centred in the Mystery of Golgotha,* to the Theosophical Society's course, which was based on a traditional acceptance of ancient Oriental wisdom.

To a greater degree than is visible at first glance, the topic that Rudolf Steiner chose for the lecture he himself was to give at the foundation conference concealed the single-minded determination and daring to introduce what was new and radical into the older framework provided. 'Practical karma exercises' may sound very simple and unassuming, but meant that Rudolf Steiner intended to present the actual results of his spiritual research straight away. He wished to oppose the Theosophists' eastern traditionalism with the sparks and lightning of direct and ever-new creation. To the cloudy nebulous talk of 'transmigration of souls' arising from a time before human individualism he wished to bring the clearly outlined view of the 'reincarnation of the human spirit' arising wholly from the free self. He wanted to do this not in any theoretical way, but by means of actual historical examples, so that there could be no evasion. The West should speak by revealing the actual historical secret, clearly distinguished from the passive lack of a sense of history in the East.

On that Monday evening when he returned to the Theosophists from the circle of the Kommenden, Steiner had evidently not actually been able to say what he had resolved to say. In any case, the further lectures which he intended to add on the topic of 'practical karma exercises' did not take place. In 1924, after the Christmas Conference, when he crowned his life's work with the wealth of the karma lectures, Steiner repeatedly returned to his intention on that evening of October 20. He said that, on account of the new esoteric stream in the Anthroposophical Society after the Christmas Conference, he was only now able to fully bring about what could not happen then in face of the opposition present.

> Our first meeting was such that I wanted to set the kind of tone for what should actually happen ... I actually intended to speak quite freely about the working of karma. Now, at this meeting were ... the luminaries of the existing Theosophical movement who at the time felt my presence to be that of an intruder and who were convinced from the start that I actually had no justification in speaking about something of an inner spiritual nature ... The 'practical karma exercises' had been announced but no one at the time would have understood anything about them, least of all the luminaries of the Theosophical Society. And so this remained a task which had to be cultivated in a sense under the surface of the anthroposophical movement, which first had to be agreed with the spiritual world. I can also remember how shocked the luminaries were at the time, that such a daring title should have appeared. (Prague, March 31, 1924)

> At the very first meeting I had ... chosen a particular title for a lecture which I wanted to give at the time ... 'practical karma exercises' ... There were certain elderly members in the German Section of the Theosophical Society at the time ...,

who began to positively tremble at the prospect of my intention to start in such an esoteric manner. And in fact there was no enthusiasm for it. It became apparent, how unprepared the souls were for something like that. The topic of 'practical karma exercises' could not be successful at all in the form which was intended at the time. The conditions made it necessary to speak in a much more exoteric manner than had been intended. But a start must be made with the actual esoteric at some point ... and so it is now possible to pick up the thread of what was intended at that time of introducing this esoteric stream into the Society. (Berne, April 16, 1924)

The lecture was announced, but could not be held [in the form intended] for the simple reason ... [that] there were the various older members ... they had their views on what could be said and what could not be said; but the whole milieu, the whole atmosphere was formed accordingly. Those who were the leaders would have been horrified if you had started to talk about practical karma exercises at that time. The Theosophical movement was simply not ready for this. A great deal had to be prepared first. And ... the preparation took two decades ... In future within the Anthroposophical Society completely open discussion will take place about that which was part of the intention from the start, but for which the Anthroposophical Society first had to gradually become mature ... (Breslau, June 9, 1924)

The first which I announced to a very small circle at the time, bore the title 'practical karma exercises' for a couple of lectures. I felt the most vigorous resistance to this intention being carried out ... These lectures did not take place. It was not possible ... to cultivate the esotericism which truly speaks in a totally open way about what was theoretically always there. Since the Christmas Conference ... the actual effect of human karma in historical figures, in individual human beings, has been spoken about here in a completely open manner ... This leads us back in a certain sense to our starting point. (Dornach, September 5, 1924)

*

Nevertheless, in 1902 Rudolf Steiner did not immediately give up the struggle. It is really moving to see how, at important moments, he repeated the attempt which had at first failed. At the first annual general meeting of the German Section — from this time onwards the same days in October on which the foundation meeting had taken place were chosen for the annual gathering whenever possible — Rudolf Steiner addressed the same subject on Sunday October 18, 1903 at 5.30 pm, this time under the title of 'occult historical research.' It is evident from the report which appeared in the journal *Vahan* that Steiner purposely muted his boldness by linking the actual karmic information to revelations by H.P. Blavatsky, amongst others. But he still did not give up and kept the means to turn the old world upside down clearly in sight:

> In the spiritual world we find that realm where the events of history *arise*. This is where we must look for the true source of all that happens on earth, this is where the leading personalities in history confer face to face with the great invisible leaders of humankind. Only if we investigate the intention which impelled them to action do we understand the often inexplicable facts of history.
>
> For example, in the fifteenth century there was a cardinal Nicholas of Cusa who possessed deep scientific insight. Long before Copernicus he had recognized and expounded the double motion of the earth ... It was a kind of preparation for that which Copernicus (born 1473) was able to convey to a generation with more insight. The occult researchers now unanimously teach (and H.P. Blavatsky also said this openly and indicated it in the third volume of the *Secret Doctrine*) that Copernicus was none other than the reincarnated Cardinal Cusa ... The speaker presented another two examples ...'

After the Christmas Conference — in one of the karma lectures in Torquay (August 12, 1924) — Rudolf Steiner once revealed the spell which he was unable to break in 1902, but which the spiritual force of the Christmas Conference had weakened. He described how, as a young man between the ages of 28 and 35, he had been present in the beginning of the new Michael age which started in 1879.

Behind a veil tremendous events were taking place which were all centred around the spiritual being whom we call Michael. There were mighty followers of Michael ..., but also mighty demonic powers which, under the influence of Ahriman, opposed what was meant to come into the world through Michael ... I had to stand inside this world behind the veil ..., in this Michaelic realm, had to go through what was taking place there ... Behind the scenes...in the Michaelic realm, the great questions about life were raised ... These questions ... continued to influence the twentieth century. And each time, even after having experienced and lived with these questions for decades, it was nevertheless as though, if you tried to express these things, then the enemies of Michael always came and stopped you from speaking. [But] recently it has become possible to speak openly about these things ... Now the connections between earth lives can be discussed openly. This is linked to the revelation of the Michael mysteries ... What has happened is that the demons which previously prevented things from being voiced have been forced into silence.

The Christmas Festivals

Our age needs to achieve a new Christmas experience. The childlike Christmas mood of the past is increasingly disappearing. Humankind will rediscover the Christmas festival on a new level, if it succeeds in moving from a Christmas mood that surrounds the *child* to a new one surrounding the *human being.*

Destiny has bestowed on us, who have the task of nurturing and unfolding the new spiritual stream, all the means for realizing this step. Those among us who still had direct contact with the last phases of Rudolf Steiner's life and work, or at least had it conveyed to us, really cannot experience a Christmas festival anymore without thinking of the Christmas Conference in 1923. There Rudolf Steiner achieved his last spiritual breakthrough for humankind's future, and took a decisive step in the history of the Anthroposophical Society. Once more, the social configuration, the dwelling for the spiritual being Anthroposophia in human beings, was formed anew. The superhuman sacrificial courage shown by Rudolf Steiner opened the heavens, and in the months following, until he departed from the earth, the wealth of his lifework was enhanced and expanded beyond any expectation. It was no coincidence that this significant step was taken during a Christmas festival. Until November an almost forlorn, tentative searching often showing doubt had coloured Rudolf Steiner's conversations. He was not yet certain whether it would be right or possible to take this step. At Christmas, however, he took it. And once again, new revelation and substance poured abundantly out of the wide open gates of the spiritual worlds.

What follows is a summary of the earlier Christmas festivals preceding this unique Christmas event. Perhaps this will also make clear why it was no coincidence that the formation of the Anthroposophical Society happened at Christmas. Beginning at a certain moment, year after year Rudolf Steiner gave significant series of lectures during the Holy Nights of Christmas.

1910

The first one took place in Stuttgart at Christmas 1910. In humble surroundings — the house on Landhausstrasse did not yet exist — Rudolf Steiner held the lecture cycle *Occult History*. In the most direct manner, he referred back to this subject in the lectures of the Christmas Conference. In 1910 as well as in 1923, the Christmas lectures were contemplations of karma that dealt with the same historical personalities. The relationships between the incarnations of these individualities spanning centuries or millennia are brought to light. During the Christmas Conference of 1923 something more than merely interesting historical information was given: it was a matter of presenting examples through which human beings meeting one another within the anthroposophical movement could begin to feel and recognize their own karma. This was also the case with the karma cycle of Christmas 1910.

In the lectures concerning *Occult History*, there is no mention made of Christmas at all. Nor does a Christological motif stand out. Christmas was the topic of a lecture Rudolf Steiner gave on the evening prior to the beginning of the lecture cycle in Stuttgart. It was entitled 'The Yule Festival and the Symbols of Christmas.' Just as he had done every year since 1904, he gave a Christmas lecture in which he illuminated the mystery backgrounds of the Christmas festival. Thus, the Christmas lecture of 1910 does not distinguish itself in a particular way from those of preceding years.

The absence of Christmas and Christological subjects in the six lectures that started on the following evening is particularly conspicuous, because the theme of the whole preceding year had been the revelation of a new Christmas event in the spiritual world. Beginning with the first days of the year 1910, travelling from city to city, Rudolf Steiner had spoken of the fact that after the passing of the first third of the century, human beings everywhere would begin to awaken to a new etheric vision; clearly or obscurely, indirectly or in a direct manner,

10. THE CHRISTMAS FESTIVALS

they would arrive at a perception of the being of Christ in the etheric realm. A new manifestation of Christ in the etheric realm was imminent; this theme persisted throughout the year of 1910. Now, in the Christmas cycle, there is no mention of it. No mention at all? Not quite. In the firth lecture there is one brief mention, but it is in order to point out that in the present historical study a completely different rhythm of evolution is focussed upon.

> ... that, coming from a different stream, a significant nodal point has been placed into our century. It is alluded to in the Rosicrucian Mystery [in the first Mystery Drama]; namely, the ability to once again see into the etheric world, and the manifestation of Christ within the etheric world. This, however, is part of another stream. I now refer more to the forces that send their influence into the broad basis of historical events.

We should be surprised that on Christmas day, after having spoken for a whole year about the new Christmas event in the spiritual world, Rudolf Steiner puts this subject aside, as it were. But — and we will come back to this in conclusion — a direct line leads from the Stuttgart Christmas cycle of 1910 to the lectures of the Christmas Conference of 1923. Rudolf Steiner would surely not have started to give Christmas lecture cycles, to schedule lectures between the days of the old and the new year, if a new Christ event had not been approaching. Later, in 1917 he did speak of the fact that, beginning with the year 1909, visible to spiritual sight, Christ had begun to walk in etheric form among men. Unnoticed by humanity, a new Christmas event had thus occurred in 1909. Just as two thousand years ago Christ walked on the earth in physical form, so he now begins to walk in etheric form among men. Here, the transition from the old to the new Christmas mood finds its basis in an event: that is, if humanity will awake to the realization of the new supersensory event.

One of the moments in 1909 when the new Christ light that had risen in the etheric realm penetrated directly into Rudolf Steiner's lecturing activity, was the Michaelmas cycle, *The Gospel of St Luke*. The unheard-of theme he spoke of now was the mystery of the two Jesus children. Though this dealt with historical disclosures concerning external events that had occurred two thousand years ago, the new aspect developed here stood in intimate connection with what had now appeared as an event in the etheric supersensory sphere. What really was behind the revelation concerning the two Jesus children? The child of whom the Gospel of Matthew reports brings with him much history. He carries the essence of the ancient historic epochs into the present of that time. The other child, however, of whose birth the Gospel of Luke tells, the cosmic child from whom emanates the magic of the Christmas mood of old, is a celestial being. He is not a human being who carries within himself the essence of earlier millennia of history. Here a being incarnate for the first time on earth and brings with him the archetypal image of man's being that has been lost through the Fall. This purest of all human beings, untouched by the Fall of man, who has undergone his development in heaven, not on earth, offers himself as the physical and soul sheath in which thirty years hence the being of Christ can incarnate. By this description of the two Jesus children in the lecture cycle on St Luke's Gospel, a new light is also shed on Christ. He can manifest himself through the sheath of this pure paradisal human being.

From 1909 onward there was a key in anthroposophy to understanding the old Christmas mood. Through this one can truly comprehend the significance of the Child of Bethlehem. Why could Rudolf Steiner reveal the mystery of the two Jesus children at this particular moment? Because the dawning light of the etheric appearance of Christ illuminated this particular secret of history. Here we are offered a key explanation for much in Rudolf Steiner's lifework. No longer was it a matter of proclaiming Christological teachings. The *teachings* change to an actual *report* of the new event just then occurring in the cosmos. What is now required is to watch the course of the drama, on the stage from which the curtain has risen for the seer. Starting in 1909, Rudolf Steiner constantly reported on the progress of this drama. It could be described as a *teichoscopy* — a description from a wall — as in scenes from Greek dramas where one person on the stage stands on a wall and describes the course of the battle that he is observing from there. Towards the close of the year 1909, two lectures were given in Stuttgart; one was on 'The Tasks and Aims of Spiritual Science,' the other was on the Gospels. In the second one of November 14, there is a passage that refers to the new knowledge of the two Jesus children.

> In the ancient Lemurian Period, an event occurred within humankind that we call the Luciferic influence. It was then that the Luciferic forces insinuated themselves into the astral

body of man. Because of this, humanity has become what it is. At that point, the guiding powers had to retain a part of man's etheric body so that this would not become infected by all that the astral body could impart to it, the latter being under the Luciferic influence. Part of the etheric body was withdrawn from the influence of the astral body by virtue of the fact that the human being could only exercise an influence upon his etheric body to the extent that he is a being of will and feeling, but not in regard to everything connected with thinking. This was, as it were, kept back and guided from above out of the spiritual divine world. This is the reason why, from the beginning of their earthly evolution, human beings have their individual desires and personal feelings, in a manner of speaking; but they could not have personal thoughts nor the expression of personal thoughts, namely language. Thinking was of a kind that was directed in the same way in all human beings by means of an all-pervading spirituality. Thus, thinking is the same in everybody. Language as well was at least guided by the Folk Spirits so that every human being would not have his own individual language. The element that expresses itself in the sphere of language was thus withheld in regard to the etheric body from the individual personality's arbitrariness. It was kept back. The paradise myth tells us what was being retained long ago during the Lemurian period. The human being ate of the Tree of Knowledge and received arbitrary power over his will. What was not given to humankind at that time, however, was now transferred by wondrous processes to this Jesus Child whose etheric body it became.

If we comprehend rightly that with the birth of the Luke Jesus child, the actual Christmas Child, a secret of the human etheric body is connected, that the child in the manger of Bethlehem possesses a special paradisal etheric body that has remained pure and which will later be offered up as a sheath for the being of Christ as the pure Grail chalice — then we also understand to what extent the cycle on the Gospel of Luke is a first result of the Christ light newly appearing in the etheric realm. Christ appears now in etheric form as he appeared two thousand years ago in physical form. Which etheric sheath is placed at his disposal? The same etheric sheath that has retained its paradisal purity and that was offered up to him by the Jesus of St Luke when he became physical man. Since the year 1909, Christ has begun to walk among men on earth in this etheric form.

In the course of Rudolf Steiner's life, Christmas 1909 does not particularly stand out. On that date he was on his way to Stockholm. There, starting on New Year's Day, he gave a lecture cycle on the Gospel of John. On January 12 he called the friends there together for a special meeting and began to unveil the mystery of the etheric Christ, the secret of the future just arising on the horizon. From then on, throughout the year 1910, travelling from city to city, he brought word of the impending etheric Christ appearance that was increasingly becoming more powerful. This message was not only in the form of lectures. In the first Mystery Drama in August 1910, the same theme is expressed in artistic form; the initial impulse for the soul development that runs through all the four dramas is the scene right at the opening of *Portal of Initiation* where Theodora mentions that, owing to her soul vision, she can always behold the etheric Christ as the pure image of man. Theodora's Christ vision triggers the dramatic developments in Johannes Thomasius as well as in Dr Strader. This is why it is so surprising that the theme of the whole year is put aside when Rudolf Steiner gives for the first time a Christmas cycle of a kind.

1911

One year later, Rudolf Steiner again gives a Christmas lecture cycle, this time in Hanover: *The World of the Senses and the World of the Spirit.* The magnificence of this series of lectures is yet to be discovered, in my opinion. In them we find, especially in the three middle lectures, a description of the nature of man: how the various bodily sheaths in the human being work into each other; how, right down into physiology, the various formations of substances are distinguished: the formation of the blood, the muscles, the bones, and nerve substance. It appears to be a strictly scientific cycle, a scientific study of man; not a word about Christ or Christmas. And yet, we only understand the significance of this second Christmas cycle, if, once again, we survey the theme of the past year and find its culmination in the days around Christmas.

Just at this time, at Christmas of 1911, when the Hanover cycle was given, a sort of midpoint in Rudolf Steiner's writing of verse occurred.

10. THE CHRISTMAS FESTIVALS   29

The first two Mystery Dramas were in existence, the other two followed in 1912 and 1913. The *Soul Calendar* with the 52 weekly verses appeared in the middle. It guides the soul in meditation through the course of the year. The connection between the *Soul Calendar* and the Christological main theme of that time is not hard to find. It bears repeating here that, to the question of how one could prepare meditatively for perception of the etheric Christ, Rudolf Steiner answered that one should meditate the course of the year, meditatively accompany its rhythms. The *Soul Calendar* an aid for a meditatively striving person to partake of the new Christmas mystery, the new Christ appearance. An additional point is that on the first day of the Hanover Christmas Conference, Rudolf Steiner for the first time presented his German translation of the Nordic epic *The Dream Song of Olaf Åsteson*. Again, this is also a gift that permits us to penetrate into the profound depths of the year's seasonal rhythms.

The lecture cycle itself appears not to present anything concerning the year's theme. But what precisely was the year's theme? The theme for 1911 continued with the new revelation of the being of Christ in the etheric realm. But now an additional chapter unfolded, namely how Christ's appearance in the etheric realm relates to the etheric streams in the human being. We are now led into the alchemy of man's inner being, especially the alchemy of blood. This way, the proclamation concerning the etheric Christ gains a direct Rosicrucian turn.

During the days around Michaelmas 1911, Rudolf Steiner spoke in Neuchâtel in two lectures about Christian Rosenkreutz. When he returned from there, he gave the lecture 'The Etherization of the Blood' on October 1 in Basle. Among the lectures concerning the new Christ revelation, this is the most moving one. It shows how, through an alteration in the human blood, in the etheric streams connected with the human blood circulation, the wall that separates us from the higher etheric realm can be penetrated; how, in the etheric streams accompanying our blood circulation, the etheric force of the being of Christ, now newly manifesting, can enter.

I should point out again that the Christmas lecture cycle in Hanover remains strictly on the scientific level and seemingly says nothing at all concerning Christology. This is the more astounding since among the lectures preceding it, there is the great cycle in Karlsruhe in October, *From Jesus to Christ*, given directly after the Basle lecture 'The

Etherization of the Blood.' Now, at Christmas, there is no mention of Christ — and yet, mention *is* made of him. One day, when this Hanover cycle will be truly discovered, it will reveal itself as the most significant contribution to Christology. After all, the human being is described showing how he has developed under the Luciferic influence, through the Fall. The map of the human being lies open before us. Since the light through which sickness can be healed, has appeared in the etheric surroundings, the map of the sickness can now be read diagnostically. The three central lectures of the Hanover cycle describe how the human etheric body is covered by a certain preponderance of the physical body and how, in this way, our sense organs come into being. Thus, we do not really see a true world with our senses. What we see with the eye and hear with the ear is a world that only reveals itself to us because our etheric body and our physical body are too deeply entwined. If they stood in the divinely intended relationship to each other, we would perceive the world differently. In the same way, astral body and etheric body are too tightly fitted into each other. The astral body preponderates over the etheric body, which results in different functions in man. Finally, there is a kind of preponderance of the I-organization over the astral body, which causes our thinking, feeling and will to be linked together too tightly. They would be a freer, more independently organized threefoldness, if the Luciferic dislocation and amalgamation of our being's members had not taken place.

The lectures go on to describe how the substances in our sheaths, the matter of our body, could only come about because of such a disarranged human form. We learn here how matter comes into existence in the first place; how spirit sparks forth and disperses and in dispersion becomes matter. Now, if something spiritual disperses into an etheric body which is under the dominance of the physical body, then nerve substance results. In the same manner, muscle and bone substance result in consequence of the human sheaths being too tightly joined together. The starting point for this is the human blood. Something comes into being in the blood that would not emerge if human nature were not subject to the Luciferic influence. From the blood, this is transmitted to the bones, muscles, and nerves. Thus we have here clearly mapped the consequences in the human organism of the Fall of man. No mention need be made of Christology which is, in a manner of speaking, the complementary form. When the influences of Christ reach the human being, they too start off in the blood. In the area where the Luciferic influence pushed one thing after the other into coarser development, the force of Christ must work to release the human being step by step from increasing coarseness, rigidity and solidification. The lectures do not say so directly, but they are preceded by what was started in the course of the year concerning the mysteries of the blood; for example, in *An Occult Physiology,* the cycle in Prague, then in *Wonders of the World, Ordeals of the Soul, Revelations of the Spirit,* the cycle in Munich, and in the lecture in Basle, 'The Etherization of the Blood.' In this last one we find the direct Christological connection. It hovers unspoken over the cycle in Hanover. One can feel one's way into it and perceive how this second of the great Christmas cycles flows out of the Christological main theme of that year. It is an application of Christology, so to speak, to the physiology of the human body; it is natural science out of the Christ perspective without the name of being of Christ mentioned.

1912

The Christmas lecture cycle of the year 1912 took place in Cologne and had as its title, *The Bhagavad Gita and the Epistles of Paul.* There was at that time a definite reason for a larger-than-usual gathering of members. For the first time, those members of the Theosophical Society met who wished to pursue new directions together with Rudolf Steiner. They wanted to leave behind the framework of the Theosophical Society which had come under Indian direction. The gathering in Cologne was, as it were, a preliminary meeting for the founding of the Anthroposophical Society, which then took place in Berlin in February 1913. The Cologne Christmas cycle, *The Bhagavad Gita and the Epistles of Paul,* has therefore a direct relationship to the later Christmas Conference, because it was then that the Anthroposophical Society was initially founded. It was founded *anew* in 1923.

Let us limit ourselves to one motif from the Cologne lectures. It is truly magnificent to observe how everything Rudolf Steiner presented always followed what, in the etheric realm, began as the drama of the new Christ manifestation. In this cycle, a comparison was made — one does not know at first, why — between the ancient Indian wisdom contained in the old epic of the *Bhagavad Gita,* and that of the Epistles of Paul. Ancient Krishna wisdom was compared to Christ wisdom as proclaimed by Paul. Something of the theme of the years 1909 and 1910 directly came to the fore. Rudolf Steiner proceeded by stating that it was not quite true to say that the Luke Jesus child was never incarnated during the course of humankind's ancient history. Though never incarnated in the sense that we as human beings are incarnated, his soul-being nevertheless came so close to incarnation once that it ensouled a great teacher of humanity through and through. This was the case with Krishna who, as the great teacher of humankind, occupies the central position in the *Bhagavad Gita*. This inspirational ensouling of Krishna by the heavenly soul, later born as the child of the Luke Gospel, was in a way preliminary to becoming a human being, something that became reality at the turn of time. In comparing Krishna's world to that of Paul, mention is made of Paul's Damascus experience. Here we must recall that in previous years, whenever he spoke of the approaching time when one would behold the Christ in the etheric realm, Rudolf Steiner always stated that it would be an experience similar to that of Paul outside Damascus. Now he poses the question: What *did* Paul experience there? Certainly, he experienced the Christ. But how could Christ appear to him in such radiant glory? What garment of light served him? The following sentences from the fifth lecture give an answer:

> As Paul journeyed to Damascus it was the Christ who appeared to him. The flood of light that enveloped him was Krishna. Because Christ took Krishna as his own soul sheath, through which he then continued to work, everything that once was the content of the sublime Gita streamed from him.

Thus, the glorious radiance, the luminous etheric body, in which Christ appeared to Paul, is none other than the etheric body and soul-being of that celestial being that once inspired Krishna and hence was born as the Jesus child of Luke's Gospel. The development that only in the twentieth century is to take on broader reality was, as it were, anticipated by Paul. The etheric sheath that Christ made use of to manifest himself to Paul and that he will use in the future, is the paradisal, radiant being that is not filled with earthly thoughts but instead is the quintessence of celestial wisdom. Thus, in the Cologne Christmas cycle, the Christmas theme that in previous years always stood silently in the background was now clearly formulated.

When, after the Cologne lectures, the founding of the Anthroposophical Society took place during the annual general meeting in Berlin at the beginning of February, the name 'Anthroposophy' only now acquires the importance that is its due, because the members no longer call themselves Theosophists but anthroposophists. Then, on February 3, 1913, Rudolf Steiner gives the lecture, 'The Being of Anthroposophy' and, for the first time, describes something that reappeared towards the end of his life with the greatest significance, namely that anthroposophy is a living being. He describes that it is the same being that the ancient world revered as the divine Sophia. But this being is no longer what it once was. It has 'passed through man.' It has become one with the image of man, and thus Sophia has become Anthropo-Sophia. It says in the lecture:

> Sophia will have moved into the human soul and will have achieved as intimate a union with the human soul as could hence be described in such a beautiful love-poem by Dante. She will again free herself but take along what man represents, and objectively present herself not merely as Sophia, but as Anthroposophia. After having passed through the human soul, the being of man, she is the Sophia who henceforth carries this being of man within herself, and thus she presents herself to cognizing human being — as once did Sophia, the objective being who dwelled among the Greeks.

We don't want to artificially construe a connection between the passage from the Cologne cycle and the one from the annual general meeting lectures that followed soon afterwards. But it is quite evident that we are dealing here with a specific being that is a human and at the same time a divine-superhuman entity. The being that was born in the Jesus of Luke's Gospel was the source of inspiration of pre-Christian eras. From it flowed the ancient wisdom. It then became the etheric-soul sheath in which the Christ newly manifested. Rudolf Steiner pointed also in the direction of this being when he spoke of the entity whose inspirational fountain is approached by him who does not perceive anthroposophy as abstract teachings but as a living being. Already in 1913, the Anthroposophical Society was not founded on a set of abstract principles; it was explicitly founded as the abode of a living being.

1913

The fourth Christmas festival in this series leads to an unheard-of culmination, Christmas 1913 — the last one before the War. Again, a Christmas cycle is given, this time in Leipzig. It was later published under the title *Christ and the Spiritual World and the Search for the Holy Grail*. Here, too, we must briefly sketch the character of this year that had as its highlight the Leipzig cycle. In August, the Fourth Mystery Drama was written and performed in Munich. Four dramas were now finished. One more was planned; however, it did not materialize because war breaks out. Nevertheless, the four dramas in themselves contain a wondrous completeness and unity. The new Christological message flowed into this work and was presented in artistic form to humankind. After the performance of the dramas, on the anniversary of Goethe's birth, August 28, the first public eurythmy performance took place. Many thoughts for the future enthused those who were privileged to participate in so much that was new.

Many gatherings were occupied with thoughts of building. Plans of erecting a building in Munich had to be given up. But then the land on the hill of Dornach awaited the building. After the conclusion of the August activities in Munich, the foundation stone for the Goetheanum was laid. The Mystery Dramas were the first artistic expression, thus the first cultural fruit, of the new immediate Christ Knowledge.

After the laying of the foundation stone in Dornach on September 20, we experience how the Christological proclamation of those years is lifted up to surprising new heights. Rudolf Steiner travelled to Scandinavia, and in Oslo — then still called Kristiania — held lectures from October 1 to 6, in which part of the Fifth Gospel was unveiled. Beginning with the profound mystery experience of the Apostles at Pentecost and the significance of the 'three years,' a sphere opened making it possible to relate events of the life of Jesus not contained in the Gospels. The life of Jesus between the age of twelve and thirty particularly was described. Jesus' profound suffering was revealed; wherever he went, he saw how all spiritual heritage and reserves of soul forces had run dry.

After Steiner's return from Scandinavia where he also had spoken in Bergen and Copenhagen, he set out on a travel schedule that intensified his activity of previous years when he had frequently spoken day after day in different towns. He criss-crossed Germany in his travels. One cannot look at his schedule without being deeply moved: Did a definite goal have to be reached before a certain time? What is essential is that the proclamation of the Fifth Gospel continued through this abundance of activity. Further chapters were presented in lectures in Berlin, though there were long breaks in between because of engagements in other cities. The six lectures of the Berlin version that are added to the five Oslo lectures extend over 3½ months, from October 21, 1913 to February 10, 1914. But during this time Rudolf Steiner spoke about the Fifth Gospel, condensing it into one or two lectures, in other cities as well (Nürnberg, Hamburg, Stuttgart, Munich, Cologne, Bremen, Hanover), The longest interruption of this group of lectures was seven weeks, between the third and the fourth of these six lectures, from November 18 to January 6.

During this break the Leipzig Christmas cycle was given and thus is embedded into the proclamation of the Fifth Gospel. With its central theme, this cycle belonged directly within the sphere of influences of the Fifth Gospel. It made this lecture cycle a culmination among the series of Christmas cycles. Within the Leipzig cycle, no mention was made of the Fifth Gospel, though the presentation of the latter surrounded it, just as in the Stuttgart Christmas cycle barely a mention was made of the theme of Christ's appearance in the etheric realm, though earlier this subject had dominated. But in 1910 as well as in 1913, the Christmas cycle that did not directly speak of Christmas was nevertheless placed in a Christmas-like framework. In 1910, it was the new Christmas event, the appearance of the etheric Christ. In 1913, the light of the Fifth Gospel — the first segments of which had already been given in the Luke cycle — newly illuminated the whole Mystery of Golgotha with the Christmas secret of the two Jesus children and the theme of the Luke Jesus and his mother. In the lectures in Oslo and Berlin on the Fifth Gospel, for example, the motif was unveiled of the farewell conversations lasting for days between Jesus and his mother prior to Jesus' wandering to John the Baptist to receive the baptism. In the higher sense this is a Christmas theme. When, in an outpouring of his soul, Jesus revealed the sorrowful experiences of his past eighteen years concerning humankind to his stepmother, a transformation occurred in this Mary similar to what then took place in Jesus himself through the baptism. Just as the being of Christ entered into Jesus, so there descended into Mary the soul of the Mary of Luke's Gospel who had died at a young age. This is the actual Christmas Mary always painted by Raphael.

The Leipzig Christmas cycle gives a vast amount of new insight concerning Moses and Paul, sibyls and prophets, and the Mystery of the Holy Grail. The expanding Christology becomes a source of light in all directions. In the third lecture, however, an unprecedented secret is unveiled. The Christ event at the beginning of our era was not the first intervention into humanity's history by the Christ; rather, three great pre-Christian Christ events had preceded it. The first occurred during the Lemurian, the two others in Atlantean times. On all three occasions, Christ was able to intervene in humankind's evolution in a helping and healing manner, because the soul-being that had remained in the pure, paradisal state, the celestial Adam soul that later became a human being on earth in the Jesus child of Luke — the actual Christmas child — put itself at Christ's disposal as his soul-sheath and vehicle. The Christ event at the beginning of our era is the fourth in the series of great redeeming deeds accomplished by the being of Christ to save humanity from the most severe crises and dangers. And each time this pure celestial being, held back by Providence in the spiritual worlds because it was to retain something of the paradisal etheric forces of the original Tree of Life, served as the Grail chalice in which the being of Christ could approach the sphere of human beings and influence them.

Afterwards, in other lectures where Rudolf Steiner repeated this central message of the 1913 Christmas cycle, particularly in Pforzheim on March 7, 1914, we are shown that a fifth future Christ event — connected with the appearance of Christ in the etheric realm, has its beginnings in our age.

All at once, not only our present age but all of Christianity is connected to pre-Christian history, because the great sources of light and revelation of the pre-Christian era appear as projections of the first three great cosmic Christ events.

The two Christological themes, the appearance of Christ in the etheric world and the Fifth Gospel, clearly come together. The first speaks of the new light arising in the present age. The second can be described because this new light illumines the events of the past. From its first mention (the two Jesus children in the lectures on the Gospel of Luke), the Fifth Gospel is the fruit of the new Christ light in the etheric realm. First, the vision into the past opens up the secrets presented incompletely in the gospels. But then it extends further into the past to the lofty sequence of Christ's great deeds of redemption. And it becomes clear that the Leipzig Christmas cycle is also a fruit of the new Christmas event inasmuch as it is a continuation of the Fifth Gospel.

It should be added in conclusion that it was in Leipzig that Christian Morgenstern, already severely ill, heard Rudolf Steiner for the last time.

1914–1922

With this, the four Christmas lecture cycles that could be given prior to the outbreak of the First World War are outlined. Then the war began and it seemed that the connecting Christmas thread was torn. The voice was silent. But it is deeply moving to observe how the Christmas initiative went on, only in altered form. Beginning in 1914, a turn is taken to unprecedented outer activity. Rudolf Steiner is in Dornach. The construction of the building continued to the distant sound of cannons from Alsace. Among the lectures held at Christmas time is 'Technology and Art' (December 28); on December 29 & 30 two lectures follow, 'Impulses of Transformation for Man's Artistic Evolution' (in *Art as Seen in the Light of Mystery Wisdom*). They describe the relationship of the various arts to each other. Everything moves towards cultural renewal; the tree of anthroposophy is to bear practical fruits for life.

In 1915 for the first time the Oberufer Christmas plays were produced in Dornach. They had been performed earlier in other cities. And now, tentatively, a Christmas cycle formed itself after all; three lectures each on two different occasions. First, 'On Old Christmas Plays,' then three lectures entitled 'Meditations on the New Year.' Each had a different theme. The third was called 'Perceiving and Remembering,' describing how man would perceive his own etheric body as a body of light, if the Ahrimanic powers did not cover it up and obscure it. Therefore, instead of seeing into the luminous world of ideas, which forms man's etheric body, he only possesses memory. Memory is the luminous world of man's own etheric body darkened by Ahriman. And in connection with certain Gnostic texts, a prayer was given in this lecture, which the Risen One taught his disciples during the forty days after the resurrection:

> O ye powers in the spiritual world,
> from out of my physical body
> let me consciously be in the Light World,
> let me be in the Light,
> so that I can behold my own body of light.
> And do not allow the strength of Ahriman's forces
> to overpower me so much
> that they make it impossible for me
> to see what occurs in my body of light.

The theme of etheric vision, the seeing of Christ's etheric body, is connected with the possibility of man's perception of his own etheric body.

Then, in 1916, we have a Christmas cycle of surprisingly different nature. The secret political activities of eastern and western Europe were relentlessly revealed. This does not seem appropriate for Christmas, and yet one must admit that just as earlier the Christ light fell on the evolving Christ events, so now the same light source falls upon Ahriman's sphere, the Antichrist. A completely different tone entered into the context of Christmas. This determined the trend of the following Christmas meetings.

Let us take 1918; we need not discuss every year. As Christmas was approaching, Rudolf Steiner gave weekly talks that each time were like an exposure, an unmasking. An obvious example is the cycle, *The Challenge of the Times,* given during November and December. In Dornach, at Christmas time, there followed the lecture cycle, *How Can Mankind Find the Christ Again?* Resolutely, the symptoms of the contemporary age were pursued, but always with the theme: How can humankind find the Christ again?

Then, in the Christmas activities of 1919, the aim of the new trend came out more clearly than ever. Rudolf Steiner was again in Stuttgart. It was the first Christmas festival since the founding of the Waldorf School. Now, he gave two courses for the teachers. The first scientific lecture course was presented in ten lectures. Simultaneously, for the teachers' seminar, there was a course on 'The Spiritual Scientific View of Speech' (published in English as *The Genius of Language*). Amongst all this, five lectures were given for members of the Anthroposophical Society. They have been published under the title *The Cosmic New Year*. In them, a subject of the most unprecedented kind was brought out, which had already been discussed in Zurich, Berne and Dornach. Of all times, on Christmas Day it was revealed that not only are we approaching a time when the Ahrimanic powers re-intensify their attacks on humankind but that Ahriman will appear in human form, just as Christ appeared in human form two thousand years ago. An incarnation of Ahriman would occur. In connection with the beginning of the threefold movement, Rudolf Steiner gives two public lectures that could not have been more to the point. The time of Christmas was used to give momentum to the struggle for cultural renewal, and to harvest the fruits of anthroposophical insight in all the different sectors.

Thus it continues during the following years. In 1920, Rudolf Steiner gives the 'Course on Astronomy,' eighteen lectures for the teachers at Stuttgart.

In Dornach, in 1921, there follows the basic course on pedagogy in sixteen lectures, *Soul Economy; Body, soul, and Spirit in Waldorf Education*, commonly called 'The Christmas Course.' The nature of these cycles is cultural renewal.

In 1922 at Christmas time, Rudolf Steiner held the last lectures in the old Goetheanum, *The Spiritual Communion of Mankind* (published in *The Reverse Ritual*). After the last lecture of this series, the building burnt down on New Year's Eve. Parallel to this series there was a scientific course, 'The Origin of Natural Science in World History and Its Recent Development.' On the day following the fire, this cycle is continued in the carpenters' workshop. One can see that it is not intimate Christology that is dealt with at Christmas time but instead applied Christology, it is anthroposophy in the arena of the issues and controversies of the day. Right into the fury of the unleashed tempest a new culture is implanted in all areas of life.

1923

We have now arrived at *the* Christmas Conference. One year after the Goetheanum fire, it brought the great culmination in Rudolf Steiner's life work. The whole of 1923 was filled with the pressing urgency with which he challenged the members to make the Anthroposophical

Society into such an organism that anthroposophy could stand in the world as a vigorous cultural force and vitalizing factor. The essence of this appeal is contained in the lectures, 'The Anthroposophical Movement,' given in June, when he said:

> Anthroposophy is actually an invisible human being who moves among visible human beings. As long as we are a small group, we have the utmost responsibility to him; he must really be considered an invisible person ... whom one must consult concerning every action in life.

So, anthroposophy is a living, invisible *being* going through our ranks; a human being, but not in an external form; anthroposophy, the image of man in person.

> If anthroposophy itself is seen as a living, supersensible, invisible being moving among anthroposophists, then there will perhaps be less talk of brotherhood, less talk of general love for humankind; instead, these ideas will live more in the heart. Even from the tone with which people express their thoughts uniting them with anthroposophy — the tone with which one says this or that to the other, you will note that it means something to him, that he too, like you, is one who follows the invisible entity anthroposophy.

Then came the Christmas Conference. There is no doubt that it was a fruit of the new Christmas mystery taking place in the spiritual world since 1909, which has been transmitted to us by Rudolf Steiner as through a great interpreter. He had the capability of transforming what occurred in the heavens into earthly deeds.

We thus return to the starting point of our study. When, in the lectures *World History and the Mysteries in the Light of Anthroposophy* at the Christmas Conference, Rudolf Steiner referred back to the first Christmas cycle, *Occult History*, the initial reason was that this earlier lecture series could actually be designated as the first karma cycle, and that on the other hand, now, during the Christmas Conference, starting from the same karma examples, the floodgates were opened for the mighty stream of karma revelations that, up until Michaelmas 1924, was to pour forth as the main expression of the unprecedented new spiritual impulse.

Now the relationships become clarified. The unveiling of the mysteries of karma are a fruit of the working of Christ in our time. Perhaps this can be illustrated by drawing upon a scene from the Gospel. The first three Gospels describe the scene on the mount. The three closest disciples become witnesses of Christ's transfiguration. They behold him in an aura of light, in a radiant glory that already then was the etheric Christ who overcame death and manifested in the physically incarnated human being, Jesus of Nazareth. After the disciples beheld the etheric Christ in his radiant power, a conversation took place during the descent from the mount. It is the conversation in which Christ instructed those disciples closest to him into the secret of reincarnation and karma, something that even penetrated into the wording of the Gospel of Matthew. The disciples ask, 'But why does it say that Elijah must come first?' And they receive the answer, 'He has come.' Then it says, 'They understood that he was speaking of John the Baptist.'

What is the meaning of this scene? When the Spirit-Sun Light of the etheric Christ arises, it illuminates the sphere of destiny, which lets the human being pass from one earth life to another according to the law of karma. Christ has become Lord of Karma. Through an inner connection to the forces that through the Mystery of Golgotha have entered the sphere of earth and humankind, man has been given the opportunity to work off karmic debts through repeated earth lives, and to reunite with the paradisal state of humankind's childhood. The Christmas experience progresses from child to man, and from man to child.

The rich abundance of the karma lectures that, beginning with the Christmas Conference, Rudolf Steiner bestowed upon us were — literally — a Christmas gift, since they flowed out of the new Christmas event of our time. And this pertains also to the first karma cycle, the Christmas lectures of 1910. Even though the proclamation of the etheric Christ, which had pervaded the whole year, was not mentioned in so many words, and there seemed to be silence just at Christmas, the inward connection was no less close. Rudolf Steiner interrupted his speaking of the new Christmas event in order to present us with the first fruits of it as a gift.

The Fifth Gospel

Michael can pave the way for the spiritual future because he is also the great guardian of the original impulse:

> What Michael desires is to keep the intelligence, which is developing within humanity, permanently in connection with the Divine-Spiritual beings ...
>
> It is the task of Michael to lead man back again, on paths of Will, whence he came down when with his earthly consciousness he descended on the paths of Thought from the living experience of the Supersensible to the experience of the world of sense.
>
> (*Anthroposophical Leading Thoughts,* No. 5 and 3)

Part of Michael's being is the wonderful broad arc which reaches from the original spiritual point of departure to the spiritual aims of the future. Through all our striving and working, he guides us to repeatedly connect with the original impulse, the idea when it first lit up, the *status nascendi* of our intentions. This Michaelic relationship between past and future is the key to the composition of Rudolf Steiner's work at some important points.

Here I wish to mention the structural form in which the four mystery dramas belong in relation to their origin. We are always given something in them which is much more comprehensive than we are able to understand at present, and this is indicated by their majestic Christological setting which reveals the polarity of future and past, of preview and review in a classical manner. The dramas have a prophetic prelude in the lectures in which during the early months of 1910 Rudolf Steiner first announced the coming of the etheric Christ. After the first third of the twentieth century, a new kind of seeing will awaken in humankind allowing people to see into the sphere of the etheric Christ. This forward-looking message forms the subject of the overture. It is clear that the mystery dramas themselves flowed from the new spring of prophetic knowledge. In the first drama, the key scene is the one in which the seer Theodora describes the shining form of light before her soul, as a forerunner of the new perception of Christ as it were. Her words flashed into the hearts of the assembled people, triggering dramatic developments which run through all four dramas, especially in Dr Strader and Thomasius.

The series of four mystery dramas also has a mighty epilogue. Immediately following the performance of the fourth drama in 1913 the foundation stone of the first Goetheanum was laid and the lectures on the Fifth Gospel, particularly those in Oslo and Berlin, were held. Both these were the results of a very special spiritual review.

*

The law of preview and review appears in the first drama like a great mystery. Significantly, the lecture cycle which followed the performance of the *Portal of Initiation* in August 1910 was about the biblical creation story which looked far back into the very beginnings. In the introductory lecture, Rudolf Steiner said:

> [This] lecture cycle longs for human thoughts to come a little nearer to what has passed through human hearts and occupied human minds for thousands of years — to lead human hearts and human minds upwards to what man can feel as the highest and most powerful which can exist for him: his own origin in its majesty.

It is a Michaelic touch which, at the moment of the most important revelations of the future, goes back to the earliest sources which alone can form the basis of the future. The etheric Christ becomes visible as the future principle and at the same time a ray of light shines far back onto the emergence of our earthly aeons out of the archetypal Word. This offers us the most important key to the inner structure of the dramas themselves. An impatient eager striving towards the future permeates everything. Strader is the modern human being. He has to struggle with the future and the problems of the new consciousness. Johannes Thomasius, the artist, also does this but in a different way. The torch of the vision of Christ which has been lit by Theodora, shines into this striving for the future. But precisely because the prophetic lights of the future are illuminated, rays of light fall onto earlier lives on earth. A piece of the past lights up along with the future. At two points in the first drama, Theodora speaks an important verse. In the first scene, when she gets ready to describe her vision of Christ, she says:

> I am compelled to speak. Before my soul
> A pictured form stands wrapped in robes of light;

In a later scene she once more speaks as a seer and begins with exactly the same words:

> I feel compelled to speak. A glow of light
> From out thy brow, Maria, upward mounts.

This parallel is extremely illuminating. The first thing which compels her to speak belongs to the future while the second is the corresponding review. What is it that she sees in the glow of light which is released from Maria's brow? She looks back on an earlier life on earth in which Maria and Johannes Thomasius were already connected to one another. Knowledge of karma arises in review when foresight gives rise to an experience of the etheric Christ.

In the introductory lecture which forms the bridge from the performance of the *Portal of Initiation* to the Genesis cycle, *The Secrets of Creation*, this principle is expressed very clearly:

> Therefore at this point something appears which — if I may put it like this — encloses a certain mystery in the spiritual world. Theodora who sees into the future on the physical plane and who is in a position to foresee the significant event which is about to happen, the reappearance of the figure of Christ — on the spiritual plane is capable of calling up the meaning of the past in front of the soul ... It is a realistic description to say that Theodora is the seer of the future on the physical plane and the conscience and awakener of past memory on the spiritual plane and therefore brings about that moment in which Johannes Thomasius looks back on his own past in which he was already connected to the individuality of Maria.

*

The spiritual structural principle, this Michaelic principle, also governs the composition of the New Testament. At the beginning the Gospels describe historical events: this is the review. At the end there is the Revelation of John, the Apocalypse: this is the preview. If a significant part of what Rudolf Steiner stated in the time after the mystery dramas were written is described as the Fifth Gospel, then this expression is correct in as far as what was said deals with experiences of looking back into the past. In the five lectures given in Oslo Rudolf Steiner proceeds by starting from an event which took place amongst the apostles, from the disciples' experience at Whitsun. From this point the lights shine backwards. The moment of darkness which set in at noon on Good Friday becomes visible. Then it goes further back. The events of the three years can be understood in a new way. Finally, the important event of the farewell conversation between Jesus and his stepmother takes place before he sets out to meet John the Baptist. The scroll of this life unrolls ever further into the past. What is contained in this conversation which is so moving? It is the young Jesus' inexpressibly painful disappointments with humankind between the age of 12 and 30: first with the Jews, then with the heathens and lastly with the Essenes. It is this scene, in which the soul of Jesus conversing with his stepmother becomes the focal point of the great emptiness, the human god-forsakenness and twilight of the gods, which brings about the great transformation in both souls. The soul of Jesus is prepared to receive the spirit of Christ at the Baptism in the Jordan. In the soul of Jesus' stepmother, the virginal spirit of the Lucan Mary can also live from now on.

From this brief description of the fundamental principle it should be clear that a spiritual review does not simply happen by itself. The spiritual researcher does not merely need to look into the past in order to have everything immediately laid out before him. This kind of spiritual review is only revealed when a courageous step into the future has first been taken.

At what moment was the Fifth Gospel actually born? In the lectures which followed the four dramas in 1913/14, Rudolf Steiner said that he had already given part of the Fifth Gospel, mentioning in particular the Luke cycle which was held during Michaelmas 1909. Steiner later said that from this time onwards the etheric

Christ had become visible walking amongst people on earth. He started speaking about this in 1910, but of what was he able to speak in 1909? Not the future element as such, although it was waiting beyond the horizon, but the corresponding gift from the past. It was interwoven in the Luke cycle because for the first time it was possible to speak about the two Jesus children. This was the first part of the Fifth Gospel.

We come to understand what view of the future is produced by the symmetry of the past. What does it actually mean, when we say that the etheric Christ starts to walk on the earth? It means that the being of Christ himself undergoes a transformation by clothing himself in an etheric body, just as he clothed himself in an astral, etheric and physical body two thousand years ago in the Holy Land. Since 1909 Christ has been present amongst human beings in a new sheath. But now it is an etheric sheath and not another physical one as it was at the time of the mystery of Golgotha.

Which etheric sheath is this? It is the miracle of that unique being of humankind whose birth is told in the Christmas story in the Gospel of Luke. The child who was born in the cave in Bethlehem was different from all other human beings. He was the heavenly soul of Adam. He brought an etheric force of such purity as humankind had not possessed since the fall into sin. It is the same heavenly etheric sheath which the Lucan Jesus child brought to earthly existence in which the being of Christ approaches humankind in the twentieth century. When we consider Christ and the pure etheric sheath in which he reveals himself, then the counterpart of the past lights up at the same time: it is apparent who Jesus of Nazareth actually was, as he is described in Luke's Gospel. This leads to the mystery of the two Jesus children. This secret actually lies in the Nathan Jesus: the double nature can only be understood by starting from this figure. We therefore see the involvement of the being of the etheric Christ at the moment of birth of the Fifth Gospel. The appearance of Christ is the future element. What is stated about the two Jesus children is the corresponding past element, the first part of the Fifth Gospel.

*

1913

September 20:	Laying the foundation stone in Dornach
October 1–6:	Oslo, lectures 1–5
October 21:	Berlin, introductory lecture
November 4:	Berlin, lecture 1
November 9 & 11:	Nürnberg, lectures 1 & 2
November 16:	Hamburg
November 18:	Berlin, lecture 2
November 22 & 23:	Stuttgart, lectures 1 & 2
December 8 & 10:	Munich, lectures 1 & 2
December 17 & 18:	Cologne, lectures 1 & 2
December 30:	Leipzig, lecture 3 from the cycle *Christ and the Spiritual World*

1914

January 6:	Berlin, lecture 3
January 11:	Bremen
January 13:	Berlin, lecture 4
February 7:	Hanover
February 10:	Berlin, lecture 5
March 7:	Pforzheim, the pre-Christian and the two 'Christian' Christ events
May 27:	Paris, summary: the Fifth Gospel and the pre-Christian Christ events
June 2:	Basle, the pre-Christian Christ events

This calendar of the Fifth Gospel begans with the laying of the foundation stone in Dornach. In the action which was performed on that evening, many things came together. First the seal was set on the revelation from which the four mystery dramas had flowed. At the same time a great eagerness for action presented itself for the future. The building would create the stage on which the 'mysteries' could be at home. In Munich the rented halls or theatres were completely inadequate and the plan for the Johannes building in Munich failed because the planning authorities had decided against it. Now in September 1913 the foundation stone of the Goetheanum was laid on the hill in Dornach. This gave rise to a fountainhead, a centre of action whose

11. THE FIFTH GOSPEL   49

task comprised much more than the cultivation of the mystery dramas. These 'mysteries' typified the future of the place only in as much as they were themselves signs for a rich new far-reaching spiritual stream. The subject of the Fifth Gospel which was uttered in a concealed manner in the words of the laying of the foundation stone, had to be felt like the call of a new spiritual principle which would inaugurate a 'new creation' on this spot. The address at the laying of the foundation stone was not the beginning of the content of the Fifth Gospel. But the core of this, the cosmic Lord's Prayer, rang out into the stormy night. We shall return to this later.

Rudolf Steiner travelled to the far north. The five lectures in Oslo — Kristiania at the time — laid out the Fifth Gospel in a clear and complete way for the first time, that is, those elements of the Gospel which are not part of the four traditional Gospels. We mentioned how the Whitsun event formed the beginning, as though the Pentecostal awakening of the souls of the disciples reopened the view into the past. Looking back, the hour of Golgotha appeared, the three years and the baptism of Jesus, and the transforming conversations before that between Jesus and his mother. The subject of these conversations was the threefold suffering of the young Jesus at the drying up of the most important spiritual streams, the Old Testament stream, the heathen one and the Essene one.

Returning to Berlin, Steiner began to describe the subject matter of the Fifth Gospel there as well. But he did not simply repeat the development which the exposition in Oslo. The sequence of scenes which unfolded this time was more linked to the historical order of events in the life of Jesus. Here it was not possible to develop the topic over a number of days. Even the weekly evenings were not always available as Steiner had a busy travel schedule at this time. As soon as he had held the second lecture in which he made a start on the description of the Fifth Gospel after the introductory evening, he had to break off on account of his activities in other cities, so that in the end the six lectures ran from the end of October until February the following year.

However the travelling provided the opportunity to lecture on the Fifth Gospel in other cities as well. The first German city where it was spoken about apart from Berlin was Nürnberg. Here Friedrich Rittelmeyer, who had been a private student of Steiner for years, was deeply moved — a spark was kindled within him. There were two lectures in each of Nürnberg, Stuttgart, Munich and Cologne, one in each of Hamburg, Bremen and Hanover. Apart from the Berlin lectures, transcripts have only survived from those which were held in Munich, Cologne and Hamburg and one of the two in Stuttgart. The version from Cologne has been available in print for many years. Wherever two lectures were held, the structure follows that of the Berlin lectures. (This also applies to the Nürnberg version as friends who were there vouch for the fact that the lectures there and in Munich matched each other exactly.) The Hamburg text follows on more from the Oslo version. This may also have been the case in Bremen and Hanover.

At Christmas the great Leipzig cycle, *Christ and the Spiritual World*, was fitted into the schedule of lectures on the Fifth Gospel. It appears to be a break in the lectures continued later in Bremen and Hanover as well as Berlin. However in reality it was a mighty intensification. The view into the past here underwent an enormous expansion, far beyond the life of Jesus, back to the primal epochs of the earth's evolution. The third lecture of the cycle describes the three pre-Christian Christ events, the first of which took place in the Lemurian time, but the second and third in the Atlantean epoch. The being of Christ had already intervened in a healing way at crucial junctions in humankind's development before he was embodied as a human being on the earth in our post-Atlantean epoch. On each of these pre-Christian occasions he had made use of that etheric-spiritual being which still retained a paradisal purity. This being was a sheath and tool which afterwards actually incarnated for the first time, was born as the Nathan Jesus child. The vision of the figure of the etheric Christ approaching humankind again by using the pure soul of the Nathan Jesus had enabled the revelation of the secret of the two Jesus children in the Luke cycle in 1909. Now this opened up mighty cosmic perspectives. A lens was formed which focused on the great prehistoric healing deeds of Christ. This enables Christ in the etheric to become visible again in the sheath of light of the pure heavenly Adam being. The life of Jesus — that is, the human healing activity of the pure soul in the Lucan Jesus-being — did not start just in the stable in Bethlehem. It had already aided the fallen human race since primal times. In this respect the Leipzig Christmas cycle of 1913 is part of the

Fifth Gospel. This also applies to the lectures held elsewhere which, like this third Leipzig lecture, describe the three pre-Christian Christ events: Pforzheim, March 7 and Basle, June 2, 1914. The Paris lecture of May 27, 1914 in particular also belongs here. This lecture is particularly important for our context as it first portrays the three preliminary stages of the mystery of Golgotha in a few words and then gives a complete outline of the Fifth Gospel, both according to the Oslo version and the Berlin one. Although it apparently interrupted the Fifth Gospel, what is revealed by the Leipzig cycle is identified here as being an intrinsic component of the Fifth Gospel.

In the address which Rudolf Steiner held for the laying of the foundation stone in Dornach on September 20, 1913, the concept of the Fifth Gospel appears for the first time with systematic clarity.

He began with a remark that building on this site was based on a deep karmic fate, because this was a point — as he stated in very general terms — through which important spiritual streams had passed:

> Led by karma, we stand at this moment at a place through which important streams of spiritual life have flowed; let us feel within ourselves this evening the full gravity of the situation.*

Now our attention is drawn to humanity: we are surrounded by souls who have lost the spirit. A thousandfold cry of longing for the spirit resounds to the heavens. May the answer to this cry be a new revelation:

---

* A remark which was both humanly touching and historically explicit on the karma of the place was contained in the letter which Steiner wrote on September 19, on the evening before, to Alexander von Bernus:

'Your very kind offer concerning a building in the grounds of your estate [Neuburg near Heidelberg] would have been immediately gratefully accepted if it could be considered in relation to the building in Dornach at this time. But this building can no longer be abandoned. Karma has pointed so clearly to this point that I would no longer give the *Johannesbau-Verein* any other advice but to build [in Dornach].

'And I have to say that each day more spiritual reasons arise in my soul which make the situation which to a certain extent was forced on us appear to be the right one. So I no longer have anything against laying the foundation stone here tomorrow after sunset. In an esoteric connection, this is a responsibility which weighs really heavily on my heart.'

On September 22, two days after the laying of the foundation stone, Steiner once again mentioned the karma of the place in the third annual general meeting of the *Johannesbau-Verein*: 'In a certain way we might say that a clear karma was expressed in this action. A karma that may only come to light gradually.'

> Feel that in our time the possibility has indeed arisen of
> adding to the Spirit-Word, four times proclaimed, that other
> proclamation which I can now present — but in symbol only.

The fourfold Gospel in the New Testament is the old revelation, it is the Gospel of the *annunciation*. Now the Fifth Gospel asks to be added, the Gospel of *knowledge*. This was described in a systematic way: the four Gospels came from the east. The answer must now come from the west:

> From the East it came — the Light and the Word of the
> Proclamation. From out of the East it passed over to the West,
> four times proclaimed in the four Gospels, awaiting the advent
> from the West of the mirror that will add knowledge to what is
> still only proclamation in the four-times uttered Cosmic Word.

It was further said that the quintessence of the four Gospels which came from the East is the Lord's Prayer. But it is the microcosmic Lord's Prayer. It is based on the human form. Likewise, the quintessence of the Fifth Gospel is the macrocosmic Lord's Prayer with its reversed structure. The macrocosmic Lord's Prayer which is the heart of the Fifth Gospel was spoken by Rudolf Steiner at this moment for the first time:

> Deep-toned rang out the undying prayer which from the
> innermost core of the human heart was to make known to the
> microcosm, in depths of soul, the secret of existence. That
> secret was to be heard in the Lord's Prayer, as we know it, and
> as it reverberated from the East towards West. Yet it waited
> patiently, this Cosmic Word which sank then into the micro-
> cosm — waited in order that one day it might resound in har-
> mony with the Fifth Gospel; for the souls of men had to ripen
> before they could understand that which, as the most ancient
> of all, because it is the Macrocosmic Gospel, is now to rever-
> berate from the West like an echo to the Gospel of the East.

It is repeatedly stated that something from the most ancient past resounds in the words of the macrocosmic Lord's Prayer. 'As a first revelation of the Fifth Gospel there shall even now sound forth the primal macrocosmic World Prayer.' Against the four Gospels' microcosmic Lord's Prayer which was prayed as the basic Christian prayer, sounds the primal macrocosmic prayer, the quintessence of the newly revealed Fifth Gospel.

11. THE FIFTH GOSPEL

We are faced with a great riddle. The four Gospels are there. Now, as it were, as something totally new from western civilization, the Fifth Gospel should be born out of the West. But at the same time this is referred to as the most ancient Gospel, the macrocosmic one. How is this to be understood? The Fifth Gospel, which is actually the oldest, has been created anew directly from spiritual sources. We may sense that this is once again a case of the significant connection between preview and review: the further Michael reaches into the future, the older are the primeval ages which are illuminated at the same time. We can feel our way towards what is meant at this moment. The four Gospels do indeed come from the East, just as the eastern wisdom which flowed into Theosophy comes from the East in a completely different way. Now western wisdom should arise, having worked its way through the intellectual culture. This is why Rudolf Steiner had to part from the Theosophical Society, because he had to bring western occultism to the outdated, unworldly eastern occultism. We really have to say that what Rudolf Steiner called the Fifth Gospel, the Gospel of knowledge which was an answer from the West to what had always been there from the East — he could well use to refer to the whole of anthroposophy. Anthroposophy as such is the Fifth Gospel in a certain way. It is the answer which the West gives to the wisdom of the East, which in the present day is gradually dying away.

We should actually give a great deal of consideration to the purposely unanswered question as to why the Fifth Gospel is the most ancient although it has just been newly created from spiritual sources. However, another quotation can be added which, though it enlarges the question rather than answering it, nevertheless provides a sense of overall connections. In the fourth lecture of the Leipzig Christmas cycle at the end of 1913, Steiner goes back to the description of the three pre-Christian Christ events, the last of which took place in the Atlantean epoch.

> And when we look back over what happened then, we must say that what was accomplished in Atlantean times flowed over into the East ... But a messenger such as Elijah worked in the after-effects of the threefold Christ-event; we might say that Elijah went ahead of the Nathan Jesus-being, who was passing spiritually from West to East in order to find his way

into the course of civilization and then to be born as one of the Jesus children.

We do not need to go into the question of Elijah here. It is primarily a case of the Nathan Jesus-being who had been involved with the pre-Christian healing events, the last time in the spiritual realm of the Atlantean stage of the earth. This being travelled from West to East in order to be born as the Jesus child in Bethlehem.

> But when we have sought out the threefold Christ-event ... which on three occasions preceded the Mystery of Golgotha, do we not see the Christ pass over from West to East, to the place where the Mystery of Golgotha was to be fulfilled? Do we not see how he had sent his messenger in Elijah, and do we not know how in his next incarnation the messenger reappeared as John the Baptist? And are we not expressly told of this in a wonderful harmony of words: 'He sent his angel before him, to herald his coming'? That can be said as well of John as of Elijah. Or even more of Elijah ... Such messengers were always messengers of the Christ, who was passing from West to East.

We can see Christ himself and the soul of the Nathan Jesus passing from the West to the East. This is the preliminary macrocosmic step. It might be said that the etheric body of the Nathan Jesus was itself the Fifth Gospel when it was in its most ancient condition, even before the mystery of Golgotha. The spiritual task of the West was foreshadowed in him back to the most ancient times. From the end of the Atlantean period onwards, it was already the bearer of the principle: *ex occidente lux.* The 'light from the west' which would one day complement and replace the 'light from the east' had already appeared. The gods had already planned anthroposophy in primeval Atlantean times. Actually, it did not have to be planned at all: the cosmic paths of Christ himself resulted in the essential Fifth Gospel being able to radiate at a later stage as a great feat of knowledge, as anthroposophy, from West to East in answer to the four Gospels, which are only a question from God to humankind to see if humankind is able to respond.

Two days after the laying of the foundation stone, Steiner again spoke about the Fifth Gospel in the annual general meeting of the *Johannesbau-Verein* (Johannes Building Association):

11. THE FIFTH GOSPEL

My intention was to put into words, that which ... could be called the macrocosmic echo of that prayer [the Lord's Prayer in the Gospels] which can be addressed as the most important event of the fourth period of our post-Atlantean development. What must be added to the other Gospels in the fifth epoch will then gradually be discovered from the mysterious writing of the Fifth Gospel. Then the eternal prayer, which resounds in the microcosm as the Lord's Prayer and occurs in the Gospels, will come towards us from the Fifth Gospel as the *Lord's Prayer of knowledge* — in contrast to the *Lord's Prayer of the entreaty for deliverance.* The entreaty for deliverance in the fourth epoch will be knowledge in the fifth epoch. If people do not absorb knowledge of the spirit in the fifth epoch, they may well wither, and belief, the fulfilment of the spiritual, may be replaced by disbelief and emptiness.

*

We would like to an observation here to illuminate the other riddle contained in the foundation stone speech: Rudolf Steiner's allusion to the karma of the place.

The four Mystery Dramas, the idea of holy festivals and a building which would serve the performance of these dramas had an obvious historical root in addition to the current stream of the new revelation of the etheric. Rudolf Steiner's Mystery Dramas were not the first to be performed in Munich. A start was made with dramas by Edouard Schuré. There a character appeared whose importance in influencing Rudolf Steiner deserves to be looked at very carefully. The effect of this person, his karmic significance in Steiner's life can be seen at first glance. Schuré had already played a role from afar from the beginning of the century. Marie von Sivers, who was later to become Steiner's wife, translated some of the works of this writer who wrote such a lofty high-sounding French that it is always a pleasure to read it. At the beginning of the twentieth century she translated Schuré's play *The Children of Lucifer.* She showed this to Steiner with whom she came into contact at that time. Among the lectures which Steiner held in the home of Count Brockdorff in Berlin Charlottenburg, which later resulted in the connection to the Theosophical Society, is one about this play. This lecture took place before the lectures which were later published as

Christianity as Mystical Fact, not long after the lecture on Goethe's *Fairy Tale*. The correspondence between Schuré and Marie von Sivers was lively, because she was also starting on the translation of his book *The Great Initiates*. It is clear that Marie von Sivers was eager to bring the two men together. This happened in Paris in 1906, where Rudolf Steiner was giving a long series of lectures. Edouard Schuré was exactly twenty years older than Steiner, but this older man who certainly felt himself to be the bearer of an esoteric task felt from the first moment that he had met his master. He described vividly how having studied the initiates of humankind, he now stood face to face with an initiate in the flesh. Crossing paths with Steiner was the greatest blessing fate could have sent him.

Much arose from this meeting which is clear to us today. In any case, in 1907 we can see the attainment of what could only be talked about at this meeting. At the great Theosophical congress which took place in Germany for the first time in Munich, and which Rudolf Steiner — as the Secretary General of the German Section — was able to organize freely, a mystery drama rehearsed by Steiner was performed for the first time. This was the *Drama of Eleusis* recreated by Edouard Schuré. Steiner wanted to counteract the overly sentimental unworldliness of the Theosophical Society by making plenty space for the artistic element. He decorated the hall with the basic artistic motifs of the 'occult seals and pillars.' But above all he placed great hopes in Schuré's drama. Edouard Schuré did not attend, as he had a prejudice against amateur actors. But now things had been set in motion.

In 1909 another play was performed, but on this occasion not as part of a conference. This time Steiner organized the event himself. In Munich he started the tradition of regular summer festivals. Edouard Schuré's play *The Children of Lucifer* was performed, followed by the important lecture cycle, 'The Children of Lucifer and the Brothers of Christ,' which is known by the title *The East in the Light of the West*. This time Schuré was present, as he had meantime heard that the amateurs had done very well under Rudolf Steiner's direction.

A year later the first Mystery Drama, *The Portal of Initiation*, was produced but before this received its first performance, Schuré's *Children of Lucifer* was performed again. So a play by Schuré and one by Steiner appeared side by side. And so it went on. In 1911 two Mystery Dramas were performed, *The Portal of Initiation* and *The Soul's*

Edouard Schuré

Probation. The recreated *Drama of Eleusis* which was first performed in 1907 formed a prelude, and Schuré was again present. In 1912, *Eleusis* was again performed as a prelude to the first three Mystery Dramas. Only in 1913, when the number of Mystery Dramas rose to four, was there no Schuré performance for the first time. When the First World War began, a tragic estrangement arose on account of a certain chauvinism from which Schuré was unable to free himself. I am only recounting facts here, but a great deal more might be said.

After the two men had met in Paris, they were together for lengthy periods every year. In the first few years, Rudolf Steiner travelled to Barr in Alsace to visit Schuré and often stayed for a whole week. Schuré's country house which is still standing lies at the foot of the Mont Sainte-Odile. If you follow the gentle slope of the Vosges mountains with your eye, you will see the ruins of Andlau Castle towering steeply above. In 1906, after the two men had met in Paris in May, Steiner spent some days in Barr in September. A year later, in September 1907, he was there again, this time for a whole week. This was after the Eleusis play had been performed in Munich in Schuré's absence. Naturally they climbed Mont Sainte-Odile together. Edouard Schuré was very involved in occultism, something which was reflected in the popular legends of Alsace and particularly in the Celtic myths and legends. So he had also taken a great interest in the figure of St Odile who lived in the eighth century. On the peak of the Mont Sainte-Odile an extraordinary conversation took place. Schuré kept on talking about St Odile. Rudolf Steiner was silent. Schuré recounted: 'Rudolf Steiner said nothing for a long time. He was sunk in silent reflection or, rather, searching. It was Odile herself whom he sought. Afterwards he said that he had not found her here, but rather, could follow her better where she turned in her flight from her father, in Arlesheim in Switzerland.' This was the first mention of the landscape in which the Goetheanum would later be built. Apart from that there was no talk of Dornach or Arlesheim at that time. But it is clear that Rudolf Steiner had already gone there from Basle.

*

Through Schuré, who was twenty years older, Rudolf Steiner came in contact with a new world, that of Richard Wagner. The young Steiner had not had a particularly high opinion of Richard Wagner. In Vienna he had been repelled in particular by the fuss in the circle of Wagnerians, although Friedrich Eckstein, who had made a pilgrimage to Bayreuth as a young man of twenty-one and whom Steiner was indebted to as he himself admitted, belonged to this group.* This time, in the encounter with Edouard Schuré, things were different. Schuré was a Wagnerian, but then again he was not one, having a free relationship to the composer. He did not see in him the writer or composer, but from the start saw the occultist, the seeker after an esoteric Christianity, and Rudolf Steiner immediately joined in this approach. In August 1906, after the meeting in Paris, he went to Bayreuth with Schuré in order to take part in the festival. It is not certain whether this was exclusively Schuré's initiative, but how things then turned out may be karmically important. In 1907 Steiner was in Bayreuth again, but this time he did not attend the festival, but was more interested in studying the milieu and the surroundings more intently. Around the time of this meeting important links were made in Steiner's destiny.

We need to cast a brief glance at the previous course of Edouard Schuré's life. He was born in 1841, so that when he first saw Rudolf Steiner he was already in his mid sixties. When he was 24 (1865), he remained in Munich after finishing his studies and there experienced the première of *Tristan and Isolde,* having previously studied the subject in depth. He attended all the performances which took place at the time and was deeply impressed by what accompanied them in the form of occult echoes from ancient Celtic spirituality. He also came into contact with Richard Wagner. But he encountered him as someone who was already crushed. A year before, the nineteen-year-old newly crowned King Ludwig II had called Richard Wagner to Munich, wishing to build a festival hall there for him. While the premiere of Tristan was taking place, at the instigation of the Bavarian ministers and the incensed public, the king unfortunately had to withdraw all the promises that he had made to Wagner. This was also the reason that only four performances of Tristan were given. Although the first meeting took place under such a dark cloud, the personal relationship between Wagner and Schuré must have been an important one. Schuré met the great man on two other occasions, the last time in Bayreuth in 1876, at the opening of the festival hall which had not come about in Munich.

---

* See Volume 1, Chapters 2 and 3.

So this had happened once before: a festival hall was to have been built in Munich and had to move to Bayreuth, just as decades later another such building was to be built in Munich and had to move to Dornach. Forty-one years elapsed between the premiere of *Tristan* which Schuré witnessed as a twenty-four-year-old in Munich and his first meeting with Rudolf Steiner in Paris. But Schuré did make the transition from Munich to Dornach in an amazing way. When it came to the building plan he took a keen interest in Rudolf Steiner's project because his plays were also to be performed there. He recognized a continuation of his own basic impulse, but on a higher level — an elevation of the entire life's work of Richard Wagner who had been the first 'great master' for him before Rudolf Steiner became his teacher. He did not come to Dornach at first. He was not present when the foundation stone was laid in September 1913. And during the war, when people of opposing nationalities worked together on the Goetheanum building, the tragic estrangement had occurred. But then, in 1922 when he was 81, Schuré did manage to overcome his resistance and took part in what was called the 'French course' in Dornach in September. He engaged in conversation with Steiner walking to and fro in front of the building, three months before the fire which destroyed the Goetheanum. The picture of the enthusiastic old man left a lasting impression on all those who saw him in Dornach at that time.

The figures who appear to us here show a purpose. A spiritual impulse arose from the circle around Richard Wagner which was aimed at a theatre for the mysteries. In this mystery drama impulse one of their number recognized the fundamental ideal of his own life. Through Richard Wagner's creativity, Schuré was encouraged to write mystery dramas himself and gave his full support to the plan for a building which then came into being in Bayreuth. In his striving for true European occultism and esoteric Christianity he actually reached beyond Richard Wagner. He himself could not achieve what he finally had in mind, but he witnessed the fulfilment which Rudolf Steiner gave this impulse in the creation of the mystery dramas and the Goetheanum.

The relationship between Steiner and Schuré hints at a mysterious swing of the pendulum between Mont Sainte-Odile and the hill in Dornach. In future discussions we shall attempt to go into more detail about how the karmic ground referred to here is connected to the spiritual landscape of the Grail. Not in the sense of a castle of the Grail in physical terms, but as part of the scene of those events connected with the Grail in the ninth century which are concealed in the legend of Parsifal. A century after St Odile, something of the destiny of Parsifal resonated in the area between the hill in Dornach and Mont Sainte-Odile. Rudolf Steiner came into contact with this karmic source as a result of the meeting with Edouard Schuré. This flowed beneath the surface into the mystery dramas and the plan for the building. As things progressed towards the laying of the foundation stone and each day brought new insights, it is moving to imagine how Steiner also had figures from the Grail legend before him with whose karma his own spiritual mission was closely connected. He spoke about the intermediate incarnations of Aristotle and Alexander the Great in the ninth century before they were reincarnated in the Dominican order in the thirteenth century: 'as unnoticed, unknown figures who died young in a corner of Europe which was, nevertheless, important for anthroposophy ... as it were only looking briefly through a window at western civilization ...' According to verbal statements by Steiner, the Grail legend contains poetic images of these two silent figures from the ninth century in the characters of Schionatulander and Sigune.

In the Leipzig Christmas cycle, *Christ and the Spiritual World and the Search for the Holy Grail*, Steiner mentioned several personal spiritual experiences which belong here. In the fifth lecture (January 1, 1914), he recounted how once, when looking at Michelangelo's *Pietà* in St Peters Church in Rome, an important insight arose about the mystery of the Grail. It was as though he could see through the sculpture to the scene in which Parsifal comes across Sigune who holds the dead bridegroom Schionatulander on her lap close to Trevrizent's hermit's cave. As Steiner mentioned in private conversations, it was this scene which led to the landscape of the Dornach building, to the caves in the Hermitage near Arlesheim, where St Odile fled from her father in the eighth century.

*

The third London karma lecture (August 27, 1924) can throw a light on the theme of the confluence of the historical stream coming from the East characterized by the four Gospels and the microcosmic Lord's

Prayer, and the stream from the West in which the elements of the Fifth Gospel and the macrocosmic Lord's Prayer point the way. This lecture describes a spiritual event in the ninth century which is of importance for the future of humankind. Around 869, an encounter took place above the heads of human beings. The cosmic impulse of the Christ sun, as it had worked before Christ's incarnation on earth and as it remained alive in north and west Europe in a particular way, especially in the activities of Arthur's Knights of the Round Table, united itself with the historical Christian movement coming from the events described in the four Gospels.

> So on the one hand we have the story of the Mystery of Golgotha, legible in the book of nature for those who were able to read it, working from the West to East. It represented, as it were, the science of the higher graduates of King Arthur's Round Table. And on the other hand we have a stream flowing from East to to West, not in wind and wave, in the air and water, not over hills or in rays of the sun, but flowing through the blood, through the hearts of humankind, on its course from Palestine through Greece into Italy and Spain.
>
> Two streams which approach one another. The *pre-Christian* Christ stream — almost as though etherized — the *Christian* Christ stream. One later became known as the *Arthurian stream;* the other became known as the *Grail stream.*

A tragic shadow of this light fell on earth at the eighth ecumenical council of Constantinople which denied the spirit. A bright clear unbroken ray from this light illuminated the moment in which Parsifal (who had previously been one of the company of Arthurian knights) as the Grail king held aloft the holy chalice above which the dove of the Holy Spirit appeared.

The confluence of the Arthurian stream and the Grail stream in the ninth century was a preparation for the confluence in which the macrocosmic Lord's Prayer sounded from the Fifth Gospel for the first time.

It is often related that Steiner referred to Richard Wagner as the reincarnation of Merlin, the inspirer and teacher of the Arthurian knights. In any case, in Wagner's compositions the mythical magic returned in the form which the Arthurian stream possessed before its confluence with the Grail stream. Lohengrin and Parsifal express a great longing for the Grail, a presentiment of esoteric Christianity.

Edouard Schuré had such a sure sense for esoteric Christianity in his soul that, by becoming a pupil of Richard Wagner, he reached beyond him. The Grail nature had clearly won predominance over the Arthurian element in him. This made him able to recognize Rudolf Steiner and his message and to be able to offer important support to the creations which in a present-day metamorphosis bring about the full synthesis between the West and East.

12

The Structure of the Karma Lectures

It is no small task to survey the karma lectures, one of the last great bequests by Rudolf Steiner. It would probably take the rest of our life to comprehend in full measure the kind of superhuman intentions that prevailed in the nine months after the Christmas Conference of 1923, while Rudolf Steiner still lectured. Let us feel our way toward this powerful complex of lectures.

Though it was evident that he had to struggle for physical strength throughout this whole time, in the following nine months he gave more than 350 lectures. Then on September 28, 1924 with his last remnant of energy Rudolf Steiner gave his farewell address. Among these lectures, the 83 karma lectures have special significance. Almost all the lectures given in those days for the members of the Anthroposophical Society were dedicated to this theme. They not only dealt with interesting revelations concerning historical relationships, but Rudolf Steiner was at pains to mould and shape the people who listened to him, as well as those who would come to this later — in other words, us. Never more than in the karma lectures, he did everything to train us to penetrate so deeply into the roots of our own being through cognition that finally we would be able to grasp our own eternal destiny, our most sublime purpose. He spoke to us specifically as anthroposophists, as human beings united through a spiritual life imbued with reality as if through a common blood stream.

In order to focus on the starting points that led to this undertaking, let us look at the two events of historical importance. Like pillars at the gateway of a newly ascending development of humankind, they are the Goetheanum fire at the close of 1922, and the Christmas Conference at the end of 1923. The flames that consumed the first

Goetheanum, this temple-building of new spiritual-artistic creation, burned away the curtain through which the vision must penetrate that Rudolf Steiner opened up to us with the karma lectures. It was this tragic irreplaceable loss that made it possible for him to conclude his lifework with such a sublime bequest. We have to relate the karma lectures of 1924 to the developments of 1923.

When the first anniversary of the Goetheanum fire occurred, Rudolf Steiner said during the Christmas Conference how significant streams of humankind's past had become visible in the flames soaring into the sky. Those ancient mystery streams which are to resurrect through anthroposophy opened up. What first became visible through the transparency of these flames was also a conflagration of a temple, namely the fire, started by Herostratus, of the Temple of Diana at Ephesus during the night in which Alexander the Great was born. Earlier, Rudolf Steiner had spoken many times of these themes. Prior to the Goetheanum fire, he had striven unceasingly for the renewal of what once lived in the ancient mysteries, particularly those of Ephesus. But as the transparency of the two temple fires arose, a breakthrough occurred. Something of the substance of the old mystery streams flowed directly into the present time.

There are essentially two streams — characteristic already of the mysteries of Ephesus — that dominate the lectures of 1923. Just as it was the main purpose of the mysteries of Ephesus to nurture the Logos-secrets of the world, distinguished in the mysteries of the Micrologos and the Macrologos, we now note two themes that, like a silver and a golden thread, unite in *one* braid. Where the great rhythms and sounds of the cosmic word appear behind nature's veil, the mysteries of the Macrologos become visible. Here, the spiritual beings that work creatively in all the kingdoms of nature show themselves ever more clearly. Tracing the direction of the Macrologos led Rudolf Steiner to present the mysteries of the year — those of the great festivals that contrast with each other, Easter and Michaelmas, Christmas and St John's Day — quite differently from the way he had earlier. The mysteries of the Micrologos concern the spiritual force that shapes the microcosm — that is the human being — as the replica of the macrocosm. And it is here that the second thread weaves through the revelations of 1923. It emerges when life between death and a new birth is described in ever new forms, when vistas open into the realms forming destiny from which human beings originate.

To view the theme of the Micrologos as it unfolded through 1923 into 1924, we must for a moment look back to the time preceding the burning of the Goetheanum. As we have seen from the course of Rudolf Steiner's life, we find that with everything new that is brought from the spiritual world, the key points of the previous path are once again brought in a new light. Looking back through the pain of the soaring flames, the brief period during which the first Goetheanum served Rudolf Steiner's work can be surveyed. After its construction over seven years, the first Goetheanum was in use only for two and a quarter years, from the opening day on September 26, 1920 until New Year's Eve of 1922/23.

The substance of these twenty-seven months was perhaps concentrated as in a focal point in the days when the French Course took place. This was in September 1922, three months before the fire, when Rudolf Steiner gave the lecture series *Philosophy, Cosmology and Religion*. Many guests from France were present, among them Edouard Schuré. This overcame much bitterness and ill will from the past and signified Schuré's reconciliation with Rudolf Steiner. It was always a specially festive atmosphere when, in the evening, Rudolf Steiner gave his lectures in the packed great hall of the Goetheanum, each time in three parts which were translated by the French journalist Jules Sauerwein.

Perhaps I may be permitted to inject a personal recollection. During the same days when, in the evenings, the lectures of the French Course were given downstairs in the great hall, we were gathered in a small room located high in the building, called the White Hall. Here Rudolf Steiner helped to bring into being what led to the birth of the ritual and the whole religious work of the Christian Community. He was really in our midst the whole day; we were, so to speak, in another world with him. We could hardly grasp how it was possible that, aside from everything that he bestowed upon our future work, he was able to do so many other things. Every morning he would even bring neatly written notes of the lecture he intended to give that evening, for the translator to study during the day.

In the lectures of the French Course, the cosmic spheres, through which the human soul passes between death and a new birth, were presented in a special way. It became clear how all striving after cosmological knowledge, both religious striving on one hand and philosophical insight on the other, has its origin in our journey through these spheres radiating into our earthly life. In all insight and knowledge transcending the merely earthly, we constantly draw from the realm in which we have lived between death and a new birth. Perhaps one can say that Rudolf Steiner's words during the days of the French Course were in most intimate accord with the architectural forms of the first Goetheanum. In these days, temple architecture truly became the vessel for descriptions of supersensory temple forms. For those who were present at the birth of the ritual, it was understandably a special event to be permitted to pass back and forth, as it were, between two realms. The uniqueness of the first Goetheanum may well have been clearly experienced during other occasions also. But during these days, this wonder revealed itself in cosmic dimensions.

Therefore, I feel that in 1923, the Micrologos description of the development of man between death and a new birth always had some connection with the lectures of the French Course. Rudolf Steiner himself often pointed out this connection. In 1923, the description of the Micrologos mysteries was continued primarily in lecture cycles given elsewhere: in Oslo in May 1923, *Man's Being, his Destiny and World Evolution;* in Penmaenmawr in August, *Evolution of Consciousness;* finally in November in the Hague, *At Home in the Universe, Exploring our Suprasensory Nature.*

During the weeks before Christmas, the two threads — the Macrologos, the lectures on the course of the year, and the Micrologos, the lectures concerning the life after death — were intensely woven together in the sequence of the two lecture series, *Harmony of the Creative Word* and *Mystery Knowledge and Mystery Centres.* The mysteries of Ephesus, Eleusis, Samothrace and Hibernia are presented vividly. It is clear evidence of what has become newly visible through the flames of the Goetheanum fire.

The lectures during the Christmas Conference itself, *World History and the Mysteries in the Light of Anthroposophy,* summarize the presentations given throughout that year: the mysteries of the Macrologos and of the Micrologos. Man enters history, and in this cycle we have the nucleus for revelations brought in the karma lecture that run through

12. THE STRUCTURE OF THE KARMA LECTURES

the whole of 1924. Themes which a decade earlier Rudolf Steiner had introduced in his 'karma lectures' in Stuttgart 1910/11, *Occult History*, emerge anew. The karmic relationships between Gilgamesh and Eabani in the Babylonian era, and those between Alexander and Aristotle in the Greek age are unveiled. The paradigm, the representative example, of the stream of destiny that we are to relate to ourselves as anthroposophists is described. These are not relationships of destiny between just any persons of the past, we are dealing with our own destiny.

Now, however, we must speak of a third thread, which runs through 1923, because otherwise we cannot fully comprehend why, for the crowning of his lifework, Rudolf Steiner decided on the karma lectures. We have often tried to make clear how, between the Goetheanum fire and the Christmas Conference, he untiringly appealed to the members of the Anthroposophical Society to do their part in actually reorganizing the Society. It was to demonstrate whether the people who had come together as anthroposophists now truly possessed the social energy to turn their spiritual community into a social factor, to find forms in which it would be possible to show a cultural unity and strength that would command the respect of the public, especially in view of the antagonism at that time.

We know that finally Rudolf Steiner took the responsibility upon himself and did what he had hoped the members of the Society would do. We were then unable to summon the strength to form a real Society out of our own initiative. It therefore belongs to the spiritual-social culmination of his lifework that in the end he placed himself completely within the earthly karma of the Anthroposophical Society. He assumed the office of president and inaugurated a society structure that was on one hand to be permeated through and through by the new, current spirituality, and on the other, stand before the world in powerful and solid unity. The karma lectures must be understood as emerging in no small part out of Rudolf Steiner's struggles of the year 1923. Why, in these lectures, did Rudolf Steiner not lay bare the roots of just any other courses of destiny, but instead our very own destiny? As we have mentioned, it had to be his goal to awaken a deeper consciousness in those who gathered around him, an awareness that penetrates to the realm of the spiritual sources that have led us together. If his students follow into the deeper layer, where they find their own as well as the destiny of others, then this will give birth to forces which build society.

Thus, I believe, the bequest of the karma lectures emerges directly from the substance of the three themes of the year 1923: the teachings concerning the Macrologos and the Micrologos, and also the impulses for the future of the Society.

*

January 25	Berne: The Gate of the Moon and the Gate of the Sun (in Vol. 6*)
Variations:	Dornach: January 27
	Zurich: January 28 (in Vol. 6)
	Stuttgart: February 6 (in Vol. 6)
Feb 16–March 23	Dornach: 12 Lectures (Vol. 1)
March 29–April 5	Prague: 4 Lectures (in Vol. 5)
April 6	Dornach: One Lecture (in Vol. 2)
April 9	Stuttgart: One Lecture (in Vol. 6)
April 12	Dornach: One Lecture (in Vol. 2)
April 16	Berne: One Lecture (in Vol. 4)
April 23–May 18	Dornach: 9 Lectures (in Vol. 2)
May 23–May 25	Paris: 3 Lectures (in Vol. 5)
May 29–May 30	Dornach: 2 Lectures (in Vol. 2)
June 1	Stuttgart: One Lecture (in Vol. 6)
June 4	Dornach: Whitsun lecture
June 7–June 15	Breslau: 9 Lectures (Vol. 7)
June 22–June 29	Dornach: 3 Lectures (in Vol. 2)
July 1–July 13	Dornach: 6 Lectures (in Vol. 3)

――――――

July 18–July 20	Arnhem: 3 Lectures (in Vol. 6)
July 28–August 8	Dornach: 5 Lectures (in Vol. 3)
August 12–August 21	Torquay: 3 Lectures (in Vol. 8)
August 24–August 27	London: 3 Lectures (in Vol. 8)
Sept. 5–Sept. 23	Dornach: 10 Lectures (Vol. 4)
September 28	Dornach: Last Address

* Vol. 1–8 refer to the English editions of *Karmic Relationships*.

12. THE STRUCTURE OF THE KARMA LECTURES

In this timetable, some lectures given in January and the beginning of February, appear as a kind of 'prelude.' It was only on February 16, 1924 that the karma lectures actually began. But the lecture in Berne on January 25, entitled 'The Gate of the Moon and the Gate of the Sun,' belongs with them as a preparation. This lecture exists in four versions. The second version originated on January 27 in Dornach as the third lecture in the book *Anthroposophy, an Introduction*. A third version on January 28 in Zurich has been published (in English) in volume six of *Karmic Relationships*. And finally we heard Rudolf Steiner on this theme in the first karma lecture in Stuttgart on February 6, 'The Significance of the Heavenly Bodies Surrounding the Earth.'

This prelude gives an introductory picture. In the world of the senses there are no analogies to our supersensory nature. At most, in the beholding of the stars we have a sort of dim sense of our etheric organism. But is there not something in the field of our perceptions that indicates our soul and spirit nature? The moon and the sun in the heavens are the two great indicators of the higher levels of our being. Behind the symbol of the moon a world can open up, from which, as though through the gate of the moon, everything representing our own past destiny streams toward us. Everything from earlier lives enters into our present life as 'material of the past' to be worked out; as such it forms the content of our astral body. In the symbol of the sun, on the other hand, that spiritual world is indicated into which we are only just beginning to grow, in which rests our future destiny, the potentials, goals and ideals, towards which we are striving. From both the moonlike karma of the past and the sunlike karma of the future, our present earth life is woven. Encounters occur with people we know from the past; but meetings also take place that are a new beginning. It is indeed possible to distinguish between past and future aspects. Through the balance between moon and sun, past and future karma, the problem of human freedom is resolved. Were we only the products of our earlier incarnations, we would be in the grip of predestination. Due to the fact that our future karma comes to meet us through the portal of the sun, we have the opportunity to freely shape the material of the past. In this prelude-like lecture, everything concerning the stream of the Micrologos as given in the French Course is once again summarized.

In this introductory lecture there is a question concerning the composition in Rudolf Steiner's karma lectures. A greater emphasis is placed on the side of the moon aspect through the extremely vivid description of the great moon teachers — those great spirit beings with whom man deals after death in the moon sphere. It is said of them that they once dwelt on earth, not in physical incarnations, but in etheric bodies. They guided men in ancient times by inspiring them with all the wisdom that they needed to know. Later, these superhuman beings departed from the earth along with the moon. As in a fortress, they now reside on the moon and in the moon sphere. Hence, when man leaves the earth as well as when he approaches it again before a new incarnation, he has to pass these guardians.

In searching for the inner symmetry of this lecture, one cannot but ask, are there perhaps beings on the side of the sun also with whom man can unite? The question remains open. An explanation may perhaps eventually be found for the apparent imbalance in this introductory lecture. Then, in the karma lectures that followed, Rudolf Steiner spoke of how man must learn to see and shape his karma in the light of the sun sphere.

February 16, 1924, the day of the first actual karma lecture, is an important date. After the Christmas Conference, Rudolf Steiner was not only concerned with bringing to life the new, structured and yet completely open form of the Anthroposophical Society. With the greatest possible emphasis and earnestness, he strove to incorporate into the Society as its safeguarding spiritual core the School of Spiritual Science which he intended to build up in three classes. Again and again, he undertook to clarify the fundamental concepts of what he visualized: to guide everything in such a way that — to begin with in a First Class — a properly conscious membership would come into being. And so he repeatedly postponed the start of the First Class of the School until the right moment had come. On February 15, the first Class Lesson was be given. And immediately on the next day, as if only then the preconditions had been fulfilled and the foundation laid, the systematic development of the karma lectures began.

*

From this important moment onward, Rudolf Steiner remained in Dornach for six weeks, not travelling elsewhere. The structure of the Society had first to be built to a certain point on the newly created foundation. Week after week, there were Class Lessons on Friday evenings, karma lectures on Saturdays and Sundays. In six weeks the lectures were held that now comprise the first volume of karma lectures. Clearly the intention was a planned pedagogical sequence. The first six lectures contain general laws inherent in the shaping of destiny; for example, how, in the various kingdoms of mineral, plant, animal, and man, cause and effect relate differently to each other. Further, how love in one life forms the karmic basis for joy in the next life; hate, on the other hand, brings suffering; and how love produces joy and an open mind to the world in a still later incarnation, whereas hate and suffering are followed by dullness of mind as a third karmic phase.

Then all at once, when the second half of this first group of twelve lectures began — to the almost shocked surprise of the audience — Rudolf Steiner started to describe individual historical figures and showed concretely what sort of earlier lives laid the foundation for the present biographies. Individuals such as Friedrich Theodor Vischer who had been professor of aesthetics at the Technical Institute in Stuttgart, or the composer Franz Schubert, appear vividly. And it is not without significance that right away the first examples thus described are of the kind that point back to earlier incarnations in the world of Arabism. At a stroke, a previously unmentioned motif appears: Arabism. Important individuals of contemporary cultural life — from the nineteenth and early twentieth centuries — were described as proceeding from Arabism. Those present felt it was courageous to express all this so concretely. We were not quite sure: what was being done with us? New disclosures followed from one lecture to the next. But Rudolf Steiner not only depicted people who emerged out of Arabism, he also describes individuals who came from medieval Christian and Greek incarnations. Yet emphasis was laid upon the karmic reappearance of Arabism. And very soon afterwards, the example was given which reappears about ten times in the karma lectures, namely Sir Francis Bacon, the great Englishman of the Elizabethan age, the reincarnation of caliph Harun al-Rashid. Here, the advanced Arab culture of Baghdad of the ninth century can be seen streaming into the beginnings of modern scientific development. The following lectures showed that there were two main paradigms: on one side Aristotle and Alexander, on the other Harun al-Rashid and his counsellor, who are subsequently reincarnated as Bacon and Jan Amos Comenius. These two pairs represent the two spiritual-historical mainstreams that battle with each other.

After the initial six weeks, the series of karma studies was continued in Dornach, but the group of lectures that later formed the second volume was subject to numerous interruptions. For from now Rudolf Steiner undertook many journeys to carry the impulse of the Christmas Foundation Conference to other centres, and to ensoul the whole realm of anthroposophical endeavour in East and West with new forces of enthusiasm. Everywhere he travelled, he spoke about karma. In the end, there are nine localities where karma lectures were held: Dornach, Stuttgart, Berne, Paris, Prague, Breslau, then Arnhem in the Netherlands, and two different places in England, Torquay and London. This message, in the nature of a bequest, was spread across Europe. In addition to this, wherever he gave karma lectures, Rudolf Steiner also spoke about individuals belonging to the history of that particular country. In France he used examples of French, in England of English history. In Prague, he spoke of Comenius, in Switzerland of Conrad Ferdinand Meyer and Pestalozzi.

Thus the regular series of karma studies in springtime in Dornach was interrupted by other lectures, among them the Easter cycle in Dornach and the Whitsun lecture of inexhaustible depth — a wonderful karma lecture in itself.

The second series of Dornach lectures began with concrete examples, as did the second half of the first series. Up to this point we still believed that Rudolf Steiner only wanted to show us humanity in a new light; we did not as yet realize that he was referring to us. But then he turned matters around, and karma exercises followed in the middle of the second series. This implied that an anthroposophist must achieve at least the elementary experiences in this area. It does not suffice only to hear of these matters in lectures or read them in books. We ourselves must penetrate into the depths where destiny reveals its truth. Therefore, a number of lectures demonstrate the kind of exercises through which we can reach a point where the physical human being allows the eternal spirit to shine through.

Of the karma lectures given elsewhere, and aside from the nine given in Breslau during the agricultural course in Koberwitz, the three lectures in Paris stand out. They are explicitly tied to the French Course. The journey through the planetary spheres between death and

12. THE STRUCTURE OF THE KARMA LECTURES

a new birth, is characterized again. One of the most magnificent descriptions of life between death and new birth thus comes into being. One can read it only with the greatest enthusiasm. An infinite number of insights dawn upon the reader. It is pictured how, after death, man passes through the moon sphere, then through the Mercury and Venus spheres. Then comes the decisive crossing: entrance into the sun sphere. In the three lower spheres, the human being has to leave behind everything that cannot endure in the eyes of eternity. In some cases it is very little that man still can bring along when he passes through the portal of the sun sphere. Now man no longer has the world around himself, instead he has the cosmos within himself. He has grown as large as the cosmos. The spheres are contained within him, as were lungs and liver during life on earth. Then, after the sun sphere, the passage opens to the further spheres of Mars, Jupiter and Saturn, and after the 'midnight-hour of existence,' the image of the human form arises as a kind of new external world around the human being. It forms itself from the head: from the realm of Mars, the area of the mouth; from Jupiter, that of the forehead; and from Saturn, the shape of the head as a whole — bearer of future speech, thought, and memory.

To perceive the image of man, the divine model, so to speak — according to which the human being can now build his future body in union with the hierarchies of the heavens — this was possible up until the time of the Mystery of Golgotha, because Christ himself was still present in the sun sphere. He helped man to bring to life within his soul the image of man as an orientating, all-encompassing ideal. But at the time of the Mystery of Golgotha, Christ left the sun sphere and united himself with the earth. Henceforth, in his passage through the planetary spheres, the human being depends on having found the connection with the Christ impulse on earth; and only insofar as he has found it can he behold the image of man after death. Only the power of Christ carries him through the upper spheres.

In the karma lectures in Paris, one of the lines of thought of the year 1923 reaches its final and most sublime fulfilment; and now it is also shown how the karma lectures actually deal with the mystery of the sun and a spiritual life through which man attains the strength, already here during his life on earth to make the sun sphere his own.

*

The third volume of the Dornach karma lectures again offers a great surprise. Rudolf Steiner began to describe the karmic origin of those human beings who encounter one another within the anthroposophical movement. With the greatest boldness, but at the same time in a matter-of-fact way, he proceeded to characterize and unveil our own important former earth lives. If until now it had not been clear, it became clear now: these were no neutral historical studies that are given to us; we were told what is to lead us to a more conscious grasp of our own spirit being. To begin with a little tentatively, mention was made of the fact that there are two different major streams that meet in the anthroposophical movement. The members of the *one stream* experienced their last significant incarnation in the first Christian centuries. Therefore, they have already been able to acquire the Christian element in a former life and now, after permeation with the Christian impulse, have a longing for the cosmic element that has been lost in historical Christianity. The members of the *other stream* had their last significant incarnation prior to the Mystery of Golgotha; they therefore bring with them something of the cosmic mood of the ancient mysteries. Now, however, they have the longing to find the Christian mysteries from the cosmic element. Both streams flow into the anthroposophical movement, because there they find what they are seeking. The lectures, to begin with, retained something of an exploratory nature, leaving matters open, and beginning again from different, new directions when naming the centuries under consideration. The statements were not pressed into hard contours; the quality of a gentle touch prevailed, as if the asking, 'Are you following me?'

The lectures of the third volume break into two groups; a fairly long time elapsed between the first six and the following five lectures, and above all, an extremely important incision lies between them. A mood of lofty inspiration and harmony poured into the first group, after the incision, this was replaced by a completely different element.

The harmony can be felt particularly strongly in the description of the School of Chartres where a Christian stream lived which, dwelling within the order of the Cistercians, could still sustain itself from the founts of Platonism. Here Christianity preserved its cosmic connection, its cosmic inwardness, up into the twelfth century.

Something else is added to this indication concerning the centuries in which these two main streams of anthroposophical souls had earlier lives on earth. The destiny that one carries within as an anthroposophist is not only traceable back to earlier incarnations; it is in particular attributable to events experienced jointly in the spiritual world between earth lives. Here for the first time, mention is made of the cosmic ritual which took place in the spiritual world at the end of the eighteenth and the beginning of the nineteenth century, and which has been the source of inspiration for the fruitful Goethean era. The kindling moment in the conversation between Goethe and Schiller in 1794 is pictured: they speak about the archetypal plant and are touched by inspiration, whose fruit in Goethe's case was *The Fairy Tale,* and in Schiller's, the *Letters Concerning the Aesthetic Education of Man.* The light rays of the spiritual world touching them together is the actual source of the friendship between Goethe and Schiller.

A second karma-forming event was the following: after the teachers of Chartres had passed through the portal of death, a supersensible council took place around the year 1200 between the Platonists who had just concluded their earthly life, and the Aristotelians who were just readying themselves to appear on earth as the great Dominicans (Thomas Aquinas and others). Many souls who are today incarnated as anthroposophists were witnesses to this spirit discussion.

The break in the development between the sixth and seventh lectures of the third volume is so decisive that it is marked in the overview of the lectures (page 70) by a line. Today we have the third series of karma lectures 1–6 and 7–11 in one volume. One simply reads on from the sixth to the seventh lecture, perhaps noting that there was an interval of several weeks, during which time Rudolf Steiner travelled to Holland and gave lectures in Arnhem. But if one becomes aware of the unprecedented force that suddenly appears from then on, one begins to understand the whole thing anew. The friends who were in Holland in those days with Rudolf Steiner tell us that on several occasions he was so near the end of his physical strength that they feared for him and were deeply concerned. If this is taken into consideration, one recognizes how, in the three karma lectures in Arnhem, Rudolf Steiner does not side-step the dangers that seem to threaten him, but faces them head-on.

Beginning with Arnhem, the karma lectures assumed a new style. From here on, the theme Michael entered into the karma lectures. Until this point, Michael had not been mentioned; now he appeared like a flash of lightning. To begin with, no longer tentatively, the two major karmic streams are summarized. The stream that received its mark from the first Christian centuries is comprised mainly of Platonic souls, whereas those from the pre-Christian centuries are mostly Aristotelian souls. Also, the terms of 'old' and 'young' souls are applied in regard to the two groups. The old souls have a greater, the young souls a lesser number of incarnations behind them. Everything is presented in condensed form. It now becomes clearly evident that we are concerned with the group of human souls who belong to Michael. A completely new theme! This is why the lectures continue to describe how the supersensible ritual, prior to and after 1800, was not the only preparatory spirit-event for the destiny that today leads one to anthroposophy. Now the sublime spirit gathering is depicted which took place in the fifteenth century above the earth-realm of humankind — the Michael School; but this was opposed by a kind of school of Ahriman below the surface of the earth, which gave rise to the mechanistic civilization and produced, for example, the art of printing. Above the heads of human beings, Michael gathers his own into a great school of teaching, just before the light of ancient spirituality was extinguished, in order to give instruction concerning the great spiritual streams of the history of humankind.

And now, surprisingly, a motif lights up which also has not surfaced until this point in the karma lectures: when, around 1200, the discarnate souls of the Platonists of Chartres and those of the Aristotelians, who then became the Dominicans, deliberated with each other — what were they planning? They agree upon a joint guidance of humankind's destiny that would culminate at the end of the twentieth century. Then the decision must come. And Rudolf Steiner added: from this follows that many of those human beings who have come to anthroposophy in a genuine way will, after a relatively short interval, return to earth in a new incarnation even prior to the end of the century, when the culmination of the great spiritual conflicts of our time will take place.

In Arnhem, the Archangel calendar was also developed for the first time. Seven Archangels take turns in guiding the various ages.

Something of this structure was revealed earlier: in 1879, we passed from an age of Gabriel to an age of Michael. The description continued: up into the last pre-Christian Michael age and for some time afterwards, Michael was the guardian of cosmic intelligence, and as such, from above, could imbue human beings with thoughts out of the spiritual worlds. But then the gods let go of cosmic intelligence and it fell to earth. Human beings must take possession of it. But this is not possible without the Ahrimanic spirits contending for it. Therefore, the present Michaelic age consists of the battle of Michael with the Ahrimanic forces, which the Archangel can only wage through the human beings allied with him.

Returning from Holland to Dornach, Rudolf Steiner retained the new apocalyptic battling style which his descriptions had assumed. Everything resounded in the new Michaelic tone. In Dornach, he again depicted the great Michael School above, in the fifteenth century, in which those human beings who are gathered around Michael listen to the teaching of Michael together with beings of other hierarchies. In Arnhem, the picture of the supersensible Michael School was filled with dramatic tension by virtue of the contrast with the subterranean school of Ahriman. Now, in Dornach, the dramatic, apocalyptic element is intensified by the description of the lightning and thunder of a spiritual thunderstorm accompanying the celestial school of instructions, which is unleashed upon humanity by higher hierarchies. The outpouring of cosmic intelligence finds continuation and intensification in a spiritual fire-storm through which the creative powers of the cosmos give earth-man the final inner structure necessary for the development of modern consciousness. Each one of us carries a sort of reminiscence of that fire storm in the depth of our soul. If we succeed in bringing to life this fire-seed within ourselves, we will find the enthusiasm that we need for anthroposophy.

The apocalyptic element intensifies toward the end of the third volume which includes the vision of the end of the century. Finally, we hear that even among the angels a division will occur. If human beings do not find the connection to the spirit, their angels will fall along with them. Human beings drag whole hierarchies of angels along into the break from the spirit. The Michaelic drama continues on through all the lectures given in Dornach to the beginning of August 1924. In England also, where, during the summer meetings, Rudolf Steiner gives karma lectures in Torquay and London, the apocalyptic Michaelic theme dominates. Here are some quotations from the lecture in Torquay:

> Michael sends his impulses through the evolution of humanity in the sphere of earthly life. He is the bringer of the Sun-forces, the spiritual forces of the sun ... The present rulership of Michael ... signifies that the cosmic forces of the sun penetrate right into the physical and etheric bodies of men ... Christ, the Sun-being, ... has lived since the Mystery of Golgotha in supersensible communion with the world of men. But before the whole mystery connected with Christ can reveal itself to the soul, humankind must become sufficiently mature.

With these belongs the passage, where, speaking about his own life, Rudolf Steiner narrates how, at the time when he wrote his *Philosophy of Freedom*, he experienced Michael's entrance into the ether sphere surrounding the earth, an event that ignited the actual enthusiasm for his lifework. The start of the Michael age was 1879. All appearances to the contrary, we are increasingly entering the sun-filled side of destiny. The Michaelic sun-mysteries of karma face the mysteries of the great moon teachers, creating the balance.

One part of the tenth lecture in the third volume needs special mention here. Within the Michael revelations that are given in these lectures there is a practical hint for our innermost life, something that should warm the heart not only of the young but also of older people. Rudolf Steiner describes that a certain nuance is karmically built into the disposition of those who gather around anthroposophy. He states as a starting point that one can readily observe that for the young people who at that time had graduated from the Waldorf School, life would not become easier but harder because it would be more complicated. One should have no illusions. Through anthroposophy life becomes more difficult, not easier. Why is that? It is because of the law that inner initiative of soul-experience is an indispensable ingredient of an anthroposophist's karma. Rudolf Steiner says that much could be gained if anthroposophists only realized this and took it to heart, but instead, all too often they acted like bees that are afraid to use their sting. Hence initiative gives way to a general fear of life. Many would become ill and would not know where the illness comes from. Illness in anthroposophists often derives from other sources than those of other people. Why are anthroposophists ill so frequently? Because they do not put into use the law of inner initiative, allowing themselves to be pushed into a defensive attitude toward life, into that of the passive consumerism. An anthroposophist cannot afford this. Only with the sting of soul-initiative and constant willingness to confront life does one come to oneself.

*

After the tremendous tension to which the karma lectures rose in the second half of the third volume, the fourth volume poses a certain riddle, inasmuch as the stormy, dramatic element appears at first glance to have been completely replaced by a tranquil, pictorial one. In great images Rudolf Steiner portrayed a number of historical figures: Strindberg, Weininger, Count Hertling, and numerous other persons of history and the present time, all the way to Karl Julius Schröer. In the third volume, Rudolf Steiner spoke specifically of us, of the 'karma of the anthroposophical society and movement.' Was he now moving away from this intimate Michaelic theme in favour of great historical descriptions? One reason this question remains in us throughout all the lectures is because from one day to the next, Rudolf Steiner kept intimating a direct continuation of the subject matter dealt with in the third volume. Thus, he said in the third lecture:

> The dominion of Michael is connected with what the anthroposophical Movement in the deepest sense intends, with what this movement ought to be and do. Thus the events of which I shall speak are not unconnected, as we shall see next time, with the destiny, the karma of the Anthroposophical Society, and hence too with the karma of the great majority of the individual human beings who find themselves within this Society.

The question of how, despite the changed style in the karma lectures, the apocalyptic element evolves during the last period of Rudolf Steiner's work, can be a key that to a profound riddle of destiny.

When Rudolf Steiner returned from England at the beginning of September, a great number of people had gathered in Dornach. Several special courses had been announced that were to be given simultaneously. Groups of actors, either belonging to the movement or close to it, together with those interested in speech formation, awaited the Drama Course. Almost all anthroposophical doctors were present, who, together with the entire group of priests of the Christian Community, had been invited to the Pastoral-Medical Course. Aside from these, many friends from far and wide had arrived for the karma lectures and class lessons that were expected in the evenings.

And now the three weeks began which, not only in anthroposophical history, but in spiritual history in general, was a unique event. On the first day Rudolf Steiner told us, as if he had to apologize for it, that unfortunately he had returned from England very ill. Each day gave four or five lectures, and each time he reached the lecture hall from the car with the greatest physical effort. By the end he had held seventy lectures in this brief timespan. Each one, in the most concentrated form possible, brought so much wealth that what was given in these three weeks alone would contain enough material and tasks for the work of many decades.

As priests of the Christian Community we experienced the breathtaking, far-reaching pace from one day to the next in a particularly clear way, not only because we were invited to all courses and evening lectures, but for another special reason: some time earlier Rudolf Steiner had promised us a course on the Apocalypse of St John. At Easter, when he decided to give the pastoral-medical course for doctors and priests, he told us, 'There will still be time for two or three lectures about the Apocalypse.' Now our course on the Apocalypse started as soon as the Drama Course and the others began. Nothing had been determined beforehand about the length of the courses. After we had received such over-abundance for nearly two weeks day after day, I was given the awkward task of asking Rudolf Steiner how long the courses would continue. After all, we did have congregations in those days that expected their regular Sunday service, and we had already once delayed our return by telegram. Rudolf Steiner answered: 'Please wait a few more days, then it can be determined how long we will continue the courses.' Finally, the Drama Course had grown to nineteen, the Pastoral-Medical Course to eleven, and our course on the Apocalypse to eighteen lectures. It was impossible not to think that this was the farewell, and that Rudolf Steiner still wanted to give as much as was humanly possible.

*

12. THE STRUCTURE OF THE KARMA LECTURES

In this connection and against this background, a direct continuation of the apocalyptic style and motivation of the second half of the third volume certainly was not needed in the content of the remaining karma lectures. In reality, a whole apocalypse of continuing revelation concerning anthroposophical karma is concealed within the ten lectures of the fourth volume. The complete series of special Michael events is entwined into the historical karma portrayals — events that have led from the last pre-Christian to the present Michael age, and that have worked and shaped the souls in the times between death and a new birth; the same souls who now, in our times, find their way to the anthroposophical movement and to the Society.

A solemn sequence of Michael events is brought before our souls. The first highlight contains the part that the followers of Michael — who by and large were not incarnated then on earth — had in the Mystery of Golgotha. They shared in the experience of Christ's departure from the sun: through a twilight of the gods, a *Götterdämmerung*, suffered above, the light then shone into the dark depths. Then, in the ninth century, when the great outpouring of cosmic intelligence from heaven to earth began, the light-filled counter-event to the spirit-negating Council of 869, a celestial council took place that planned the future of exoteric and esoteric Christianity for the centuries in which Ahriman's influence would increase. The third highlight was the spirit conversation between Platonists and Aristotelians around 1200, where the vista opened to the end of the twentieth century. Then followed the great school of instruction by Michael in the fifteenth century, and the supersensible ritual woven of divine imaginations that bestowed its inner sun-quality on Goethe's time. After these preparations, and after the dawn of the new Michael age, anthroposophy came into being as the great gift of Michael, and its culmination was reached during and after the Christmas Foundation.

In two versions, one spoken and one written, Rudolf Steiner put a seal on the bequest that he left us especially in the karma lectures. One is the Last Address which, after twice having to cancel the lecture, he wrested from his failing body on Sunday September 28. The double mystery of John and Michael shone forth in a deeply moving way, seed of countless future perceptions. The invocation of the hierarchies allied with Michael in the concluding Michael verse was at the same time a call to the whole present and future age.

The letters concerning the Michael Mystery that Rudolf Steiner subsequently wrote for us on his sickbed relate to his whole lifework and specifically to the lectures of the last nine months in the same way as does the Apocalypse at the end of the New Testament to the preceding texts. Here, the apocalyptic element, which since Arnhem imbued the karma lectures, continued directly, but in such a way that it must be 'done.' It cannot merely be read and received as a teaching. In the Michael letters, the great intention out of which Rudolf Steiner gave the karma lectures continues. In these letters, Michael works directly on those souls who earnestly try to work with them.

13

Resurrection of the Word — Logos and the Word of Man

Rudolf Steiner's entire lifework stands under the sign of the resurrection of the word. To regain the 'lost word,' to awaken the word that has died, was the core of his life's effort. This all-embracing endeavour led him to coin the expression, 'the Easter Word.'

Let us examine that brief segment in Rudolf Steiner's life, immediately preceding the final crowning event, that brought the decisive impetus regarding the mysteries of the word.

We return to the fateful year between the Goetheanum fire and the Christmas Conference. It stands under the sign of the flames that consumed the first Goetheanum. These flames, however, not only destroyed but also revealed. As the year 1923 drew to a close and the Christmas Conference event was already in the air, Rudolf Steiner described in a lecture (December 2, 1923) how the flames of the burning Goetheanum had become windows to deeper spheres of looking back into spiritual history. In particular, he pointed out the moment when the flames appeared coloured by the melting metals of the organ pipes:

> When we turn to that tragic night, to the flames of the burning Goetheanum, did we not see, do we not still see, the molten metals of the musical instruments? And do we not have the metals of the musical instruments uttering in clear tones their holy speech, enchanting the flames into the most marvellous colours, eloquent colours, colours that speak, colours that are akin to the metals? Through uniting with the metallic element there rises up within us something that is like memory in the earthly sphere.

Through the flames, coloured by the melting metals, a special Akashic record appeared, the 'Fire Akasha of New Year's Eve.' Through the flames of Dornach there appeared the flames of Ephesus, that destroyed of the Temple of Diana. And through those flames in turn the archetypal fire appeared from which the creation itself emerged. To begin with, they became windows to the great Logos mysteries that were nurtured in Ephesus, the mysteries of the Micrologos and the Macrologos, of the human word and of the cosmic word. I should like to recall briefly the essence of a number of lectures. This lecture contains a brief, but most powerful mantric verse sounding forth like a revelation

> Behold the Logos
> In the burning fire;
> Find the answer
> In Diana's House.

December 2, 1923

This magic verse bursts the rocks of the past, and the view becomes clear. We learn how in Ephesus the process of speech was experienced as a window to the archetypal process in which God created the world through the Word. Speech uses the element of air. Air streams upward and downward when something is spoken. It radiates upward to where thought manifests within the word like a phenomenon of light, into the warmth element. Streaming downward from the airy into the watery element, into the human organism, the word becomes feeling. And this process — the word streaming upward to the fire and downward to the watery element — becomes transparent for the very beginning of the earth. Then, however, everything took place at a lower level: the process began in the fluid element, radiating upward into the airy and downward into the solid state. The whole earth was still a fluid globe, and out of the fluid body of the earth, fluid calcium arose in a resounding of the universal Word, in a great cosmic symphony. It evaporated, in so far as one can speak of evaporation then, into the albumen atmosphere, which was also still fluid, and only later would evolve into the airy element. However, as the element of calcium thus rose into the albumen atmosphere, a new level of existence began below through precipitation: solid calcium formed the skeleton of the animals. The skeletal structure of the animal kingdom is, so to speak, the first coagulated cosmic sound. The Word, the Logos, became an actual fact on earth. The solid element separated out of the fluid element.

In the Micrologos, in human speaking, we find a process that begins in the element of air, radiating upward to warmth and light and downward to the element of water. In the Macrologos, the resounding of the archetypal Word, we find a process that occurs one level lower: in the element of water, radiating upward into the nascent atmospheric element and downward into the nascent solid element. In the earth's ancient past, we find the condition of which it can truly be said that the cosmic mystery is *heard*. It is a process that resounds, that expresses itself in tones. As an illustration, Rudolf Steiner related how he once visited a museum of natural history in Trieste and looked at the skeletons of antediluvian animals. This, he said, had been a musical experience for him; through the forms of the bone structure of such prehistoric creatures, the archetypal resounding tones, the creative Word, the Macrologos that is *the* creative force of the earth, could still be discerned.

He then described how the sound that ascends from the fluid to the airy, which simultaneously brings about the solid substance, the earth's ground, is like a great cosmic question. And the cosmos answers this cosmic Word with cosmic thought. Along with this, the silica element trickles into the calcium process, and the foundation of the plant kingdom is thereby implanted in the newly arising ground of the earth.

This is one of those powerful lectures that should be studied not merely for content; we can become sensitive to Rudolf Steiner's indication that a pain-filled moment of destiny opened vistas more clearly for him, the 'Fire Akasha of New Year's Eve.'

Through the whole year of 1923, unlocked by the key of that night of conflagration, runs the theme of the Word, the Logos. We need only think of the lectures on music that Rudolf Steiner gave for the teachers of the Waldorf School (March 7 and 8) in Stuttgart, and of the significant lecture which he added in Dornach, 'The World of the Hierarchies and of Tones' (March 16). During this year, he unveiled the secrets of music. We need mention further only the lecture that he gave in the week before Easter at the educational conference in Stuttgart,

'Sounding of Syllables and Speaking of Words' (March 29). In it Rudolf Steiner attempted to pierce through the prose into which the whole mystery of the word had fallen. He showed how one must take hold again of the syllable within the word, in order to set the Logos free.

We can also recall how in the fourth lecture on the seasons of the year, given at Easter, Rudolf Steiner described the mystery of midsummer, thereby pointing to the secret of the song of birds. The secret of the birds chirping and singing in midsummer is that the sounds ascend into the spiritual world and then return as the formative forces that sculpt the body of the bird. A similar principle was true to human life in ancient times, when the festival of the summer solstice was celebrated with great ritualistic roundelays and musical performances. The purpose of these festive sounds at the highpoint of the year was to call down upon man a celestial echo, namely the premonition of the I, the dream of the I. Through those ecstatic celebrations in music and song, ancient humanity experienced the first contact with the I of the single human being.

These are only examples of how the secrets of sound, of the Logos, run through the year 1923. The titles of some of the lectures indicate this fact. The June lectures, *The Arts and their Mission*, bear the subtitle, 'The Genius of Language and the World of Revealing Radiance.' Rudolf Steiner's creative activity revolved around this theme day after day up to the lecture cycle, *The Harmony of the Creative Word*, in October and November 1923. The title of this cycle refers particularly to the ninth lecture, which describes, among other things, how, out of the kingdoms of nature, the elemental beings — gnomes, undines, sylphs, and fire beings — speak in unison and together constitute the Logos. They are the constituents of the Logos, and man is the concentration of this many-tongued cosmic speaking. Just as in spirit the Logos comprises the resounding voice of the universe, so man on earth is the symphony of the cosmic Word.

*

I would like now to select a number of lectures from the second quarter of that year that show how the new creative contact with the Logos mystery is at the same time the source in the following year for the crowning achievement of Rudolf Steiner's lifework: the whole series of karma lectures.

It is interesting to note that these lectures, which, as it were, unfold the karma mystery out of the *Logos mystery*, were not given systematically in Dornach. In Dornach, Rudolf Steiner began the theme and developed it further when he spoke to members elsewhere. The following lectures belong to this group:

Dornach	March 11/12	*The Driving Force of Spiritual Powers in World History* (lectures 1 & 2)
Berne	April 6	'The Forming of Destiny in Sleeping and Waking'
Dornach	April 13	'The Recovery of the Living Source of Speech'
Prague	April 28	'Three Stages in the Waking of the Human Soul' (lecture 1)
Stuttgart	May 2	'The Individualized Logos'
Oslo	May 18	'Man's Being, his Destiny, and World Evolution' (lecture 3)
Berlin	May 23	'The Riddles of the Inner Human Being'
Stuttgart	June 21	'Our Thought Life in Sleeping and Waking'
The Hague	Nov 18	*At Home in the Universe* (lecture 5)

Something really new began when Rudolf Steiner gave the lecture of March 11 in Dornach. His emphatic efforts toward a living reorganization of the Society had evolved to a first stage during the Stuttgart meeting of delegates. The basic lectures given in Stuttgart, 'The Principles of Forming Communities' (February 27 and 28) were offered again in Dornach in more elaborate form (March 2 and 4). Now, in the lectures, 'The Driving Force of Spiritual Powers in World History,' he began anew.

March 11 and 12, 1923

The following is a brief summary of the contents. Our life does not consist only of what is ordinarily designated as our biography, namely, the sequence of days. An equally important biography consists of the sequence of nights, namely, those segments of life that we spend asleep. What do we find in this second biography? Here he focused on the following significant secret: when with the onset of sleep the astral body and the I emerge from the physical and etheric bodies, the astral body in particular contains the after-effects of what the human being has spoken during the day. The echo of the words spoken during the day is carried aloft during the night by the astral body. In the night biography, man must use as speech the soul-spiritual essence of what he spoke during the day; during the nights, he must come into conversation with the Archangels. The Archangels await what the astral bodies of sleeping human beings bear toward them as the soul-and-spirit content of all that was spoken during the day. If this soul-and-spirit substance is meagre, there can be little contact between the human soul and the Archangels. The less we bring with us of the soul-spiritual after-effects of our spoken words, the less we are regenerated by creative contact with the Archangels. To the degree to which we bring such after-effects, we find ourselves during the night in a creative, regenerative exchange with the Archangels. If, however, we have been unable to imbue with idealism the words we have spoken during the day, if we have allowed ourselves to be overwhelmed by what spreads so rapidly today into all spheres of life, so that only the dead buzzing and noise of the mineral and vegetable worlds extend into our speech, then our soul has no wings at night. It is deaf and mute to the spiritual world. In his verses and meditations we find a mantric formulation, which, although Rudolf Steiner did not give it in the lecture itself, he obviously recorded in direct connection with it. It is dated March 1923.

> In the present earth-time,
> Man needs anew
> Spiritual content for the words of his speech;
> For from speaking
> Soul and spirit retain,
> For the period of sleeping
> Sojourn outside the body,
> What from the word points to the spiritual.
> For sleeping human beings must
> Arrive at an exchange
> With the Archangeloi.
> They, however, take up only spirit content,
> Not material content, of the words.
> If man misses this exchange,
> He suffers damage to his whole being.

Here a new thread has been added to the loom.

The second lecture of the same cycle offers a supplement, although only in the form of a first glimpse. Just as we live during the day in the three kingdoms of nature — mineral, plant, and animal — so sleeping human beings live in three elementary kingdoms. From there they look up longingly to the hierarchies, because they wish to be nourished by them. Rudolf Steiner described how today sleeping human beings actually long for the Archai, the primordial forces, and how they are increasingly incapable of coming into contact with the Archai during the night.

What is the task of the Archai? They cause human beings to enter their body properly on waking. Human beings today move further and further from the Archangels because of the coarsening of their speech. They are thus increasingly unable to find contact with the Archai at night and therefore can no longer properly take hold of their bodies on awakening. As an example of this, Rudolf Steiner mentioned Goethe, who as a young man suffered particularly from not being able to achieve this Archai-contact. This is why he had to go to Italy. The journey to Italy was the jolt he needed to come at night into a productive relationship with the archetypal forces. Upon awakening, he could then properly take hold of his body again and unfold the unique Jupiter-nature of his creativity. We are told that the human being can improve their relationship with the Archai only if they acquire quite definite, inner activity and initiatives and turn them into lifelong habits.

April 6, 1923

Let us now follow the thread as it continues to develop. During the week of Easter, the previously mentioned lectures on the course of the year were given in Dornach. Between his lectures, Rudolf Steiner travelled to several towns in Switzerland, making use of the attention that had been aroused in the general public by the Goetheanum fire, speaking on 'What was the Aim of the Goetheanum and What is the Aim of Anthroposophy?' On the evening preceding the public lecture in Berne, he gave the lecture to members that we shall now summarize. He called what he gave there a 'karmic study.' The theme of the following year appeared clearly on the horizon.

Rudolf Steiner described how, at the beginning of life, the human beings sleep their way into incarnation. In the first three years, after all, they are not fully awake in the sense that they are later on. In this early dream state, they bring the endowment and sustenance of the spiritual worlds into earthly life. What they thus bring from pre-earthly existence and weave into their physical existence, though obscured to them, can be observed in the way the child learns first to walk, then to speak, and finally to think. As the description of the trinity of walking, speaking, and thinking unfolds, an important moment of revelation is referred to, namely, the theme of the lectures given in Copenhagen in 1911, which formed the basis of the book, *Spiritual Guidance of the Individual and Humanity*. Walking, speaking, thinking — these are the basis, as it were, of education. Learning to walk encompasses many elements: learning to stand upright, finding a sense of balance, perfecting the manifold uses of the hands. From the spiritual world something is brought that is recast into an earthly capacity through learning to walk. Out of this ability to walk, the child then learns to speak. This can afterward be traced in the intonation of the voice, the rhythm of the word. Learning to walk continues in learning to speak. Learning to think emerges finally not from thought but from the spoken word. As the child learns to talk, the seed for the capacity of thinking also develops.

Now the investigation continues. When with the onset of sleep the astral body and the I loosen themselves from the physical and etheric bodies, the astral body carries aloft the soul-spiritual essence of the spoken word and the I bears aloft the soul-spiritual essence of every bodily movement, every action, every deed. The feelings with which man has accompanied his actions during the day — contentment or discontent — are carried into the higher world by the I (in the same way that the astral body carries the soul-spiritual essence of the spoken word). If idealism has pulsed through the word, conversation arises between the human being and the Archangels. Insofar as human actions were imbued with love of one's fellow human being and concern for the other person, the I attains a relationship with the Archai. From this exchange with the Archai, the I derives the strength to penetrate and take hold of the physical body upon waking. Man is a free being and can be in control of himself if, during the nights, he has brought his I close enough to the Archai to have received strength from them.

Rudolf Steiner states clearly that while the I rests at night within the arms of the Archai, karma is formed. The contentment (or discontent) taken along each night produces the strength for the shaping of karma. This strength is gathered for that realm that is traversed after death. When man later enters anew into incarnation, the process of learning to *walk* demonstrates how much positive contact with the hierarchy of the Archai he has had in his last life through his love for his fellow human beings. Here, many hints are given for educators: how, through observation of toddler's learning to walk — whether they remain upright or tumble over again and again, and so on — and hence, through the child's development of the nascent capacity for movement, the moral substance of the last life on earth can be deciphered. It is as if the love or the hate with which man in his earlier incarnation permeated his bodily activities, actions and deeds, emerges in the way in which a child learns to walk. And the way in which a human being learns to *speak* in childhood corresponds to the life between death and a new birth, now referring back to the nights of the previous earthly life. The human being weaves his karma during the nights, but he only harvests in the nights what has been accomplished in the day through permeating speech, as well as action, with soul and spirit. Into what the Archangels and Archai give human beings, the higher hierarchies also pour their influence. The *voice of conscience* is thereby implanted into human speaking and inner experience.

Finally, a third aspect is considered. We have spoken of walking and speaking, but what is the situation regarding thinking? Thinking belongs to the etheric body, which remains connected with the physical body at night and is not carried into the higher worlds. This means that man can learn to exist in thinking without the help of the higher worlds and thus attain freedom; whereas in feeling and will, the spheres of speech and of action, he depends on the Archangels and Archai in order to weave freedom into his karma.

April 28, 1923

After Easter, Rudolf Steiner was in Prague. There, in the lecture, 'Three Stages in the Awakening of the Human Soul,' he presented a simplification of the panorama shown in the preceding lectures: man sleeps his way into life during the first three years of life and brings the extract of his karma into the processes of learning to walk, to speak, and to think. How does it happen that on earth he learns to think? It is the fruit of his living exchange with the Angels during the time between death and a new birth. There he communicated with the Angels in a direct thought-language, and thus, when he enters into life and as a child learns out of the experiences of walking and speaking to think, he is inspired, as it were, by his own past association with the Angels. When he learns to speak, which concerns his rhythmic system, he benefits from the relationship he had before his birth with the Archangels. And when he learns to walk — as the 'I' brings about the upright gait — he benefits from his association before birth with the Archai. 'For my thinking, I thank the Angeloi; for speech I thank the Archangeloi; for my being placed into earthly existence in accordance with physical and moral forces I thank the Archai.'

Now that walking, speaking, and thinking have been considered as they originate in the world before birth, our attention is directed to how they present themselves in the condition of sleep. When the human being falls asleep, the conceptual life becomes dim, speech is silenced, action is at rest. As thinking grows dim, man draws near to the Angels in sleep and this to the extent that he has been idealistic, inclined toward the spirit, in his thinking during the day. In a side remark that is most significant for educators, Steiner said in this lecture that the child's thinking, especially that of the very young child, is so filled with spirituality that when the child falls asleep it then shoots, so to speak, straight toward its Angel. The child's soul approaches its Angel as if on the wing; this is due to the spirituality of thought that is as yet untarnished by the adult's mode of thinking. The idealism of thought-life therefore leads to communion with the Angels during the sleeping condition, though unfortunately not to the same degree with adults as with children. Idealistic dispositions and intentions lead to contact with the Archangels; love of one's fellow man leads to contact with the Archai.

If during the night human beings cannot communicate with the Angels through their thinking, with the Archangels through their life of speech, with the Archai through their life of deeds, then Ahrimanic beings appear, and today they gain ever greater power over human beings. The influences on karma take hold because in the first period after death the human life is repeated backward from the end to the beginning, yet it is not the course of the days but of the nights that is recapitulated. Because the life of sleep amounts to approximately one third of the whole life span, the backward life after death also takes up about one third of the lifetime. In clear outlines, we see what causes must be active in order that human beings have the possibility between birth and death, as well as beyond death, to associate with the Angels, Archangels, and Archai. If they do not have that, in a subsequent life they will be born paralysed in thinking, devoid of speech, or paralysed in limbs and moral impulses.

May 2, 1923

The next lecture to be spoken of here is the one given in Stuttgart, 'The Individualized Logos.' The lecture began with the term 'etheric body.' What is the etheric body? Its essence appears more clearly in the sleeping than in the waking human being. It is not as if during the night the etheric body were at rest. On the contrary, its activities are intensified. Where the human being's senses have functioned during the day there are now after-effects; for instance, a phosphorescent radiance in the eyes; a resounding music, a ringing sound, around the organs of hearing and speech; and the skin as a whole radiates streams of warmth within the etheric body. These reflections of day-life in the etheric body of sleeping man are revelations, as if something were mirroring itself in them. The Exousiai, the Spirits of Form, who are also called 'the Revealers,' draw these streams of reflection out of the sleeping etheric body and make use of them for their revelations.

All this concerns the etheric body of the nerve-sense human being. What does the etheric part of rhythmic human being do? Here the etheric body is composed of thought-forms. This is, in fact, the individualization of the thought-forms of the cosmos, contracted into a single entity. This is the 'individualized Logos.' The silent language of universal thought can be read in it; the inner word spoken during the day sounds in reverse once again in the etheric body. Earlier, we spoke of what the astral body carries aloft; here it is a matter of how the spoken word continues its effects at night in the etheric body: it is taken hold of and used by the Dynameis, the Spirits of Movement, the group of beings in the middle of the second hierarchy. And finally the will, the part of the etheric body that relates to action, manifests at night as a counter-spine. The etheric spine is not in the back but in the front; and here, just as the ribs ray out from the physical spine, the streams of the etheric body flow in the same way — although in reverse direction — to this frontal etheric spine on which, as on a staff, the lotus flowers are lined up. This is the revelation sphere of the Kyriotetes, the Spirits of Wisdom. The etheric body of the sleeping human being is thus described in a threefold manner.

Now a further question was raised. How can we approach the essence of the astral body, since the activity that finds its reflections in the sleeping etheric body exists as such also in the astral body? Rudolf Steiner focused our attention on the condition a few days after death, when the etheric body is already laid aside and human beings, who now possess only the astral body as a sheath, begin to live through their past life in reverse order. A length of time equal to one third of the past lifetime is taken to repeat the experiences of the nights from the end of life to the beginning. Here, the distortions and meagreness that a person has carried into the realm of the Angels, Archangels, and Archai, because of his lack of spirituality, are corrected and made good; also everything detrimental that the human being has caused even to the higher hierarchies through inadequate nocturnal discourse with, for example, the Archangels.

When this period of retrospection has ended, the astral body is laid aside, and the human being passes from the soul world into the spirit land. There he is directly surrounded by all kinds of spiritual entities. At first he has only a quite general impression. Rudolf Steiner frequently made use here of the image of a swarm of gnats or midges. As he approaches more closely, however, he discovers that they are all separate entities among whom he too is now accepted as separate being. The universal resounding of the flowing together of all entities, which man at first perceived as a cloud, is the Logos. The human being therefore finds himself in the sphere of the Logos during the most essential part of the time spent on his journey between death and a new birth. As long as the Logos is only understood to mean the sum of all spiritual entities, however, this sphere of the Logos is still illusory. It is not yet something in its own right. Then Rudolf Steiner indicated that only through the Christ event, Christ's passing through the Mystery of Golgotha, has the illusory Logos become the real Logos. Henceforth after death man can experience the whole spiritual world concentrated in one individual being, in the being of Christ.

May 23, 1923

In the third lecture of the cycle given at Whitsuntide in Oslo, 'The Human Being, Human Destiny, and World Evolution,' the whole subject is once again treated in a similar way. On his return trip, Rudolf Steiner passed through Berlin. It was the only time after the Goetheanum fire that he visited Berlin, where earlier he had been able to carry out so much of his work. It is understandable that in his lecture, 'The Riddle of the Inner Human Being. The Approach of the Michael Force,' he referred to the Goetheanum fire and tried to communicate as much as possible of what he had worked out in recent months. He condensed and inserted the essential points of the music lectures, the great stages of evolution: the interval of the seventh in the Atlantean age, the interval of the fifth in the first post-Atlantean age, and the interval of the third in the age now already belonging to the past. In conclusion, there followed a discourse on the Michael festival of which he had also spoken in Oslo.

Still, the essence of the lecture is the continuation of the line of thought traced by us. Much is already familiar: dreamlike sleep of the child during the first three years, learning to walk, to speak, and to think; the after-effects of these three activities during sleep; the more-or-less refreshing exchange with the Archangels regarding his life of speech, with the Archai regarding his actions, with the Angels regarding his life of thoughts. During man's life after death, after having shed the etheric body and while reliving in reverse order his night experiences, the Angels, Archangels, and Archai become his inspirers, just as they were earlier during the nights of his earthly life. But then, when man lays aside the astral body and passes over into the spirit land, he arrives in the realm of the higher hierarchies, bringing with him the results of the triad that expresses itself on earth in walking, speaking, and thinking.

Then follows the time that Rudolf Steiner described as the 'reverse world view.' What is outer world for us on earth when we look out into the cosmos becomes then inner world. And what is inner world here on earth becomes outer world there; for in every organ — liver, heart, and so on — the cosmos is contracted, as it were. Thus we experience the 'riddles of man's inner being' in spirit land. They are now his outer environment. Here, together with the higher hierarchies, he may construct his future human body, which is therefore called a temple of the gods. From images similar to those of our dreams, but much more real, the human being, together with the gods, weaves the prototype of his future body, the image of man that will be implanted as spirit seed into the earthly seed within the mother's womb. In this way the human being passes through the world of creative deeds, which afterward on earth is itself symbolized in the process of learning to walk. In learning to walk, in raising himself upright, in his whole life of actions, the human being experiences the echo and result of the creative construction of the temple of his body that he was allowed to carry out in the spirit land together with the higher hierarchies.

Then the human being reaches a stage in which the creative companionship with the higher beings diminishes. The opposite of what happened just after death now occurs: the multitude of beings again appears as a unity. It is as if one moved away from a swarm of gnats and no longer saw the single entities but only the whole. He thus arrives in the sphere where he experiences the Logos as the sum of all beings. This is the region where cosmic speech implants in him the seed for earthly language. When later he learns to speak, this is again a symbolizing imitation of what he has undergone within the realm of the Logos during this advanced phase between death and new birth. And only when he has traversed this sphere as well, does he, in the last period before birth, reach the point of drawing his etheric body together. This stage is afterward expressed in the process of the child's learning to think.

In the Berlin lecture, Rudolf Steiner pointed with special emphasis to the significance it can have for the further development of Waldorf education, if, in the child's first years, one observes from month to month how the child learns to walk, speak, and think. The year 1923 was truly a kind of culmination to the series of instruction that served to establish the educational movement.

June 21, 1923

Finally, this line of thought is continued further in Stuttgart in 'Our Thought-Life in Sleeping and Waking and in the Existence after Death.' This lecture was obviously given with special enthusiasm, so that sometimes the connecting thoughts are missing. As he had done in the earlier lecture in Stuttgart, Rudolf Steiner referred back to the condition of the etheric body in the sleeping human being. Just as dream and sleep are present in the waking human being through feeling and will, so are the elements of the waking state present also in the sleeping human being, for man does not simply cease to think when he falls asleep. There is never a time when he does not think. The etheric body of the sleeping human being continues to think (but of course in a different way from when the 'I' and the astral body are within it). The etheric body thinks even better then. The continuous thought activity in the etheric body of the sleeping human being is here described. After all, the environment of man in both sleep and after death is that of the higher hierarchies.

Here it is not Rudolf Steiner's concern to describe once again how thinking, speaking, and walking — or thinking, feeling, and will — are experienced in their after-effects in relation to the Angels, Archangels, and the Archai, be it at night on earth or in the soul land after death: he already did this in Stuttgart on May 2. Here he is concerned with the description of a new living thinking in which thinking and will work together and which therefore is linked not merely to the Angels but to a large extent also to the Archai.

Rudolf Steiner raised the question: how do Theosophy and anthroposophy differ from each other? He stated that the Theosophists always pictured the higher members of the human being as if these were merely more rarefied than the physical body; hence, the etheric body not quite as dense and compact as the physical body, and the astral body even thinner. In this, the Theosophical thought-forms coincide with spiritualism and are therefore not suitable to be taken along through death. What thought-forms can be taken along? What form of human thinking produces a continuity of consciousness?

This is not answered in a theoretical way. Rudolf Steiner asked: what is the etheric body really, if what the Theosophists say is nonsense? The physical body fills out space, the etheric body sucks in space. The etheric body is therefore, so to speak, the opposite principle of the physical body. For this reason it is also absurd to think that in the new seed, which is prepared for the human being in the course of the generations, protein, an albuminous substance, represents the beginning of corporeality. On the contrary, protein is, in fact, chaotisized matter; that is, matter that develops in the reverse direction to material evolution. Thoughts that can think this are *living* thoughts.

From here Rudolf Steiner went on to describe the difference between the 'nerve human being' and the 'blood human being.' The 'nerve human being' is spirit that has become matter. The 'blood human being,' on the other hand, is nascent spirit, hence a seed on earth from which new existence constantly arises. To conceive this polar relationship between blood cells and nerve cells is also a thought, a kind of thinking, that does not become lost when one falls asleep and when one dies; rather, a continuity of consciousness is achieved through such thoughts. This kind of thinking is related to the thought movement that continues at night within the sleeping etheric body. Freedom, the balance between 'nerve human being' and 'blood human being,' between the thought-life in sleeping and waking, is attained when the will really engages in the thinking, when the otherwise sleeping element of will streams into the waking element of thinking. A kind of thinking thus comes into being whereby a continuity between day and night, between life and death, is made possible. Rudolf Steiner continued, 'If you were true anthroposophists, you would jump for joy about such thoughts as I am developing here, namely that the etheric body sucks in space, whereas matter fills out space. But you are all still sitting in your chairs.'

Here Rudolf Steiner referred back to the lectures of the beginning of the year, 'The Night Human Being and the Day Human Being' (Dornach, February 3 and 4). If the 'night human being' is placed into the 'day human being,' then anthroposophy arises. This is why this lecture repeats what had already been outlined shortly before in Dornach: then, anthroposophy becomes a living being that moves in our midst.

The circle will be completed if, in conclusion, we discuss two more lectures: the next lecture continues our theme developed up to now; the last one, the Dornach 1923 Easter lecture, belongs thematically to the earlier lectures of the beginning of that year.

November 18, 1923

In the lecture cycle given in the Hague toward the end of the year, *At Home in the Universe*, the fifth lecture contains the following: if a person who is on the way to supersensible knowledge and on the verge of developing imaginative perception, for instance went on a hike through the Alps and saw some rock crystals, it could happen that his inner development thereby received its final stimulus so that the crystals become spiritually transparent for him. Imaginative perception for the cosmic breadth, for the etheric world, awakens in him. Similarly, the inspirational element can come to bloom when a person attains a certain experience of metals. Then, the metals begin to speak and tell of earth's past ages. Not the cosmic breadth but the earth's depths tell him their cosmic recollections through the vehicle of the metals, and inspirational consciousness is thereby enkindled. Finally, intuitive consciousness comes about when a transition from prose to cosmic poetry takes place in the spirit cosmos.

Is there a possibility in nature to receive an impetus also for intuitive consciousness? Such an impetus exists for a person who sees metals melting in fire. The flame that is coloured by the melting metal gives the corresponding final stimulus for intuitive consciousness. And what shows itself then? The spirit-form in the child that leads to walking, speaking, and thinking reveals itself.

An astounding panorama opens. Through the rock crystal, imaginative consciousness awakens to the cosmic breadth. Through the speaking of the metals, a person may attain the inspirational retrospection of the earth's past. By looking into the flames of molten metals, however, man comes to the creative powers of earth's beginning. Through the fire in which metal melts, man beholds the Thrones, who in the age of Saturn had dominion over the element of fire. Simultaneously, the human being perceives the karma-creating power in the cosmos; it is this power that becomes effective in the child's learning to walk, speak, and think.

This is indeed a lecture that can close the circle of our study in a wonderful way. The kinship is experienced of the fire forces that take hold of the metals and those forces that make man into man.

> The comprehension of human destiny, the comprehending penetration into karma, lies between the child's learning to walk, speak, and think, and the melting and vaporizing of the metals in the fire's power ... This comprehension lies between the trials of the metals in the fire and the correct transition in the child of the animalistic element to the human by means of learning to walk, to speak, and to think.

This means that what volatilizes in the metal streams out into the cosmos and returns in the form of light and rays of warmth, making the child, as yet unable to speak and walk, into a human being who stands and walks erect.

Finally, Rudolf Steiner described how this is the significance of the sacrificial flame that in all ages has been lit on the altars of humankind; the flame brings down karmic insight from heaven. The flame is the question addressed to the gods, and the gods answer with a true valuation of man that knows him as the being that passes through repeated earthly lives: in the child's learning to walk, speak, and think. This is a profound cosmic secret. (Perhaps I may mention here that when Rudolf Steiner entrusted us with the renewed Christian sacraments for this age, he set us the task to seek for the transparency in the proceedings of the ritual through which knowledge of karma shines into humankind.)

Is it not a deeply moving motif that Rudolf Steiner spoke here of the metal melting in fire, and shortly afterwards, on December 2, 1923, he described what happened to him when during the night of the Goetheanum fire he looked into the Fire Akasha?

April 13, 1923

A word concerning the Easter lecture, given by Rudolf Steiner in Dornach, can serve as the conclusion of this study. It is entitled 'The Recovery of the Living Source of Speech through the Christ Impulse.' Throughout three great stages of humanity's development, the Archangels were always the genius of language. During the last Atlantean age they transmitted a language of *will* to human beings.

They were able to do this because they stood in an intuitive relation to the beings of the second hierarchy. Through intuition, they were given speech by the Exousiai, Dynameis, and Kyriotetes, which they then passed on to humankind. In the second epoch, which falls within the Post-Atlantean age and lasts into the Roman era, humankind lived with a language of *feeling.* This too is transmitted to man by the Archangels; now, however, not through intuition. The way the Archangels now receive language and pass it on lies one level lower: they are now dependent on inspiration; but for it, they must reach one level higher: to the first hierarchy, to the Thrones, Cherubim, and Seraphim. There is a preordained darkening.

Beginning with the Roman era, humankind has arrived at an age — we still live in it — in which only the language of thought remains. Language has become merely symbolic; the Word dies within the human being. Why? The Archangels, who earlier used intuition and then inspiration, can now make use only of imagination in order to be the bestowers of language on humankind. Now, however, they would have to reach one hierarchy still higher, and there they reach emptiness. There is no further hierarchy above the Thrones, Cherubim, and Seraphim. And so the Archangels, who are still the geniuses of language for humankind, would have to reach back into the ancient stock of language. Language is dying, and it would continue to be subject to death forces if there were not, standing above the hierarchies, the being of Christ who passed through the Mystery of Golgotha. Only through the Christ who dwells within human hearts can the Archangels now re-enliven the dying language. Through him, the genius of language can be resurrected. Although the genius lives only in imagination, in Christ a new fountain of life has arisen. Now, if it happens — and with this, we return to the first part of our study — that during the night human beings bring the Archangels something that originates in a nascent Christianization of speech, they can thereby keep the language of humanity from dying and give it new life. Here we have come to one of the quietest yet most decisive Easter motifs. This motif was expressed by Rudolf Steiner in a true Easter verse:

> Into human souls I would direct
> The spirit feeling, so that willingly
> The Easter Word awakens in the heart.

With human spirits I would think
The soul warmth, so that powerfully
They can feel the Resurrected One;
There brightly shines against death's semblance
Spirit knowledge's earthly flame;
The Self becomes World-Eye and Ear.

From Theosophy to Anthroposophy

In 1910 the December issue of the Theosophical Society newsletter carried an announcement about a book which at the time may have largely been skimmed over but which, in the overall view of Steiner's life's work, is of great importance. The few words read:

> In press:
> *Anthroposophy*, by Dr Rudolf Steiner
> Philosophisch-Theosophischer Verlag, Berlin-W, Motzstr. 17.

Two basic works by Steiner were available at the time: *Theosophy* (1904) and *Esoteric Science* (1909). Now publication of a third book bearing the title *Anthroposophy* was imminent. What a trilogy was about to be completed! Two books would frame the great work of *Esoteric Science* — *Theosophy* and *Anthroposophy*. This trinity alone would have provided the outline and the future plan for an entire cultural development. But it did not happen, the third book was not published. Neither was the announcement repeated in subsequent issues of the newsletter by Mathilde Scholl. Only a few people paid serious attention to what was going on there. Even before the Anthroposophical Society came into existence, Steiner had written a book entitled *Anthroposophy* which had gone to press but in the end was not published.

The years passed. Occasionally something was heard about the mysterious book. This happened when younger people who were working on a philosophical doctorate at one of the universities came to Steiner. On one or two occasions, in order to provide a tip for their dissertations, he gave them some printed sheets from the unpublished little book, for example Walter Johannes Stein, who approached him in 1917 with a request of this kind. Finally, at the important moment when the first Goetheanum was opened with a wide-ranging lecture programme where many members who had been working on various scientific topics presented their results, Steiner himself talked about the book which he had written years before but had never released for publication. He said that in this book he had attempted to present people with the theory of the human senses, which he wished to expand beyond the usual view of the five senses, as an important element of a spiritualized natural science. As long as he had done this verbally, it had been possible,

> ... but when I then — as I said, this was many years ago — wanted to write this down in order to put into book form what I had given in lectures as actual anthroposophy, strangely it turned out that outer experience became something so sensitive when internalized, that language could not produce the words and I think that the first part of the printed material, several sheets, lay in the printers for five or six years. I could not continue writing, because I wanted to continue in the style in which I had started and the language was at first no use for what I wanted to achieve at my stage of development at the time. Later I had an excessive workload and up until now I have been unable to complete this book.

This statement was made in 1920, in other words, ten years after the book *Anthroposophy* was announced.

> Anyone who is less conscientious about what he conveys to his fellow human beings from the spiritual world might well smile about this kind of stalling over a temporarily insurmountable difficulty.

This presents us with an important riddle in Steiner's biography. Some time ago, in the middle of the twentieth century, this little book was found in Steiner's papers, all printed apart from a small part which was present in handwritten form. It is obvious that those now responsible for these matters should be delighted at the discovery, and so the book *Anthroposophy*, written by Steiner in 1910, was published in the spring of 1952. The text was designated a 'fragment.'

The observations which I would like to make here arise from the feeling that this book requires a protective cover. Behind it lies the hardest of human destinies. It would be a great blessing if this were known and felt by at least a few people. Anyone starting to read this will at first understand very little beyond the first half. Few will be able to understand it completely straight away. You soon start to say to yourself: yes, I think I know why Steiner did not have this book published. But there is no doubt whatsoever that there is much gold to be mined here in future decades. Until his death, Steiner believed it impossible to publish the book. If it has now been handed over to the public despite this, it is to be hoped that a great many people clearly understand the spiritual responsibility connected with it.

What Rudolf Steiner attempted to formulate in writing in crystal clear concentrated language, he had already presented verbally in October 1909. It must be borne in mind that year after year the annual general meetings, which always took place around the date on which the German Section of the Theosophical Society had been founded in 1902, had the character of a special event. The annual general meeting in 1909 was marked by four lectures which at first did not appear to differ from the others. But a specific precise step was being taken with these lectures, given under the title 'Anthroposophy.' What kind of step was this? Steiner expressed his views clearly on this at the start of the first lecture:

> [Up to now] we have heard a great deal from the whole realm of Theosophy which was taken from the high regions of clairvoyant consciousness, as it were, so that the need had to arise at some point to do something towards a serious and worthy foundation of our spiritual movement. This general meeting which unites our members following the seven years in which our German Section has been in existence, is the ideal occasion for contributing to a firmer foundation of our activities. This I shall attempt to do during these days in the four lectures on *Anthroposophy*.

Seven years had passed since the founding of the German Section of the Theosophical Society in October 1902. Steiner himself again mentioned the fact that at the time, when Annie Besant was in Berlin to present him with the certificate as Secretary General, he had abandoned the illustrious company for an entire evening and given a lecture elsewhere. And this of all lectures, given to non-Theosophists, had borne the title 'Anthroposophy.'* As far back as 1902 Steiner had given a lecture on 'Anthroposophy' to writers and literary figures of the day and he said that at the time he had dealt with the *historical* aspect of anthroposophy outside the circle of Theosophists, whereas this time he intended to tackle the *scientific* angle.

> After seven years the time now appears to have arrived when one cycle has been completed and it is now right to speak in a more comprehensive way about what *anthroposophy* is.

This is therefore a matter of taking the step from Theosophy to anthroposophy.

In passing it should be mentioned that much was embarked upon with a great deal of energy at the time, for example during the days of the annual general meeting. While the lectures on anthroposophy were in the mornings there was also an evening lecture on the sphere of the Bodhisattvas. This lecture attempted to put into manageable concepts for Europeans the fanciful, half-superstitious ideas which prevailed in the Theosophical Society about the spiritual beings who lead humankind, the so-called 'masters.' In these few days the basic public lectures on the Mission of Anger, the Mission of Religious Devotion and the Mission of Truth took place. Along with the four lectures on anthroposophy, a really robust assault on the world situation was intended. The lecture 'The Nature and Origin of the Arts' was also given during this time. A sortie from the fortress was undertaken through many gates at the same time.

Humankind was in a special situation spiritually at that time. The year 1909 marked not only the formal passing of the first seven years of the work of the Theosophical Society but at this point a highly important event took place in the spiritual world. Seven years later, at the beginning of 1917, Rudolf Steiner spoke about this in a very vivid way: 'Since this point in time, the etheric Christ has walked amongst human beings on the earth.' In other words, a new incalculably important phase of development in the influence of the being of Christ himself had begun. It was inevitable that in 1909 new sources of knowledge, new rays of inspiration appeared in the field of spiritual activity. In 1910 Rudolf Steiner began speaking about the mystery of the etheric Christ in one city after another, but this had actually

---

* See Chapter 9, 'Rudolf Steiner and the Theosophical Society.'

emerged in 1909. The first trace is to be detected in the cycle on the Gospel of St Luke in September 1909. The moment must have occurred exactly at Michaelmas that year, when the new force which had entered the world could be sensed particularly strongly. We know what powerful currents of activity have flowed from this event. In 1910, encouraged by the occult sunrise in the etheric, the step was taken to make anthroposophy culturally productive, first in the artistic realm. This Christ impulse gave rise to the first of the four mystery dramas, which linked in to this spiritual event right at the beginning in the scene with Theodora. Theodora appeared as one of the first people to see Christ in the etheric.

Now the following is of significance: at first the great new element which arose in 1909 was also applied to the area of Theosophy, of Christology, leading the gaze upwards to the spiritual plane. This makes it all the more surprising that, in October 1909, Steiner took steps to anchor the spiritual stream which he served firmly to the physical earth. This was achieved by those four lectures, by the step from Theosophy to anthroposophy. The subject was the theory of the human senses. Not the spiritual human being but actually the *physical* one who, out in the world, is exclusively the object of natural scientific knowledge, became the object of spiritual scientific knowledge. Attention was focused upon the physical organism of the human being and, within this, the arrangement of the senses. The step from Theosophy to anthroposophy was made in that spiritual science now no longer related only to the spiritual worlds, therefore existing *alongside* natural science, but was an object of natural science to be studied in itself, in order to let a new natural science arise out of the spiritual science. The point on which everything turns is a true knowledge of the human senses. First and foremost it must be made clear that natural science also pays attention to the human senses, but it does not really recognize that the human being has a much larger number of senses than the usual five. A broadening of the field of vision is the first contribution made by anthroposophy, or spiritual science, for natural science.

We know that at a later date Steiner spoke clearly of the twelvefold nature of the senses. I do not need to describe the theory of the senses as such, but only wish to say that, in the lectures given in October 1909 and also in the unpublished book from 1910, Rudolf Steiner's description of the twelve senses was still very cautious and tentative. He actually only talked of ten senses and not twelve at first. At one point the circle of the twelve senses was not yet complete. At the point where Steiner described the sense of touch on the one hand and the sense of the 'I' on the other, he did not yet have the final succinct formulation and so at first only ten of the senses were clearly described. Something like a veil remained at one point. What is usually counted as the sense of touch amongst the five senses, appears there as the sense of warmth. Whether what be experience in touch is really a proper sense perception, remains open. A theory of the senses was developed with a powerful approach, which nevertheless remained uncertain. Then Steiner set out to put into book form what he had expressed verbally in the four October lectures. This not only dealt with the *sense organs*, in as far as they could be clearly recognized, but also described the sevenfold human *life processes* identified later. The life processes include, for example, breathing, nourishing, growing. These are processes which are more closely connected to the etheric body whilst the twelve senses constitute the real mystery of the physical body.

We must remember what the background was to the writing of this book. It is only necessary to cast a glance at the enormous amount of travelling which Steiner did in 1910. Even disregarding the incredible new subject of the revelation of the etheric Christ, it is amazing what distances Steiner covered in a purely physical sense. At the start of the year he was in Scandinavia and gave a cycle of lectures on the Gospel of John in Stockholm. Then he had to return to Berlin. After a short break he went to Strasbourg and cities in the south of Germany, then had to return to Berlin once more. In February he went to Dresden, Weimar, Frankfurt, Cologne, Wuppertal, etc. and again returned to Berlin. Then a trip to Stuttgart and back to Berlin. In March and April came Munich, Vienna, Klagenfurt, Rome, Palermo. He reached the far south of Europe. We shall come back to the karmic significance of this Italian journey. In May he went from Berlin to Hamburg for the cycle *Manifestations of Karma*. Then to Scandinavia for the second time that year, to Copenhagen and Oslo where the cycle on folk souls was given. In July and August came the great conference in Munich with the performance of the first Mystery Drama, *The Portal of Initiation*, which was actually only completed there. Along with this was the cycle on the

Creation. In September, the cycle on the Gospel of Matthew took place in Berne, and so on. Then back to Berlin again.

This was a year filled with such activity that it begs the question: what was the source of this? Which brings us back to the fact that in the spiritual sphere something unprecedented had happened which had to be matched by what was happening on the earth. During all this activity the book *Anthroposophy* was written, but was not published although it lay almost complete at the printers. One of the avenues which emerged from the new element in 1909 — if it is permissible to call this avenue the Theosophical one in a specific sense, although it would be better to speak of a 'Christological avenue' — was successful and led to the production of the mystery dramas. It reached a complete fulfilment. But the specifically anthroposophical avenue, the attempt to lay a foundation on the ground which had been taken possession of outwardly by natural science and so found western occultism in its own right, this avenue came to a standstill at first.

*

This standstill about which Rudolf Steiner said very little is a mystery drama in itself. It did not arise from any personal weakness, but from the situation in the world. Steiner had to struggle with a world suffering from inertia, a world which did not want to be moved. The third Mystery Drama which was written in summer 1912 definitely contained a trace of the other mystery drama which must have been taking place in Steiner's soul in 1910. Even though such references can naturally only be made and received with the utmost caution and considerable sensitivity, it may nevertheless be permitted to make mention of them. In the opening scene of the third Drama, *The Guardian of the Threshold*, we see a number of characters belonging to the outside world gathered together. They have been invited by a Rosicrucian mystery society to a conference, the content of which they can naturally only have a very general notion about. The brotherhood of the order wish to take a step involving those who have worked in the esoteric circle up until that point making contact with the outside world. 'Publicizing the mysteries' has presented itself as a spiritual necessity, as an order from the spirit. Some of the guests are sceptical and even make derisive comments regarding what these mystics intend to do. But there are two amongst them who do have a relationship to the spiritual. These are Dr Strader, who is following a path towards the understanding of nature and Felix Balde, who is striving on the path of inner natural mysticism. These two try to mediate and point out the significance which it would have if these people would henceforth communicate some of their results to the outside. Dr Strader says:

> The brotherhood in future will bestow
> Its highest treasures freely on humankind

He believes that what had been previously preserved amongst a few people should be made freely available. Ferdinand Reinecke who is a sceptic, talks about the fact that an event has occurred in the mystery society which has prompted this step to be taken. He says:

> It hath indeed already reached mine ears
> That an occurrence of a special sort
> Hath forced the league to turn and think of us.
> Thomasius, who came some years ago
> Beneath the influence of a spirit-stream,
> Which sets itself to follow mystic aims,
> Hath learned just how to use such forms of thought
> As in our time compel men's confidence,
> And hang them, as a mantle, round that lore
> Which, it is claimed, to seers is revealed.

The situation is that Johannes Thomasius, who has sought the spirit as a painter, has now, on account of a change in his destiny, come to the point of expressing the spiritual through ideas and of writing a book. The fact that this book was able to be written, not in the language of occultism but in that of natural science, a language which the outer world could speak; the fact that the former painter could now emerge as someone able to understand and teach, was the reason that this order was willing to relinquish its closed way of life and make its treasures freely available. This is the point at which the discussion took place between the members of the order and the invited representatives of the outside world. It is really because of Johannes Thomasius' book that the members of the order have announced their decision on the significant step into the open. They are solemnly resolved to bestow on the book's publication the whole blessing of the rose cross. At this point, to everyone's surprise, Johannes Thomasius enters and explains that he cannot allow the book to be published.

The reasons that Johannes now offers from his inner struggle are naturally completely different to those which led Rudolf Steiner to the decision not to publish the little book *Anthroposophy*. In Thomasius' case, everything has more of a personal nature. He says that he himself is still so beset by the storms of human passions that he is unable to put himself fully and steadfastly behind his book and so must withdraw it, no matter whether it is good or bad, in order to avoid attaching the defects of his character to it. If he were to do it — as he had learned in an important spiritual encounter — then the thoughts which he had expressed in this book in the language of the outer world would fall victim to Ahriman.

Despite all the differences in the inner situation, is not this scene — which was incorporated in the Drama produced in 1912 — fed by the tensions of Steiner's own inner struggles? However in his case, the reasons were not to be found in his personal situation like Johannes Thomasius, but in the times he lived in. The era did not provide appropriate language for the concepts. If something is expressed from spiritually derived knowledge without the concepts and words being adequate and fully developed, then this can fall victim to Ahriman. It is probably not inappropriate to look into Rudolf Steiner's own biography through scenes like the one at the beginning of the third Drama.

But let us take a look at Steiner's literary work after the unnoticed but real tragedy of the book *Anthroposophy*. Up to that point in 1910, Steiner had written a great deal. The long book *Esoteric Science* had been finished shortly prior to this. The pen was there to be taken up, but at this point he stopped writing. This is not hard to imagine, because if he had written something at this point, then he would first have had to complete that book, and this was simply not possible. In the years which followed, small cautious literary works appeared, above all continuing the theme in *Knowledge of the Higher Worlds and its Attainment*, the two precious books *A Road to Self-Knowledge* and *The Threshold of the Spiritual World*. In addition, the Mystery Dramas were written, but there were no books along the lines of *Theosophy* and *Esoteric Science*.

In 1914 Steiner again set to work on a larger book. The result was the two-volume edition of *The Riddles of Philosophy*. However, this was a work which had already existed in a shorter version at the turn of the century and, in addition, it portrayed historical figures. But if we look at these two volumes in the light of this biographical enquiry, then we discover the full significance of the so-called 'appendix,' 'A brief outline of an approach to anthroposophy.' The word 'anthroposophy' comes up again. It often means more than simply anthroposophy and this is especially so in this case. This extra chapter in the second volume of *The Riddles of Philosophy* is very closely related stylistically to the book *Anthroposophy*. It is equally difficult to understand and contains a highly condensed form of the ideas which led from the theory of knowledge works before the turn of the century to the real spiritual scientific works after the turn of the century. It builds a bridge from the *Philosophy of Freedom* to *Knowledge of the Higher Worlds*, but it appears as an appendix, cautiously, so that there is no repetition of the previous situation.

Afterwards, with the exception of some less important material, it was only in 1916 and 1917 that the next two books appeared. We shall see that this is the point at which the process which had got stuck was released again — what had not been fully developed previously now came to fruition. But even the two books *The Riddle of Man* and *Riddles of the Soul*, published in German in 1916/17, only consist of individual essays. *The Riddle of Man* describes Hegel, Schelling and Fichte and all manner of forgotten philosophers from Austrian intellectual life, still somewhat in the style of *The Riddles of Philosophy* — it is not a large new book in its own right. *Riddles of the Soul* assumes a similar form: besides an essay on Dessoir who was an opponent of anthroposophy, it appears to contain only essays on individual topics. But suddenly the crucial essay appears, the metamorphosis of the book which could not be published in 1910: totally inconspicuous and scarcely recognizable for those who do not know it, in the chapter 'Anthropology and Anthroposophy' and in the 'Sketches of some of the ramifications.' 'Anthroposophy' again means more here than is usually connected with this word. It can be seen how, after the mysterious experience of 1910, Steiner turned to writing other things, not only because of the work overload, but also for inner reasons. He had to wait until it was possible to speak the language which was required for the real matter in hand.

*

The period of waiting which Rudolf Steiner accepted so patiently from 1910 onwards was the time when the great storm began its raging. The destiny of Europe entered a period of dramatic change. War broke out in 1914 and a large part of Steiner's activity had to be abruptly interrupted. The esoteric events held in intimate circles stopped immediately. The Mystery Dramas could not be continued. The lectures on the Fifth Gospel were cut short. The times put a hold on the real esoteric element. The circumstances of the day necessitated giving way outwardly, as it were, withdrawing from the esoteric realm and working into the destiny of the outer world. With inescapable necessity, this destiny itself urged a step which Rudolf Steiner had inwardly wished to take back in 1909, in other words, the step from Theosophy to anthroposophy. This now happened on a grand scale and begs the question: was this inevitability a help or a hindrance? If we are aware of the existence of higher hierarchical powers behind humankind, then we can also begin to sense that Steiner undertook the step from the inner to the outer — as he had wished to do in 1909/10 — from a prophetic consciousness, knowing that if this step was not accomplished inwardly, it would have to befall humankind in a catastrophic manner through outer inevitability.

How did things continue from this point? Nowadays it could be said without being cynical that the first years of the War in 1914/15 took an almost idyllic course. The world had not yet fallen into ruins. Even in the countries where the war was being fought, many things remained as they had been. This only changed at the point which I shall focus on here, in other words the transition from 1916 to 1917, when everything became fundamentally different.

We have arrived at the moment when Rudolf Steiner spoke in a fully developed form on the theory of the twelve senses. Things which had remained tentative in the lectures in 1909 and could not be expressed in their full form in the book from 1910 were now imparted in a fully mature way in the third lecture of the cycle 'Cosmic Being and Egohood' on June 20, 1916. But fate intervened, because before he began to introduce the topic planned for this lecture, he first had to honour the memory of someone who had died. Two days previously, on Sunday, June 18, the former Chief of General Staff, Helmuth von Moltke had died in a dramatic way. In the morning he had given an address in the Reichstag at the funeral of Field Marshal von der Goltz, someone who had been one of Moltke's close friends. In his play, *The Head of the General Staff*, Albert Steffen called him the Field Marshal of the East. After Moltke had given this address he collapsed unconscious and died immediately afterwards. This event threw its shadow on the branch meeting on the following Tuesday.

General von Moltke was a true exponent of Central European destiny. He was Chief of General Staff when the First World War broke out. After the First Battle of the Marne he became the victim of tragic confusion and intrigue which led to his being relieved of his command at the end of 1914.

Without his clear critical power of judgment suffering even the slightest loss, he was a man of soul through and through — someone who approached life through his heart rather than his head. His soul not only had a wide interest but was filled with light. In him this did not emerge as intellectual ideas but in the form of warm insight and a heartfelt longing for knowledge. His wife was a member of the Theosophical Society and the Anthroposophical Society from early on, so that through her he also came into contact with Steiner, if only in a casual way up until the end of 1914. Even after his removal from office he did not join the Anthroposophical Society, though there was a deep emotional connection there. Then, after the difficult years of 1915 and 1916 he died in this dramatic way. Rudolf Steiner began his lecture on June 20, 1916 with an obituary. He said:

> I see this man and this man's soul like a symbol of the present and the near future, born of the developments of our time. A symbol for that which ought to happen and must happen in a very real and very true sense of the word.

What he meant by this was that in this human figure Central Europe was personified as it were. Entering into such dramatic destiny and under the effect of this suffering, Central Europe was to start asking about the spirit.

> A soul which, seeking after knowledge, seeking after truth, sat here with us, ... with the most burning earnest desire for knowledge ... Hence this soul is ... an outstanding historical symbol.

This man's destiny revealed something akin to a reflection of the entire destiny of Central Europe.

When the obituary was over, Steiner began to develop his subject matter and this was the moment at which he spoke on the theory of the twelve senses in a fully developed way, where he was able to take the step from Theosophy to anthroposophy in full certainty and full accord with the course of time, the step which had not been possible in 1910. Though only a short sketch was possible after the obituary, he described how the human being's twelve senses can primarily be divided into five and seven, into the five senses assigned to the night and the seven assigned to the day. Now all twelve were present. What is the significance of this?

We need to remain with the figure of Helmuth von Moltke a little longer. In the final days of 1914 (December 20), when Moltke, who was no longer Chief of General Staff was deeply depressed on account of the completely unproductive military strategy and was inclined to despair of the future altogether, Steiner wrote to him, saying that from the course of events it might appear as though certain sanguine thoughts which he had expressed were now disproved by the facts. But that also current failures — however serious they might be — could not shake the conviction that important tasks awaited the German people in the future. Rudolf Steiner turned the focus on the future and encouraged Moltke by telling him that his destiny was connected to that of the German people.

Steiner added to this letter a few weeks later (on January 26, 1915). He spoke vividly of the spirit of the German people. He portrayed it as a shining beacon showing itself to those who turn their thoughts to it in love for this people. Those who seek to join together in love for the spirit of the German people may experience this gesture as a silent answer, as a word of strength and optimism.

Fate ordained that Rudolf Steiner's circle should include a man who was an exponent of the Central European destiny. Steiner saw the spirit of the people soaring above him. By empathizing with the personal destiny of this man he also obtained a new avenue to the guiding powers who led the entire destiny of the era.

What Steiner says about the telling gesture of the folk spirit, is said by Michael in the fifth letter of *Anthroposophical Leading Thoughts* (1924). It is a little different, but it nevertheless recalls this.

> Michael can unfold that which is to be revealed as a majestic exemplary action in the spiritual world which initially borders the visible world. Michael can reveal himself there in an aura of light, in the gesture of a spiritual being, in which all the radiance and magnificence of the past intelligence of the gods is revealed.

The Archangel Michael also reveals himself by this kind of shining gesture and it is not hard to at least imagine the possibility that, behind the folk spirit which was described as a shining beacon, the lofty being of the Archangel was visible, also speaking in a language of this kind. We are also able to see from what creative sources Rudolf Steiner was working when he had to take the step which has just been described.

*

It was rather surprising that Steiner was in Berlin when Moltke died. If we look up the lectures 'Towards Imagination,' Steiner says at the end of the first lecture that it is questionable whether he will still be in Berlin in the coming weeks. Steiner was awaiting the first copies of the book *The Riddle of Man* but was actually trying to return to Dornach. He was still in Berlin when Moltke died only because publication of the book was delayed week after week. This is not irrelevant. The reason for wishing to return to Dornach was because he wanted to work on the statue. This he then did. But from the present viewpoint can be seen that forces were at work from another dimension, and in the second half of 1916 another apocalyptic wave arrived. The outbreak of war had been ushered in by a wave of this kind. But then, in the transition from 1916 to 1917, the real collapse took place. The determination to do what he could so that a new spiritual element could arise made it necessary for Rudolf Steiner to go to Dornach. By 1916 a further seven years had passed since, in 1909, the new coming of Christ had begun behind the veil of the sense world seven years after 1902.

In 1916 a new spiritual element entered in a hidden form, but it came at the same time as the waves which bore the outer disaster. Such are the remarkable paradoxes of fate. I only need to mention that, in 1923, after another seven years, the disastrous burning of the Goetheanum finally heralded the powerful new spiritual stream of the Christmas Conference. A magnificent compositional development unfolds before us and we can look into the plans of divine providence.

Moltke's death was naturally not the reason that, two days later, Steiner presented his teaching on the twelve senses to the membership for the first time. This had been planned all along, as is apparent from the fact that the basic lecture on 'Blood and Nerves' had been held for members on the previous Tuesday, June 13. It addressed 'anthroposophy' in a special sense, that is, those forms of spiritual science which are dealt with by natural science in its own field.

At some points we are permitted to be witnesses of the advancing process of maturation between 1909 and 1916. One such point is Whitsun 1913. This was when Rudolf Steiner developed what was now a clearly organized conception of the twelve senses and the seven life processes, first in Cologne and then in Stuttgart in small intimate groups. It was no coincidence that he did this only for a closed group at the start. The fact that this was possible at Whitsun 1913 is once more connected to a great secret of the age. Rudolf Steiner had come from London where, on Ascension day in the lecture 'Christ at the time of the Mystery of Golgotha and Christ in the twentieth century,' he had spoken to the members openly for the first time of Michael as the time spirit. Prior to this he had occasionally described the transition from the age of Gabriel to that of Michael in an esoteric manner. But in London he revealed the mystery of the changing guidance of the Archangels during different ages in front of a larger audience for the first time. Then, on his return to Stuttgart in May 1913, in the lectures on the 'Michael Impulse and the Mystery of Golgotha,' he spoke on German soil for the first time about the secrets of the Archangel ages and about the transition between the ages which began in 1879.

The impulse behind the unpublished book now emerged clearly. To claim this is no fabrication. The clouds of the First World War had already started to darken the skies. Steiner reached prophetically into the Apocalypse which had become clearly tangible through the outbreak of war and proclaimed the Michaelic secret. Michael was the one who provided the apocalyptic light for what was approaching. Simultaneously, the starting point for 'real anthroposophy' — the theory of the senses — became visible in Michael's light. In 1916, when the new wave of destiny was approaching, Steiner was so connected to the Archangel of the time and the German folk spirit that, before the storm broke, he was able to express prophetically what was trying to enter humankind from the spirit. This was coloured by the meeting between Rudolf Steiner and Helmuth von Moltke. The realm of Michael and the folk spirit revealed themselves and finally enabled the step to 'anthroposophy' to be made.

Rudolf Steiner stayed in Dornach for six months. First he developed the extensive lecturing work which contain a detailed examination of the twelve senses and the seven life processes. This material now existed and could be developed in all directions. However, from December 4, 1916, Steiner gave a series of lectures which stand out from all the others. A different tone was adopted from the start. With unsparing determination, Steiner illuminated what was going on behind the scenes of the political life of the day. Things had become really serious and this can be gleaned from the style of these lectures.

In view of the increasingly acute danger, Rudolf Steiner made a series of demands, for example calling for the full publication of Moltke's documents on the course of events in Berlin in the early days of the war. Instead of general talk about the war guilt, only if everything was revealed in full could Europe still be saved from the chaos. Nothing happened, but Steiner had tried his hardest. The lectures from December 4 onwards can only be described as sword strokes clearing the clouded view once again. At least the weapons of the spirit could achieve something. We can sense the spiritual impact of 1916. Steiner was forced to become involved in the realm of Ahriman, entering the arena which was already occupied by Ahrimanic powers. Everything which happened illuminated the tragic change. The death of Emperor Franz Joseph in November 1916 was symbolic in the same way as that of General von Moltke had been. Something came to an end. In November that same year, Wilson was elected as president of America and put forward his ideas for improving the world. Everyone believed that the war was now over, but things only worsened. In March 1917 the Russian Revolution broke out and in April America joined the war. The universal conflagration widened as seen by the tongues of flame in the East and West, and the catastrophe was sealed for the time being.

These events again clarify what Steiner had tried to achieve with that little book in 1910. For where did all the chaos stem from which led to the collapse? It was the consequence of a wrong way of thinking. Incorrect thinking led to incorrect action and to a mistaken social order, that is, to the disorder and chaos. But what was the source of the incorrect thought? The source lay in that kind of scientific attitude which is only interested in seeing the outside of existence. If you wish to get to the root of all the disaster including the catastrophe of war, then the step must be taken not only from natural science to spiritual science, but primarily from spiritual science to the *new* natural science.

Because only through a different kind of natural scientific thinking, through a spiritually enlightened knowledge even of the physical human organism, will the starting point be created for better social action.

When Rudolf Steiner returned to Berlin after these six months he did not develop the twelve senses representing the human physical body, and the seven life processes which serve the etheric, but took up a third element: the threefold human organism which, in its physical development, is the bearer of the sentient human being through thinking, feeling and will. In Berlin he spoke about this third element, lecturing on the key findings of the new natural science derived from the spirit: the threefoldness of the human organism. This was then published in the book, *Riddles of the Soul,* in September 1917. It was written on Steiner's return to Berlin. He often remarked that this depiction of the threefold human organism was the result of his entire spiritual research up to that point, a new basic principle in natural science, contained in the step from Theosophy to anthroposophy.

*

Steiner returned to Berlin at the beginning of February 1917. The great European calamity hung clearly in the air. It is extremely informative to observe how Steiner then resumed his activity within the Berlin membership. The impulse which, in addition to the Christological one, had not been able to enter fully in 1910, had now matured. Whilst the Christological impulse had been able to emerge in 1910, now the other side, the specifically anthroposophical, could be presented in full. Nevertheless, Steiner started with Christology once again: 'In 1909 the etheric Christ began to walk amongst human beings.' This could be stated clearly from then on. In the first lecture of the cycle 'Cosmic and Human Metamorphoses' given in the Berlin branch, he described how anthroposophy is the language of the etheric Christ, that is, the one in which we can turn to the etheric Christ. This is clearly stated later in the sixth letter of *Anthroposophical Leading Thoughts:*

> But if at the present time we speak in such a manner that our thoughts can also be the thoughts of Christ, we set over against the Ahrimanic Powers something which can save us from succumbing to them. To understand the meaning of Michael's mission in the Cosmos is to be able to speak in this way. In the

present time we must be able to speak of Nature in the way
demanded by the evolutionary stage of the Consciousness Soul
or Spiritual Soul. We must be able to receive into ourselves the
purely natural-scientific way of thinking. But we ought also to
learn to feel and speak about Nature in a way that is according
to Christ. We ought to learn the Christ-Language — not only
about redemption from Nature, about the soul and things
Divine — but about the things of the Cosmos.

This actually means a 'Christ-filled natural science.' To know nature in such a way that the language of this knowledge corresponds to the etheric Christ. This makes it clear why 'anthroposophy' in this specific sense leads to the overcoming of untruthfulness or the un-Christian approach which had pervaded human thinking and understanding.

Finally I wish refer to a particular twist of destiny. The six months during which Steiner was absent from Berlin are framed by two great human figures. Immediately prior to Steiner's leaving, Moltke died. When Rudolf Steiner returned to Berlin, Friedrich Rittelmeyer had moved to Berlin. He had held his inaugural sermon at the end of August 1916. Steiner was not there and Rittelmeyer had to wait until he could at last hear whole lecture cycles from the teacher he admired so much, something which he had been greatly looking forward to. He had gathered his own congregation; it could be said that his arrival stirred the whole of the educated circles of Berlin. A brand new note was struck. University professors sat below the pulpit where Rittelmeyer was preaching. The psychological mood of the city changed. On the first evening, when Rudolf Steiner spoke before the Berlin members once more, the difference in attitude in the branch was tangible due to Rittelmeyer being amongst the audience as a member of the Society for the first time. The conditions were cramped, with 120 to 150 members gathered in three adjacent rooms. As already mentioned, the first lecture dealt with the etheric Christ who had appeared amongst humankind since 1909 and whose language is anthroposophy. In his book, *Rudolf Steiner Enters my Life,* Rittelmeyer says:

> The first private lecture I heard from Dr Steiner after I had moved to Berlin, was on the subject of Christ. The impression it made was one of the most vivid experiences of my life. ... I realized then how a man in the very Presence of Christ speaks

of Christ. There was something more than devotional reverence in the words. In freedom and reverence a man was looking up to Christ whose Presence was quite near, and in that Presence his being changed of itself into an embodiment of noble prayer. The lecture had nothing of the style of a sermon or a prayer. It was a spiritual-scientific communication of facts of a higher world as they had revealed themselves to research ... Not a priest nor a prophet, but a knower of reality stood there before us and let us gaze at this reality in and through him ... The many hundreds of sermons I had heard about Christ came up in the background of my mind. They faded into shadows ... A new proclamation of Christ was there. A new Christ-era was dawning.

Just how much destiny was at work can be gathered from a point in the third lecture of the cycle 'Cosmic and Human Metamorphoses' which later, in 1921, gave a group of young people the courage and certainty to approach Rudolf Steiner with a request for help in setting up a movement for religious renewal. There it says:

At this point I feel obliged to make an interpolation which is of importance and which ought to be thoroughly understood, particularly by the friends of anthroposophy. It ought never to be represented that our attempts at spiritual science are a substitute for the life and exercise of religion ... for we ought to be clear that religion in its ... living practice enkindles the spiritual consciousness of the human community. If this spiritual consciousness is to become a living thing in man, he cannot possibly remain at a standstill, stopping at the merely abstract ideas of God or Christ, but must stand renewed amidst the religious practices ... as something which provides him with a religious centre ... For spiritual consciousness is acquired through religious feeling and spiritual knowledge by spiritual science, just as knowledge of nature is acquired by natural science. Spiritual consciousness leads to the impulse to acquire spiritual knowledge. It may be said that an inner religious life may today subjectively drive a man to spiritual science.

It stands to reason that this interpolation was prompted not least by the presence of Rittelmeyer, because he was the representative of the Christian religious movement which, through anthroposophy, now had an unhindered view to a new era. The year 1917 was the fourth centenary of the Reformation. In the circle of those who joined Rittelmeyer and became pupils of Rudolf Steiner along with him there was already a spirit which was intent on bringing about a new reformation rather than celebrating an old one. But it was only a number of years later that things had progressed to the point where a new movement for religious renewal through anthroposophy could be begun. Very soon after the war came to an end, through the descent of anthroposophy to stimulate and renew the cultural life in the battleground of contemporary life numerous practical activities were at the point of being founded.

In 1917 the gravity of the situation rapidly intensified. In June and July politicians approached Rudolf Steiner with the question as to whether he could see any way out. He answered with the idea of the threefold social order. This was a further legacy which the striving for a specific 'anthroposophy' had produced: Knowledge of the threefold human organism; renewal of natural science; knowledge of the threefold social order; social renewal. This key knowledge was used in the attempt to save the future of humanity from the apocalyptic avalanche. The whole wealth of impulses for applying anthroposophy to the most diverse practical professional areas belongs to this. It gave rise to all the new undertakings and foundations in the social, educational, scientific, medical religious and artistic fields.

The Preparation for Esoteric Circles 1904–6

Rudolf Steiner's death is connected to a great riddle of life. Did we not experience him after the Goetheanum fire and, in a deeply moving intensification after the Christmas Conference, in such a limitless giving of his own resources, that death could only be a sealing of this obvious self-sacrifice? The essence which sacrificed itself was clearly revealed in the style in which Steiner spoke. After the Christmas Conference in particular, Steiner's lectures took on a completely new style. The uniqueness of this lay in an intuitive element which accompanied them, in which Steiner's surrender of his being combined with that of higher powers. During the last year each word was filled with intuition. This was also the time when Steiner formed a closed circle for cultivating a specific new esotericism. What he presented there contained the culmination of the intuitive element which at that time pervaded not only the content but also the style and sound of every word he spoke.

There is a kind of correspondence to what was revealed at the end of his life in the years when Steiner first began his work as a spiritual teacher. This concerns a particular style of speaking which was in evidence in 1904 in particular, but also prior to this and again afterwards. If you mention the 'old lectures' amongst friends who have been involved with anthroposophy for a long time, this instantly awakens quite specific feelings, because the fact is that many of the oldest lectures have an openly esoteric character. They display an *imaginative* element in contrast to the element of intuition in the final period. The style is overflowing with images due to the fact that the old pictorial symbolic, traditional occult mode of expression had not yet been fully reworked. Steiner was still making frequent use of Theosophical terminology.

The style at the beginning, filled with imagery, the style during the final period blessed by intuition are the two pillars, as it were, between which Steiner's rich *inspirational* teachings were able to unfold through which knowledge of the spiritual was expressed in the language of thought of our time. The initial period in which the richness of the imaginative pictures almost seemed to burst out of the lectures was filled with Steiner's efforts to develop particular esoteric groupings. With the aim of forming a core community within the Theosophical Society of which he had taken over the leadership, he was busy building and expanding what was to be called the Esoteric School (ES). What was added to this later was at first called Free Masonry (FM), but was changed after a few years into Mystica Aeterna (MAe or ME) because of possible misunderstandings and confusion. I should like to attempt to describe historically some of what has become clear to me about the preparations for the development of these esoteric circles.

*

An ES had existed within the Theosophical Society for a long time. It had been founded by H.P. Blavatsky and was originally called Eastern School for Theosophy (EST), which indicated that the 'old wisdom' from the Orient was to be schooled. This title was later changed to Esoteric School. In Berlin on October 20, 1902 at the foundation meeting of the German Section of the Theosophical Society, after Steiner had been appointed as Secretary General of the new section, Annie Besant accepted him and Marie von Sivers, later Steiner's wife, into the ES on October 23. Things were organized in such a way that ES membership was automatic for anyone assuming a leading role such as that of section leader.

With the greatest seriousness and energy Steiner took up the double responsibility for the German part of the Theosophical Society as a whole and also for the esoteric circle which, however, consisted of relatively few members in Germany. Naturally it did not occur to him for a moment to see his task with regard to the ES as a straight continuation of what had been cultivated there previously. Just as he set about bringing something of his own — and therefore something new — into the Theosophical stream as a whole, so it was clear to him that he should take the material needed for the smaller esoteric circle directly from the outpouring revelation of the spiritual worlds, entirely new and independent of all traditions.

It is clear that he accorded the smaller circle the greatest of importance from the start. The society which was responsible for 'spreading the teaching' should do everything possible to reach ever wider circles. But it could only venture and take responsibility for its appearance before the world if, at the quiet centre, there was a reliable circle which lived in direct connection to the guiding beings of a higher world. Steiner made contact with those already accepted into the ES but consistently held back from all official ES work. As far as the form of the work was concerned, he valued correct adherence to the responsibilities transferred to him, while, as far as the spiritual material was concerned, he remained resolute not to let anyone tell him what to do.

In conversations and an exchange of letters with a small number of people he expressed his concern: 'The success of the German Theosophical movement depends on having a core of Theosophists who undertake esoteric work. ... In Germany we definitely have reliable people, but only four or five' (to Mathilde Scholl, 1903). Furthermore, the approach led to a personal teacher/pupil correspondence, because those belonging to the ES soon became the ones who came to trust Steiner and to ask him for guidance for their meditative efforts. At the end of 1903 he began to write down an 'interpretation' of the little book *Light on the Path* by Mabel Collins intended for individual meditative work, and planned a continuation which would be sent to the members of the ES from time to time. He still refrained from taking new members into the ES.

Further important progress was made in 1904. In May in London, where he was participating in the annual general meeting of the whole society, Steiner was able to speak to Mrs Besant about the leadership of the ES in Germany and took on the office of 'Arch Warden of the ES.' This enabled him to admit new members from then on.

The month of August was mainly devoted to developing the ES. *Theosophy* had appeared in June. At the same time, the description of the Akasha Record in the monthly journal, *Lucifer-Gnosis*, had been completed. Next, in the June (the thirteenth) issue, the essays began from which the book *Knowledge of Higher Worlds and its Attainment* was later compiled. What Steiner wrote there lived in a realm that was particularly well suited as the basis for further development of the teacher/pupil relationships amongst members of the ES.

From the middle of July until September he gave all lecturing activity a rest. If you notice the gap in the list of lectures, then you might think that Rudolf Steiner had perhaps allowed himself a holiday for once. But there was no question of any such thing. He remained in Berlin and used these weeks primarily for an intensive ES correspondence. Numerous letters have been preserved from this period. Some of these are letters dealing with the admittance of new members, in other words, regular enrolment letters. In addition there are letters of invitation with which Steiner approached certain figures and encouraged them to apply for membership of the ES. A particularly lengthy and sincere letter was sent to Michael Bauer in this respect. There are also letters to those who, though they were already members of the ES, now wished to become so in a new sense. These letters, which were very personal, were accompanied by a document which was by and large always the same, but which Steiner set down carefully for each individual on special sheets of paper with a cover. These were the 'rules of the Shravana order.' Anyone who wished to become a member of the ES was first admitted to a preparatory group, the 'order of testing,' which was also called the 'order of Shravaka or candidates.' The document which the candidate had to sign, likewise handwritten, was enclosed so that everyone could copy it and send it in as an application. Steiner always used one part of the admission letter to speak about the purpose of the school and the spiritual guidance under which it stood. I shall quote a few sentences from the letter of January 2, 1905 to Günther Wagner's wife:

> You know that highly evolved beings whom we call 'Master' or 'Mahatma' are behind the whole Theosophical movement. These noble beings have already trodden the road which the rest of humankind still has to travel. They now work as the great 'teachers of wisdom and the harmony of humankind's perceptions' ... The masters neither found outer organizations or societies, nor do they direct such. While the Theosophical Society was established by its founders (H.P. Blavatsky, Olcott and others) with the aim of promoting the work of the masters on the physical plane, these masters have themselves *never* had an influence on the Society itself as such. Its existence and

leadership are the work of human beings purely on the physical plane. It is a different matter as regards the Esoteric School which was founded by the masters themselves and is under their guidance.

Steiner made it clear in every letter how he felt himself to be merely a tool of these masters, when he then cautiously set about making the ES a structured organization. Each letter closed with the emphatic request that the addressee should henceforth turn to Steiner with any questions they might have. He said that, from now on, he would always set aside a specific time for answering these questions. Some of the pages with such answers to questions have been preserved. Steiner brought complete devotion and readiness to help to this task.

There was a specific reason for Steiner approaching the work in this way at this particular time. A lecture tour by Annie Besant through a series of German cities was planned for September. Steiner, who was to accompany Mrs Besant in order to give a brief summary of the English lectures in German, planned to talk to her about a new step which he had decided to take, as she was the 'Head of the School' at that point.

The last stop on the tour was Cologne and it was there, on September 23 and 24, 1904 in the house belonging to Mathilde Scholl, that the crucial conversation took place. Marie von Sivers and Mathilde Scholl were present. Steiner announced that he now wished to start on the real work in the ES. Mrs Besant immediately agreed, but added that because his specific task was Christian occultism, he could base the planned work on her book *Esoteric Christianity* which had just been published.* Rudolf Steiner could not agree to this suggestion under any circumstances. First he was determined that Mrs Besant should not speak about Christian matters. He had had difficulty in dissuading her from the Christian topics for the lecture tour which had just ended. Furthermore, in the book *Esoteric Christianity* she supported the most serious errors, including the customary confusion of Jesus of Nazareth with Jeshu ben Pandira. But above all, Steiner could not continue on the sterile doctrinaire path which the Theosophists followed, instead wishing to courageously draw on the newly-released

---

* There is a report by Mathilde Scholl where she says that Annie Besant had recommended Leadbeater's *The Christian Creed* as study material.

current springs of revelation. He stated that he needed a free hand to lead the ES creatively from the revelations which would be available to him, to which Annie Besant agreed. This was like a preliminary step of the further one which, in Steiner's own description (in his autobiography) was made in 1907 when Mrs Besant was again in Germany at the major conference held in Munich:

> It was always my wish to link what I did with things already in existence ... I had done this in relation to the Theosophical Society and I wished to do the same in regard to the Esoteric School. Thus my limited circle came into existence first in connection with the School.

He wanted to proceed correctly, linking formally to the existing framework and working with the agreement of those whose decision it was.

> But the connection had to do solely with the *external arrangements*, not with the supersensible knowledge I imparted. Thus in the early years my smaller circle appeared as a section of Mrs Besant's Esoteric School. Yet according to its inner nature it had no connection with that School. And in 1907 when Mrs Besant was present at our Theosophical Conference in Munich the external connection also was severed completely by mutual consent.

Later, at an ES meeting in Kassel in 1909 when Christian Morgenstern and his wife were admitted to the ES, Steiner referred to this again. He said that from that point onwards, subordination had been replaced by coordination.

*

Soon the circle of those admitted to the ES by Steiner grew. He was no longer able to write out the detailed documents for everyone. So, in June 1905, he began to duplicate at least the 'basic rules.' He himself wrote the text on the wax plates from which the copies were made.

Finally, at the annual general meeting in October 1905, a crucially important step was taken: after several ES classes had already been held, on the Tuesday evening after Sunday's general meeting, the first ES class was held on a larger scale. Up until then what was to serve the development of the ES in a new sense had taken place in the context of a private teacher-pupil relationship, Steiner attending to each individual who had joined the ES or wished to do so. But now all ES members present who had come to Berlin in greater numbers at Steiner's request, were gathered in a class like a proper meeting.

The programme for the October conference in 1905 gives a view of the intentions and expectations with which Steiner worked at developing the central inner circle. This shows the outline of the structure which he wished to develop:

Oct 21 Sat	evening	Lecture for members: Atoms and the Logos
Oct 22 Sun	10–3.30 pm	General meeting, Business meeting
	6 pm	Lecture for members: The relationship of the Theosophical Society to the ES
Oct 23 Mon	10 am	for men: members lecture on Freemasonry
	11.30 am	for women: members lecture on Freemasonry
	evening	Lecture for members: East-West problem
Oct 24 Tue	evening	ES lesson
Oct 26 Thu	evening	Lecture for members: The social question

It is astonishing to see that on the day before the annual general meeting a lecture was held on the topic of 'Atoms and the Logos.' On the evening prior to such a festive occasion and before such an important step in the most personal of endeavours, why was this topic, which evokes almost alarming feelings in the era of the atom bomb, chosen? At that time the topic was more mysterious than frightening. We shall return to this.

After the official part of the annual general meeting, Steiner gave a lecture on the ES for all members of the society, but he did not call the ES by its name but described how the esoteric core ought to behave towards the society as a whole from thence onwards. Some things were also put before the whole membership which were reminiscent of what had been expressed in the personal letters:

> When we work in a practical way to expand the Theosophical Society, then the great individualities whom we call masters are always at our side: we can turn to them and let them speak through us. But when it comes to disseminating the occult life, then it is the masters who speak. If it is only a matter of organizing the society, then they leave that to those who live on the physical plane. This is the difference between the occult stream

and the framework of the Theosophical organization ... When it comes to the spiritual life, then the masters speak, but when it is simply a matter of organization, then mistakes can be made for the masters are silent there.

The point that Steiner wanted to make was that the spiritual element of Theosophical work, above all the ES, the core or 'heart' of the society, should be clearly distinguished from the more open realm where everyone carried joint responsibility.

Steiner then closed this lecture with an important announcement:
I should like to repeat the announcement, that I shall hold a lecture early tomorrow on certain current occult matters related to Freemasonry and this will take place separately for men and women in accordance with the ancient occult practice. The lecture for men will take place at ten o'clock and that for women at 11.30. You may be asking why this is so? This practice exists and will only be overridden through the Theosophical view of the world. This will follow from the content of the lectures and I should also like to add that tomorrow evening the Besant branch will hold its regular meeting.'

Why is the topic of Freemasonry suddenly brought up in this connection? We shall leave this question unanswered at present. The lecture for members on the Monday evening also stood out in a particular way, because in it Steiner spoke for the first time about the East-West problem, which was later to become such a problem for humankind. We are taken aback at the contrast: on the one hand the doors to the innermost circle were opened and on the other the tense and disastrous outer world situation was explored. But the key lies in this very contrast: the justification for an esoteric inner space lies in the fact that the ideas and strength to be gained from the outer world are no longer adequate for mastering the tasks which come to meet humankind.

This lecture makes us aware that we in Central Europe need to find the way between the Slavic peoples in the East and the Anglo-American peoples in the West. Both are developing peoples at the start of their development. But both the Slavs in the East and the Americans in the West have to deal with the streams who remained in Atlantis. This gives rise to a one-sided spiritualism in the Slavs and a one-sided material psychism in the Americans. We in Central Europe are charged with finding the balance.

15. THE PREPARATION FOR ESOTERIC CIRCLES

But more was to come. After the first ES lesson had taken place in a wider circle on the Tuesday evening, on the Thursday Steiner returned to a discussion on the subject of 'The Social Question.' This gave another instructive comparison: when esoteric work is carried out, another step has to be made in the outer world at the same time.

Let us first follow the ES thread a little further. The early members included Günther Wagner, who was 62 in 1905, his two older sisters Amanda, who was already 75 and Amalie, who was 68 and also his wife Anna. On October 24, when the ES lesson took place within the annual general meeting, Anna Wagner was ill and could not take part. So Steiner wrote down the entire ES lesson for Anna Wagner in his own hand. Destiny gave rise to a wonderful manuscript of over seven sheets. This ES lesson is an example of how Steiner gave all the assembled members of the ES personal meditation instructions. Mrs Wagner died soon afterwards, on December 30. On the occasion of her death Steiner wrote a classical letter on the question of how to help those who have died once they have crossed the threshold. This letter, dated December 31, 1905, was addressed to a friend of the Wagner family, Paula Stryczek, the adopted daughter of Hübbe-Schleiden.*

The following then took place: Steiner was holding lectures in some Swiss cities, so on January 9 and 10, 1906, shortly after Anna Wagner's death, he arrived in Lugano where he stayed with Günther Wagner, who had by then retired from the Pelikan-Werke. There he set down on paper a further important part of his exegesis of the book *Light on the Path* by Mabel Collins. What Steiner wrote in Günther Wagner's house and handed over to him dated January 9 along with the parts written earlier, for his own use and for passing on to some other friends, was a truly objective letter of sympathy for Günther Wagner.†

A strange event then took place on January 9, 1906, the date of the 'exegesis.' In Lugano, Steiner received a visit from a somewhat dubious character by the name of Theodor Reuss, who was responsible for the leadership of the Yarker Freemason lodges in Germany and England. This man handed him a certificate giving him authority to lead the grand lodges within the Ordo Templi Orientis, the Grand

---

* See *Esoteric Lessons 1904–1909*.   † See *Esoteric Lessons 1904–1909*.

Lodge of the Order of the Orient. The charter agreement bore the date January 3, 1906.

Here is the quote from Steiner's autobiography where he talks about the mysterious assignment which he was handed on January 9, 1906:

> Some years after becoming involved in the Theosophical Society, Marie von Sivers and I were offered the leadership of a society of the kind which has survived to preserve the ancient symbolism and ritual in which the 'ancient wisdom' was embodied. I did not have the remotest intention of working in the mode of such a society. Everything anthroposophical should and must spring from its own sources of knowledge and truth. I did not intend to deviate in the slightest from this aim. But I had always felt a respect for the historical heritage. This contains the spirit which evolves in human development. So I was also in favour of linking what was new to what already existed, as far as possible. I therefore accepted the diploma of the society referred to, which belonged to the movement represented by Yarker. It had the Masonic form of the so-called high degrees; but I took nothing else — absolutely nothing — from this society except the purely formal authorization to myself establish a ritual symbolic activity linked to what was there before.

Later, Steiner was greatly disadvantaged because in Switzerland offence was taken at his association with Theodor Reuss, whose bad reputation was apparently not totally unjustified. Because of having had this entirely marginal and formal contact with the Freemason leader, Steiner was later refused Swiss citizenship. But he had reasons for taking this course. After the historical occult streams had lost their meaning, his aim was to produce a transformation, a modernization, a direct enriching of occult life and he steered towards both the ES and an entirely transformed type of Freemasonry in a completely new framework.

This sheds light on the fact that, immediately before setting out on this Swiss journey, Steiner had held another lecture on 'Freemasonry' in Berlin on January 2, 1906. At the start of this lecture he had expressly stated that something quite new was to be attempted in that the subject was no longer to be dealt with separately for men and women, but for everyone together. This was a clear indication of the intention to break with the strict practice of traditional Freemasonry in which the participation of women was out of the question.

We have tried to follow the preparations for building up the ES. Next, a new development was woven clearly into what was already present. It was no coincidence that, during the days of the annual general meeting which inwardly moved towards the ES lesson at the close of the conference, Steiner had already brought up the subject of Freemasonry. So a second iron was added to the fire in the forge of progress. What was the aim of this?

I must first say a final word about the further development of the ES. From October 24, 1905 onwards, Steiner was very involved in holding ES lessons. He held repeated ES lessons in twelve German cities and ten outside Germany. It is estimated that almost two hundred and fifty of these lessons were held until they were halted at the outbreak of the First World War. The last ES lesson took place in Norrköping in Sweden on July 14, 1914.

No writing was allowed in the ES lessons, something that Steiner was very particular about, and in the first six months, scarcely anyone dared to make any notes afterwards. But from Easter 1906 onwards, Steiner permitted participants to make notes afterwards and exchange these with one another. Only a very few ES members who possessed these kind of notes ensured through their will that papers of this kind would be destroyed after their death. In time many such transcripts were in circulation and indeed, often those into whose hands they fell did not really know what they were about. There were five or more variations of some ES lessons. This was the reason that, during the last part of her life, Marie Steiner was convinced that the only way of protecting what remained of these recollections and notes was through publication. In 1941 she started having transcripts of the ES lessons printed, first in *Das Goetheanum*, then in the newsletter. She did this under the title of 'From Rudolf Steiner's thoughts,' so that anyone who did not know otherwise, would be unlikely to recognize the source of these texts. However, after a short while she discontinued this publication.

The attempt made here to portray something of the history of this matter is done in the hope of contributing something to the organization and cultivation and also to the protection of something which needs no less respect and care nowadays than it did then.

It was only in 1907, in other words, two years after the beginning of the ES lessons, that Steiner actually began proper Freemasonry meetings, which contained ritual elements but also teaching of the so-called 'Instructions.' When war broke out in 1914 all meetings of this other small circle stopped along with the ES lessons.

*

What was the relationship of these two circles to one other? At first it might be imagined that they were two completely different matters: first one was founded and then the other. But in reality the connection was much closer and more intimate. The outer course of events already make it clear how thoroughly the subject of Freemasonry was woven into the formation and early existence of the ES. Steiner himself attached great importance to a clear distinction. In the Theosophical Society led by Olcott and Besant, particularly in the English-speaking countries, there was a fairly undifferentiated mixture with traditional Freemasonry. The role which Freemasonry played there had been largely underestimated since the days of H.P. Blavatsky. The real state of affairs can be seen especially well in Leadbeater's books (for example *The Hidden Life in Freemasonry*). This approach took the easy route: you only needed to abandon any efforts at transformation or renewal and be happy with accumulating as many occult traditions as possible. Steiner had to insist on the clearest distinctions and most exact regulations being made. This is obviously the reason why, from an early stage, he ceased to allow the members of the ES to be promoted from the lowest stage, the 'order of testing,' through various grades within the ES as had been customary before his time. The possibility of promotion was available in connection with what was at first known as FM, but had next to nothing in common with traditional Freemasonry, or at most certain suggestions of its form.

The fact that Steiner was aiming not for a twofold, but for an organically structured but internally unified esoteric movement will become clear to us if we follow another specific thread in the important preparatory year of 1904. During the same time that Steiner planned a considerable lecture-free period to devote to ES correspondence and the discussion with Mrs Besant was imminent, he started a lecture cycle which can only really be understood when seen in this context. Monday was always the Berlin branch evening. On Whit Monday,

May 23, 1904, Steiner gave a lecture which was overflowing with the imagery which I mentioned at the beginning. It really is one of Steiner's hardest lectures to understand. But it did not simply describe the Whitsun festival — this lecture inaugurated something important.

A series of twelve lectures followed on Fridays, lasting until the end of the year. But before the long break occurred, only one Friday lecture on 'Cain and Abel' was held after the Whitsun one. So, what is the content of this lecture series? It can be said at the outset that towards the end of this series the subject of Freemasonry appeared clearly in the foreground, a whole ten months before the two lectures at the annual general meeting in 1905. The final four lectures before the one on the festival of Epiphany (December 2, 9, 16 and 23) deal with Freemasonry and reveal the secret element which it contained in earlier centuries.*

A biographical detail might be inserted here. We know from his autobiography that the subject of the Freemasons' order played a role in Steiner's development as a youth. In Neudörfl, from where he went to school in Wiener Neustadt, important Freemasonry meetings took place and the church there launched a fierce attack against the Freemasons. At the time, the Freemasons were banned in Austria but not in Hungary. The border between Austria and Hungary was the River Leitha and Neudörfl was the first village in Hungarian Transleithania. The Viennese Freemasons therefore went to Neudörfl to hold their meetings there. Such a coincidence in Rudolf Steiner's destiny may not be entirely irrelevant.

If it were possible to describe the whole lecture series, we should be able to see how Steiner achieved a specific goal, step by step.

The lecture on the festival of Whitsun takes as its main subject the publicizing of occult traditions. Right at the start Steiner states: 'What I shall say today comes from an old occult tradition.' The way in which Steiner boldly pulls back the shrouds to see what is hidden there can be read from the wording of the first part:

> What the festival of Whitsun actually symbolizes, what it is based on and what it means in a deeper sense is only written down in one manuscript ... still in existence ... and is guarded in the most careful manner. However, this manuscript does not

---

* See *The Temple Legend and the Golden Legend.*

> describe the festival of Whitsun, but rather that for which it is only the outer symbol. Hardly anyone has seen this manuscript except those who were initiated into the deepest secrets of the Catholic Church or were able to read in the astral light. One copy is owned by a figure who was badly misjudged by the world, but who has begun to be interesting for the observer of history. I might have said 'was owned' rather than 'is owned,' but this might cause confusion. This is why I say: one copy is owned by the Count of Saint Germaine ... The ancient teachings on this are contained in secret manuscripts which lie in hidden rooms where scarcely anyone has ever been. They are accessible to a few people who are able to see into the astral and also to some initiates.

Steiner proceeds to the attack as it were, aiming for something important. Briefly, the content of the lecture is that the Holy Spirit should be born in human beings as the redeemed reborn Lucifer, so that an arc reaches from the Fall into sin to the event of Whitsun, because without the Fall humankind could not be free. The second Friday lecture dealt with Cain and Abel, the crucial dual nature in humankind: on the one hand are people like Abel who work with what nature provides in a finished form; on the other side the Cain people who work creatively on material, metal and other earthly substances in order to produce something new. This provides an introduction to the discussion of the temple legend, the central symbol of Freemasonry.

In October four lectures followed on the legends of Prometheus, the Argonauts and the Odyssey, Siegfried and the Trojan war. The occult meaning of the ancient myths which were always an open pictorial rendering of the mysteries was revealed. The two November lectures on the 'Rosicrucians' and the 'Manicheans' followed next. This revolved directly around the temple legend in which the polarity of Cain and Abel appears personified in the master builder Hiram and King Solomon. Steiner makes a direct connection between the Manicheans and the Freemasons: 'Before it is possible to understand the Freemasons, the original spiritual stream to which they are connected must be examined. Manicheism is an even more important spiritual movement than that of the Rosicrucians.' At the end of the series, the lectures of December 2, 9, 16 and 23, 1904 deal in a surprisingly bold revelation with 'the mystery schools and their connections,' especially Freemasonry. The time for practising esotericism in a closed circle, as it then came to life in the ES and FM lessons, had not yet arrived. Steiner was still merely providing the historical background, although this contained a specific aim. So the problem of whether Freemasonry should be spoken about in front of men *and* women did not arise, as it would in October 1905 and January 1906.

Steiner provided a glimpse behind the curtain of Masonic life. He said that, as a non Freemason, he could only speak about Freemasonry from a Theosophical standpoint. Really, it required a Freemason to speak about Freemasonry. But someone of this kind, who had really gone through the various grades by means of actual experiences of his soul did not exist on the continent of Europe.

Since Freemasonry had led into rationalism, its form had become an empty shell. Previously, the symbolic objects and procedures awoke intuitive connections to the spiritual in the participants involved in the rites. This was also the time in which the Freemasons were still master builders in a real cultural sense and, with intuitive vision, built temples and cathedrals in accordance with cosmic dimensions.

One day a resurrection of the Freemasonry movement will take place and new building will therefore arise. The prospect of this future led Steiner to speak about the secret of the atom: 'The mode of thinking which has taken hold of humankind since the sixteenth century must be reproduced into the very atoms,' and: 'Only when rational thinking has grasped the atom again, can Freemasonry be revived.' This really means that the route of thinking which at first leads to superficiality and disintegration must be courageously followed right to its end until new fundamental spirituality can be acquired. Humankind will have to realize that atoms are concentrated electricity and also the same as human thinking. 'At the moment when humankind has recognized this most basic occult truth about thought, electricity and atoms, then it will realize something which will be of the greatest importance for the future ... humankind will be able to use the power of thinking to build with atoms.'

In future the meaning of occult striving will increasingly be to outwardly overcome the problems of civilization and the social life rather than people being enlightened by the occult. Nevertheless, this will not spare humankind from a harsh judgment and division. Industry will become completely chaotic and only a struggle for existence as long as people do not know what thoughts must be poured into the empty shell (FM etc.). There are only two options: complete chaos or union with the good spiritual leadership of humankind.

During the fifty years which have elapsed since then, these cultural perspectives have gained the highest relevance. Work on the atom proceeds at a frenzied pace but we are still far from understanding what the atom actually is. It often appears as though a change for the worse is much more likely than one for the better.

I shall quote a few sentences from the last of the four lectures, on December 23, 1904:

> Our task is to permeate this mineral world through and through with the spirit within us ... If you build a machine, you have put a part of your spirit into the machine. The machine perishes and turns to dust ... But what it has done, what it has achieved, passes into the very atoms and does not vanish without trace. Every atom bears a trace of your spirit and will carry this trace with it. The atom itself has undergone change as a result of having once been in a machine, and this change that you have wrought in the atom will never again be lost to it.
>
> ... When the Freemason was working with his fellow-builders, he knew: In future times the mineral world will be spiritualized; to build means nothing else than to spiritualize the mineral world. He knew that the construction would one day become the content of his soul ... Spiritualizing the four realms of nature ...To bring spirit into the whole external world — that has been the task of the secret societies of every age.
>
> ... Before the end of the fifth cultural epoch, science will have reached the stage where man will be able to penetrate into the atom itself. When the similarity of substance between the thought and the atom is once comprehended, the way to get hold of the forces contained in the atom will soon be discovered and then nothing will be inaccessible to certain methods of working. A man standing here, let us say, will be able by pressing a button concealed in his pocket, to explode some

object at a great distance — say in Hamburg! Just as ... wireless telegraphy is now possible. What I have just indicated will be within man's power when the occult truth that thought and atom consist of the same substance is put into practice.

Then Steiner goes on to speak about how one day this will bring about the decline of the post Atlantean culture. Just as Lemuria perished by fire and Atlantis through water, so the post Atlantean culture will be lost because people will not have a sufficient counterbalance to the form of the ideal of selflessness.

A tiny handful of people will survive into the sixth epoch of civilization. This tiny handful will have attained selflessness. The others will develop every imaginable skill and subtlety in the manipulation and use of the physical forces of nature, but without the essential degree of selflessness. They will launch the War of All against All and this will be the cause of the decline of our [present civilization].

It is therefore terrible if these discoveries are made without humankind having made an equivalent amount of moral progress.

Why did Steiner talk about such matters? Because he was on the point of founding a new esoteric movement for working towards a balance between the manipulation of substance and selflessness.

*

This series of lectures had a sequel in 1905. The way in which Steiner systematically built up his thoughts is astonishing. The titles of the lectures should be mentioned here at the very least. On Whit Monday, linking in to the lecture of the previous year, Steiner again began to talk about occult movements. Four lectures concerning 'the Temple Lost and Rediscovered' began on Monday May 15 and were continued on the following Mondays: 1. The great allegories, 2. The temple orders, 3. The symbol of the cross, 4. The redeemed word. The basic idea was that if you need to dig a tunnel and the work is not organized properly, then the two ends of the tunnel will not meet. This is what people do. They believe themselves capable of developing culture and solving the social question, but they have no proper plan for this. Anthroposophy is the blueprint for culture as a whole, above all for solving social problems. You should not seek in anthroposophy something lying beyond life: it is nothing other than the blueprint for what should be built on earth. The rejuvenated concept of Freemasonry comes into play here.

In this connection it is clear why Steiner held the lecture on 'Atoms and the Logos' on October 21, 1905, the evening before the annual general meeting, in other words, during the days when the important ES lesson took place.

The lecture was far-reaching. After death the human being at first moves on the astral plane. Because this is the realm where animal consciousness lives, he has an effect in the animal kingdom. During his further journeying, he moves in lower Devachan, in the sphere of consciousness of the plant kingdom and so has an effect on the plant kingdom for a while. Lastly the time comes when he influences the mineral world and takes part in the transformation of physical material. This happens in upper Devachan, where mineral consciousness lives. Those who have died thus take part in working on the mineral world: all the more reason for the living to work on the mineral world in the sense of the Logos.

Steiner next introduced the concept of the atom saying that it should be imagined that an atom grows until it is finally as large as the earth. 'The occultist is in a position to make the atom grow and to observe it internally.' If you have the ability to observe the processes which constitute the atom, then you reach the blueprint of the white lodge, those masters who are leaders of the spiritual stream, especially the ES.

> It is part of the plan of the leaders of humankind that the mineral kingdom should be progressively transformed by human beings in order to make the whole mineral world a pure work of art. Electricity for a start points us to the occult depths of matter. Finally, a point will come when humankind has transformed the whole mineral world. The special plan lives in the lodge of the masters. If you can see into this, then it is apparent what wonderful buildings and machines are still to arise from the mineral world.

But I should add — only if grave misuse does not ruin progress. It is of significance that Steiner always returned to speaking about the atom in situations where he was dealing with the development of the inner circle, in other words about the rebirth of the Masonic ideal.

A review of the lectures from the morning of October 23, 1905 (two lectures) and January 2, 1906 on Freemasonry is not absolutely necessary at this point.* Here I only wish to point out again that in these lectures 'the fight against the female spirit in favour of the male spirit' is stated as a basic tendency of traditional Freemasonry. The ancient spirituality and wisdom which, in historical times, radiated from the East towards the centre and then Westwards, came from the era before the division of the sexes (the middle of the Lemurian period) or from the time of the matriarchies immediately following and is therefore referred to as 'female spirit' by western occultists. It was brought into the advancing cultural development by the ancient priest movement. This generally misunderstood one-sidedness was now to be opposed by the male spirituality from the West which expressed the new knowledge and wisdom from working on material, above all on the mineral world. This is the reason that early Freemasonry had strictly refused to accept women into its lodges. You could also say that western occultism wished to bring out the Cain principle in contrast to the Abel-Seth principle which was still dominant.

This is basically the main source of the spiritual East-West problem. This problem became a human drama in the biography of H.P. Blavatsky. Starting out from the ancient eastern spiritual tradition, she was sucked into the wake of spiritualistic experimentation arising from western occultism, being a particular kind of medium.† In the West she fought for equality for women in the lodges of the Freemason orders, which gained her wholehearted hostility and vigorous resistance from western occultists until she finally returned completely to the influence of the eastern stream.

Steiner could never even remotely contemplate seeking the solution to the problem between the eastern and western spirit by superficial addition. Filled with Christ's impulse, he had to prepare the way for the direct spiritual activity of the present. Both what was justified and capable of serving the future in the ancient eastern wisdom and the new western spiritual impulse would naturally come into their own. On January 2, 1906 he said: 'The Abel of the past must be joined by the Abel of the future.' All one-sidedness will be transformed in the creative fire of the spiritual voice of the present.

---

* See *The Temple Legend and the Golden Legend*.

† See the lectures, *The Occult Movement in the Nineteenth Century*.

Steiner clearly showed destiny to lie on the western path, in that it must proceed from science. In view of the coming technical age, he also looked towards the West throughout his life with the gravest concern for humankind. If the stream flowing through the western secret societies was allowed to continue without implanting the Christ impulse into its justified goals, then the outcome could only be the age of atomic physics and the atom bomb in a terrible form. These may well be some of the visions which governed Steiner in his efforts to develop the inner esoteric circle, particularly in view of the renewed ideals of Freemasonry.

It is really one of the greatest tragedies of our age, that the outbreak of war in 1914 destroyed the fruitful development to build up a core in the inner circles which had been going on over more than eight years. Supported by activity at the centre, the anthroposophical movement would have dared to increase its activity outwardly both by expanding and by launching individual cultural projects for renewal. Unnoticed, a serious test of anthroposophical life took place and this test grew enormously, without people everywhere being clearly aware of it. Because the war and its aftermath themselves then heralded the need for anthroposophy to bring forth the wealth of special cultural movements: the threefold movement, the school movement and all the other offshoots arose. It became necessary to stride into the arena of the cultural struggle in a variety of ways without the presence of the supportive heart of a special esoteric circle. Can our gratitude and admiration be great enough in view of the moment when, after the Christmas Conference, Steiner once again created a heart from which living blood might flow, not only through the body of the society, but also through all the active professional communities which were at the cultural outposts? We may always fill ourselves in a special way with the secret which was and is and remains connected to Steiner's final period of activity and his death.

The Creation of Mantric Verse

The wealth of verses we owe to Rudolf Steiner is far greater than we can survey today. Each verse emerged out of a definite individual context, and was given as an aid for the inner striving of a single individual or group, with no thought of their being published someday as a collection. The attitude of the sower prevailed who freely gives of the seeds to be sown, trusting fully that from each something living will spring forth and grow. The main reason, however, for the impossibility of surveying this wealth is different. The womb from which these verses spring is the substance in Rudolf Steiner's lifework that arose from and was nurtured by the mystery-background. The most important part of Rudolf Steiner's verse creation was not intended for the world, nor even for all the members of the Theosophical or Anthroposophical Societies. It arose as spiritual preparation for strictly guided esoteric circles who were to safeguard the spiritual substance of the entire movement. An undiscriminating collection and application of this precious heritage can therefore easily violate the tact which we owe to Rudolf Steiner's creative intention, which was in each case completely specific.

The first strict condition for arriving at an overview of this verse creation consists in developing a feeling for the essence of a verse by Rudolf Steiner and what it requires from the soul. A simple reflection can make us aware of the particular body of forces characteristic of these mantric verses. In the first creative period of his life, in Weimar and Berlin up until the turn of the century, Rudolf Steiner lived wholly within the pulse and breathe of the literary world of that time. He stood in the midst of the life of writers and poets of his time. Everything that was written then, particularly the poetry at that time, found a sympathetic focus in his soul. It would be natural to ask what sort of poems this young friend of all writers and poets would try to write. The astonishing fact is that the young Rudolf Steiner composed no poems. In the circles with which he associated up to the turn of the century, one could hardly find a man more poetically unproductive than he was. All the others composed poems; only he did not, apart from at best a few occasional humorous verses, which distinguish themselves primarily by making no claim to poetic style. Later, when a boundless fountain of rich verse creation began to flow, it is possible to perceive already from the coherence of his life's course that we are not dealing with ordinary poems, whether lyrics or any other sort of verse. It is something entirely different.

Even after the turn of the century, indeed even after Rudolf Steiner had actively entered into the circles of the Theosophical Society in the years 1901–2, and had become General Secretary of the German Section in October 1902, still no mantric verses seem to arise; at least he does not come forward with any. If one observes this development more closely, one has the greatest respect for the discretion and conscientiousness which Rudolf Steiner has allowed to prevail in this sphere from which the mantric verses spring. They are in fact not verses merely brought into a metre or perhaps simply rhymed.

As last we come across a definite moment in which Rudolf Steiner for the first time steps forward with such a verse: Christmas of 1906. He brings to the circle of friends, as an unpretentious yet ultimately momentous gift, the verse:

> Behold the sun at the midnight hour,
> In the lifeless ground build thy rocky bower ...

He does this with all gravity, in that he has Marie von Sivers recite the verse. In her preface to the German collection of verses and meditations (*Wahrspruchworte*), Marie Steiner said about this significant moment:

> The moment when, at Christmas, he gave his first meditative verse, 'Behold the sun at the midnight hour ...' is one of the striking events of our lives; and the power had to be found to transform this fullness of experience, this impact of the word chiselled in stone, into resounding spoken tone. It was a turning point for the inner soul.

This was spoken personally; but in the sense of the entire cultural development it would be justifiable to call this a turning point of spiritual life. For much was inaugurated in this moment. From this seed grew a large tree, for it was also the moment of birth of a renewed speech formation, which now for the first time shone in the sky like a morning-star.

Of course at that time there were already a number of verses, but without being in the foreground of the anthroposophic work. However, today it is not only justified but even necessary that the members of the Anthroposophical Society occupy themselves with what had begun to develop at that time in a quiet, secret context. If we look at what had been prepared in the background, we become aware with reverence and respect of all the manifold conditions which had to be quietly fulfilled so that Rudolf Steiner could come forward at Christmas 1906 with the first mantric verse. The womb of all the mantric verse that he gave is the Esoteric School (ES), which at that time was in its initial stages. Already at that time there was a more intimate circle within the Society composed of members of this Esoteric School.

For a long time, an ES had existed within the Theosophical Society. It had been founded by H.P. Blavatsky and was originally called the Eastern School for Theosophy (EST), which expressed that here in particular the 'ancient wisdom' coming from the Orient was to be cultivated. Later this name was changed to Esoteric School. Rudolf Steiner was admitted as a member into this school in October 1902, when Mrs Besant was in Berlin for the founding of the German Section of the Theosophical Society and the appointment of Rudolf Steiner as General Secretary. October 20 was the day of the founding of the German Section. On October 23, Rudolf Steiner and Marie von Sivers were accepted as members into the ES. From the sequence of dates it can be surmised how resolutely, yet how correctly, Rudolf Steiner made his way. He did not want to disregard the existing links of a chain. He wanted to forge a clear connection to earlier striving on the spiritual path. But he did not for a moment consider his task regarding the ES as a direct continuation of what had previously been cultivated there. He was at pains to carry that which was inherently his, and therefore something radically new, into the Theosophical stream; thus for him it was especially important that he bring to the more intimate esoteric circle the contents taken directly from the current springs of revelation of the spiritual worlds, new and independent of all tradition. Also, he became a member of the ES without any particular instructions or contents being passed on to him. Only in this way could he follow his path.

Today it is possible to survey how Rudolf Steiner's activity in the ES took shape. Very soon an intimate teacher-pupil relationship between him and a number of members of the Theosophical Society developed. He spent an astonishing amount of time and energy cultivating these intimate teacher-pupil relationships. There was a circle of people with whom he corresponded extensively. He practically demanded that any questions one had be submitted to him, and he used these questions which emerged in their cognitive life, in an individual, careful guidance of souls. Nevertheless, we also observe for a whole year a certain careful holding back in this. But by the end of the year 1903 this clearly changed. From the attitude of the letters, and in particular from the way in which he now gave detailed instructions for meditation, one can see that he now believed it possible to take a step. He took a further step two years after his admittance into the ES. Perhaps this was related to the condition that, as a rule, only those who had been members for at least two years in the Theosophical Society could become members of the school. In a kind of analogy, it could be that Rudolf Steiner also imposed on himself a kind of two-year restraint.

From September 15 to 24, 1904, Mrs Besant went on a lecture tour through a number of German cities, beginning in Hamburg, going on to Berlin, and finally to Cologne. Mrs Besant spoke in English and after the lecture Rudolf Steiner gave a brief summary of the contents in German. Several conversations about the ES took place during this journey. Some of those present, particularly Mathilde Scholl, have related this. The decisive conversation took place in Cologne, in Mathilde Scholl's apartment, where she was present along with Marie von Sivers, when Rudolf Steiner formally presented his request. He now intended to begin work in the ES officially. Mrs Besant emphatically agreed adding: 'Now, your task is esoteric Christianity, and I recommend, therefore, that you take up my book, *Esoteric Christianity*.'

This had been published about a year before. The lecture-theme about which Mrs Besant had originally wanted to speak in the German cities was, 'Is Theosophy Anti-Christian?' Letters of that time reveal

16. THE CREATION OF MANTRIC VERSE

that this theme had caused Rudolf Steiner a great deal of consternation, for it had already become clear to him that Mrs Besant did not have the ability to speak competently about the mysteries of Christianity. At Rudolf Steiner's urging she had abandoned the original theme. This was the background to Rudolf Steiner's firm reply, when Mrs Besant said that he should connect the ES work with her book. He said that he must have a free hand in creatively guiding the Esoteric School from the revelations that were open to him. To this Mrs Besant could not withhold her assent.

This conversation was a kind of prelude to the further step which, according to Rudolf Steiner's description, was taken in 1907 when Mrs Besant was again in Germany for the big Munich congress:

> It was always my wish to link what I did with things already in existence, with what was there historically. I had done this in relation to the Theosophical Society and I wished to do the same in regard to the Esoteric School. Thus my limited circle came into existence first in connection with the School. But the connection had to do solely with the *external arrangements*, not with the supersensible knowledge I imparted. Thus in the early years my smaller circle appeared as a section of Mrs Besant's Esoteric School. Yet according to its inner nature it had no connection with that School. And in 1907 when Mrs Besant was present at our Theosophical Conference in Munich the external connection also was severed completely by mutual consent.

After that first conversation in the year 1904, Rudolf Steiner used mantric verses in his teacher-pupil relationship with individual members. He does this after he has specifically accepted a small number of people into the Esoteric School. The verses that appear from now on are given as personal meditations with detailed instruction as to their use. So after the autumn of 1904 an organism of members of the ES gradually develops. The exchange of letters intensifies, giving exact instructions for meditating on the mantric verses. Soon, to ease the workload, some letters containing what was for everyone, not just for individuals, were duplicated.

The next step follows after another year of intensive work. We can discern that everything was a preparation for a specific event. This occurred at the annual general meeting in 1905. (The annual general meeting always took place in October, the month when the Society had been founded.) The Sunday was filled with the proceedings of the general meeting. On the following day, October 24, an ES lesson took place, apparently for the first time, in which all the members of the ES that were present met together. Until then, Rudolf Steiner had only worked with individuals; between the teacher and the individual pupil a soul-bond had been formed through conversations and letters. Now for the first time the members were united in a group. Many preparations leading to this had taken place. Something wonderfully methodical manifests in Rudolf Steiner's lifework, especially concerning the esoteric element.

From then on he held such ES lessons in close succession, in Berlin as well as in other places where he was present for a lecture cycle, and in Munich on the occasion of the annual summer performances. The last was on July 14, 1914 in Norrköping in Scandinavia. At the outbreak of war this work was discontinued. The subject of all these lessons is meditative work; instructions for meditation in connection with a particular symbolism or with mantric verses. This is the fountain from which Rudolf Steiner's verses flow. These verses are not to be valued only for their pleasing sound and their thought-content, but are to be meditated. They have no other purpose. At that time great care was taken that the verses were not generally available, but only used for the purpose of meditation.

Now in these ES lessons there were also 'structure-verses' because each lesson began with the reading of verses for the specific days of the week. There were also verses with which the lessons were concluded. Thus a sacred treasure of mantric verses gradually came into being. Everything preserved from this time shows how these verses were held sacred. On the whole, Rudolf Steiner was still very prudent at that time. A greater number of verses were given in total intimacy to individual persons; in the community context of the ES, however, there was only a small number. And this prudence and care were by no means accidental but were conscious in the extreme.

Rudolf Steiner has spoken in detail in his autobiography (Chapter 36) about an additional esoteric context that arose outside the framework of the ES. The gatherings in this circle had a ritual character. But as Rudolf Steiner stressed, this ritual element was only of an illustrative nature. The gatherings therefore served the purpose of instruction and imparting knowledge. Here too Rudolf Steiner showed the highest degree of exactness and correctness. Although he drew the content and substance completely from his own spiritual power of authority, he nevertheless preserved the formal method of procedure and in January 1906 he established a certain connection with the traditional succession. He himself describes that he did this because he was approached from this side. At this time a certificate, an authorization was issued to him and also to Marie von Sivers. But here especially he placed the greatest value on drawing nothing from tradition, but only from his own spiritual vision and spiritual research. Opponents have directed their attacks here, because injurious statements could be correctly made concerning the representative of the traditional stream who issued the certificate to Rudolf Steiner. But Rudolf Steiner had nothing to do with this man except in the one moment in which he received the certificate. The whole world in which this man moved Rudolf Steiner never touched inwardly even in passing.

After January 1906, Rudolf Steiner waited quite a long time before beginning to convene such ritual gatherings. This probably occurred first in 1907. In this connection, his creation of verse advanced then, in addition to the meditation mantras verses bearing a ritual character were added which accompany texts for celebrating ritual-symbolic acts. Rudolf Steiner formed no verse that was not read directly from the spiritual world. The content of higher spheres mirrors itself directly in a 'word-body.' This should be there as a feeling of reverence and commitment to care in those who have such verses in their books or perhaps only among their papers. The mantra is composed in a wording that is not of this world, and cannot therefore be spoken or gone through in thought without a living spirituality being touched. We leave behind the everyday world which includes the poetry books by our great poets.

The ritual esoteric gatherings continue from 1907 until the outbreak of the First World War. As friends who were present have related, they often lasted many hours; and since there were many such gatherings, one marvels yet again at all the activities that found a place in the unceasingly creative and busy course of Rudolf Steiner's life.

Now let us return to the point of Christmas 1906, when Rudolf Steiner gave the Christmas mantra, 'Behold the sun at the midnight hour.' This verse was much more than an artistic enrichment of the

Christmas festival. It represented a spiritual new beginning of the first order. Rudolf Steiner only gave it after the ES had been nurtured in quiet for a whole year. The spiritual foundation was there. Something could now take place through which a principle of the most far-reaching significance could be applied. This first verse was the beginning of an unveiling of the mysteries, which later, where the wealth of verses is concerned, swelled into a broad stream. But this mystery-revelation does not emerge until the mysteries themselves are established and secured to a certain extent.

*

For a time, the development continues in a certain stillness: individual people are given verses, and other verses emerge in lectures, alongside the verse-treasure which grows in the background in the esoteric context. But then, all at once, the great stream of mystery-revelation breaks forth: the Mystery Dramas come into being. Of course they are no ordinary stage plays; from first to last they are of a mantric nature and can really be comprehended only in the context which we are now contemplating. The special meditative mantras in the Mystery Dramas naturally stand out, for example, the two verses in the first play which Benedictus gives to Johannes Thomasius: 'The light's weaving being, it radiates through widths of space ...' and 'The light's weaving being, it radiates from man to man ...'

But beyond this the Mystery Dramas as a whole have a mantric character, and we cannot fully understand their intention if we do not consider that in the background of what is placed on the stage — as a kind of gold standard — the work in the Esoteric School has been intensely cultivated. The Mystery Dramas are a conscious opening of mystery-revelation, and hence the name 'Mystery Drama.' Such a revelation was only possible because real mysteries existed.

It has often been mentioned here that these Mystery Dramas were the first cultural fruits of anthroposophy, that they signified the first emergence of the movement into the arena of cultural life. Not only were there the distinct buds of a new dramatic art as well as of speech formation and eurythmy, now the thought of a building arose. For the first performances of the plays were in ordinary halls and theatres in Munich. One of the four plays arose each year from 1910. When the fourth play was completed the first public eurythmy performance took place at the same gathering in August 1913 in Munich; and immediately following this, on September 20, the laying of the foundation stone for the building in Dornach occurred. One thing grew out of another. With the Mystery Dramas we have, not only in verse form, but as a fructification of all spheres of culture the appearance of anthroposophical work in the arena of cultural life: mystery-revelation.

Here something else must be recalled: if the cultural fruit of anthroposophical work flowed out of the Mystery Dramas in the first place, we see the Mystery Dramas themselves in the year 1910 flowing directly out of the announcement of the approaching new Christ mystery. The first months of the year 1910 brought almost daily lectures in which Rudolf Steiner announced the imminent appearance of the etheric Christ. Through the Theodora-scene in the first scene of the *Portal of Initiation*, the mystery that appears at the dawn of a new Christ-era becomes the source of all dramatic developments that run through the four plays. Thus the emergence of the anthroposophical work, first in the artistic realm, has the most intimate and direct connection with the new Christ mysteries of the age.

An extremely important stage in the formation of the verses falls exactly in the middle of the creative period to which we owe the Mystery Dramas and all that resulted from them. The *Soul Calendar*, that outwardly unassuming little book with the fifty-two weekly verses, is truly the fulcrum of a certain aspect of Rudolf Steiner's lifework. Images arose that are of overwhelming cosmic beauty. The *Soul Calendar* came into being as the quiet centre of the Mystery Dramas, between the second and the third: two are finished, two are still to come. Thus the fifty-two weekly verses flow directly out of the very centre of the same source.

It is worth looking a little more closely at the moment of the *Soul Calendar's* birth. One can clearly see then that the *Soul Calendar* is, as it were, an extract of the mystery-revelation of which we are speaking. Looking back to the last third of the year 1911: the second Mystery Drama, *The Soul's Probation*, was completed; a decision was coming to a head within the Theosophical movement. Invitations had been issued for a congress in Genoa in October. Everyone was awaiting the inevitable controversy because of the lack of understanding with which those in Theosophical circles saw the Christian mysteries. It was known that in Genoa Rudolf Steiner would sharply oppose the announcement of Krishnamurti as the reincarnated Christ. At the last moment the congress was cancelled. What had been prepared now bore positive fruit. The second series of lectures concerning the etheric Christ-event began. The first series had filled the beginning of 1910; now, in the autumn of 1911, followed the second series, filled with such profound secrets!

As he was going to go to Genoa, Rudolf Steiner instead began the lectures in Milan, Locarno, and Lugano. The unprecedented intensification in these lectures first occurred in Neuchâtel, where on September 27 and 28 for Michaelmas he revealed secrets about Christian Rosenkreutz in an astounding manner. After the theme of the great spiritual leaders of humankind had been raised in a distorted way by the Krishnamurti affair, Christian Rosenkreutz and Jeshu ben Pandira as well as the appearance of Christ in the etheric were spoken of again and again in Rudolf Steiner's lectures in the weeks that followed. In a certain sense he took hold of the spiritual realms in a new and productive way, bringing forth knowledge about the masters, the leaders of humanity, and placed these figures in the light that streams from the appearance of the etheric Christ. The lectures in Neuchâtel were immediately followed by the important lecture in Basle on October 1, 'The Etherization of the Blood,' which was a kind of central core in the announcement of the new Christ-revelation. And the Basle lecture was followed in Karlsruhe by the great lecture cycle, *From Jesus to Christ*.

After completion of this cycle, the dedication of the building on Landhausstrasse 70 took place in Stuttgart on October 15. We see that the idea of a building was not first realized only after the fourth play with the laying of the foundation stone in September 1913; it found a small prior realization in the special home for the spiritual striving of the Stuttgart branch in 1911.

In passing, I want to mention how the wealth of verses always grows on such occasions. In the pithy verse which Rudolf Steiner gave for the dedication of the house lies hidden a mighty force.

> May he who enters bring love to this home,
> May he who stays within seek knowledge at this place,
> May he who leaves take peace from this house.

16. THE CREATION OF MANTRIC VERSE

To this dedication verse Rudolf Steiner added a transposed Old Testament temple-dedication verse.

But we want to outline the whole configuration of destiny of the end of 1911, the time when the *Soul Calendar* originated. Since the annual general meeting could not take place that year in October because of the planned Genoa congress, it was held on December 10 in Berlin. Two moments stand out from the proceedings. The first meeting of the *Johannesbau-Verein* (Johannes Building Association) took place on December 12. The whole initiative for the main building came to expression, planned originally for Munich, but then constructed in Dornach; and through the figure of Johannes (John), after whom the building was to have been named, the focus was again directed to the great spiritual leaders of humankind. The building that then arose in Dornach took its name from the great spirit of Goethe. At the end of the meeting of *Johannesbau-Verein* members, an imaginative motif arose which stood behind all the spirit-impulses of these months, when Rudolf Steiner said: we Theosophists must struggle to attain knowledge; that is not possible without a descent into the forces of death. That is the cross which we as Theosophists must carry about with us; but artistic activity must be woven as a wreath of radiant red roses around the black cross of cognition. The second lecture at the dedication of the house in Stuttgart had had the theme, 'In what sense are we Theosophists and in what sense are we Rosicrucians?' This was the time in which the great revelations concerning Rosenkreutz occurred.

On December 14, Rudolf Steiner called together a smaller circle and, in the sense of a foundation out of the spirit, he appointed a committee whose task was to encourage artistic activity as an unfolding of anthroposophical work. This endeavour was soon abandoned, because one of the members who had been entrusted with an official position entered into fantastic side-roads. But at this moment, the intention of the most sacred mystery-revelations in the artistic sphere became visible. Rudolf Steiner said: 'A way of working is to be founded which ... has as its point of departure the individuality who took the name Christian Rosenkreutz in past ages of western history.' The association that was to be founded, the 'Society for Theosophical Methods and Art,' had the task of 'artistic representation of Rosicrucian occultism.' These were the words of Rudolf Steiner himself.

Thus in the sign of the etheric Christ, the mystery-source of western spiritual life is approached with all intensity. The *Soul Calendar* originates during this period.

A Christmas cycle in Hanover followed the annual general meeting in Berlin. These are the lectures, *The World of the Senses and the World of the Spirit.* They concern the mysteries of blood. What becomes especially clear is the distinction between man's physical nature before and after the Fall and, although not expressed in so many words, the transformation that is made possible through the connection with Christ. The Rosicrucian thread that appeared in the Basle lecture, 'The Etherization of the Blood,' is developed. On January 1, 1912, in the days of the gathering in Hanover, Rudolf Steiner first presented his verse translation of *Olaf Åsteson.* He rendered into German verse this great Norwegian ballad, which illuminates from the esoteric aspect the days from Christmas to Epiphany. In a certain way, this creative translation also belongs to Rudolf Steiner's treasure of verses. This is still more instructive from a biographical standpoint, as we are dealing here with the days and weeks between the Mystery Dramas, during which the *Soul Calendar* came into being. As a component of the great calendar that was intended for the year 1912/13 ('the year 1879 after the birth of the I'), the *Soul Calendar* was probably completed and sent to the printer around the turn of the year, appearing then at Easter. The first copies surfaced in Helsingfors (Helsinki) during the cycle on the hierarchies (April 3–14).

We have now gathered sufficient material from which it becomes evident how a kind of fulcrum, a point of equilibrium, formed itself in Rudolf Steiner's lifework, wonderfully adorned by the *Soul Calendar.* This calendar was not simply meant to beautify the course of the year with its verses. What was its essential meaning? Here there is a connection with a great secret. In accompanying the course of the year through the polarities of summer and winter, the human being arrives at stations resembling those that must be crossed by the soul on the inner path. Instead of merely taking a spiritual path, we can add a life of the soul with the course of the year. What emerges is a tremendous possibility offered by nature herself, to add to the intimate teacher-pupil relationship a meditative realm of life accessible to anyone, where everyone can become their own hierophant, their own esoteric teacher, if only they make the right use of what is given. Behind the unassuming link with the metamorphoses of nature in the course of the year, something profound is concealed. When Rudolf Steiner was asked once, in what way the soul could most effectively prepare itself for the experience of the etheric Christ, he answered: through the meditative experience the course of the year. The mysteries of the seasons are nature's gift to the meditating human being who seeks the Christ-sphere. Is this now not a pattern which, if discovered and contemplated, must inspire us: that the fifty-two verses of the *Soul Calendar* fall exactly in the middle of the Mystery Dramas?

There is a kind of divine timetable in all that Rudolf Steiner created. For in that period, in all that he said or did, his concern was the announcement of the etheric Christ. And in adding the *Olaf Åsteson*, is it not opening the same breach that he first made in the walls of the world to allow a breakthrough for man? From this viewpoint one sees the Mystery Dramas very differently, for the Mystery Dramas not only contain the mantras, but also, for example, the fairy tales of Frau Balde. As Rudolf Steiner said in those years, fairy tales were originally the Rosicrucians' means of bringing humankind onto the spiritual path. He described how, as folk imaginations, fairy tales flowed out of earlier rhapsodical streams into the Rosicrucian mysteries. And when he fostered the Christmas plays in our circles, this is the same world as that of *Olaf Åsteson* and the *Soul Calendar*. Why? Because through the nuances echoing in them of the year's seasons, the Christ-mysteries of our age become accessible to humankind.

A large portion of what Rudolf Steiner gave from now on in the way of verses is related to the seasons. One moment stands out here, August 1915. One evening in Dornach, a great new treasure poured out: the 'Twelve Moods,' the great verses for the months that have become so full of significance for eurythmy; and as a parallel parody, 'The Song of Initiation,' a satire for sentimental anthroposophists with soul-egotism; and finally, the 'Dance of the Planets.' All are mantric verses for the seasons of the year. Year by year this treasure is enriched by verses, above all those given for Christmas, so that finally a direct line leads from the first Christmas verse, 'Behold the sun ...' all the way to the verses of the Christmas Foundation Conference, 'At the turning point of time the spirit-light of the world entered ...' The wonderful golden chain of Christmas verses, to which another link was added almost every Christmas, is at the same time like a spine in the organism formed of the riches of mantric verses for the seasons of the year.

*

The incision in Rudolf Steiner's lifework, caused by the outbreak of World War I, was an extremely significant one, especially regarding our topic here. What now came to a sudden end had been neither slight nor unimportant. At the beginning of the war, the rich work in the esoteric circles immediately ceased. The certificate Steiner received in 1906 was torn to pieces. Just as the esoteric work had been cultivated quietly in the background, so now its cessation remained invisible to those outside of it, that is to the majority of the members. Yet the more one understands that an important substance had flowed out of the esoteric background into the common work, the more clearly one perceives the decisive change that now occurred. Performance of the Mystery Dramas also ceased. It was not only that there were no longer the annual Munich performances; the fifth play that had been planned for the year 1914, and that was to have been set in the Greek age, failed to materialize. Finally, the stream of the unfolding of the Fifth Gospel which had begun to flow during the laying of the foundation stone of the Goetheanum after the Fourth Mystery Play, also ceased. If one considers the great amount of time that Rudolf Steiner reserved for what took place in the background, one can ask, What took its place now? To what does he devote the sum of strength and time, which has now become free? We recognize clearly: Rudolf Steiner steps aside to *move forward*. The emphasis shifts to a coming to terms with the destiny of the age. The great turn to the outside commences, from which then flowed all the later daughter movements, all the foundings and fructification of practical and cultural aspects of life.

Now for example at every members meeting, Rudolf Steiner began with a mantric verse. He spoke it for those who were on the battlefield and for those who had fallen. This is part of what occurs in place of the former background activity. It is quantitatively little, but into this lesser remnant flows all that formerly had its own esoteric existence. Through what was thus spoken, the branch-meeting began with a moment of consecration. This came about through the treasure of verses. Now the number of verses given for particular deceased persons increased. A wealth of gifts unfolded, especially from the year

1915 on. Much in the background which had become silent now flowed into the relationship of the living to the dead, a relationship which had been altered by the war. In addition, mantric verses for the current time arose, including the verse, 'The German spirit has not completed ...' and the one addressed to friends in Berlin. These were verses that not only expressed something relevant to present destinies, but were intended to be sources of strength in mastering these destinies.

After the war, the richly diverse cultural fertility and activity of anthroposophy, which manifested in the various daughter movements and training institutions, brought the emergence of completely new kinds of mantric verse. Aside from the specific verses given for speech formation and eurythmy, Rudolf Steiner gave shorter and more detailed occupational meditations, for teachers, medical doctors, and those active in other fields. Each group which took up a particular cultural task thereby became inwardly equipped. Just as verses arose earlier for a mother to say with her child at bedtime, he gave verses to the Waldorf School which the teachers say with the children at the beginning of a lesson, and in addition, a wealth of verses arose for the pedagogical work.

The world now called out in manifold ways. Thus in the Waldorf School the first ritual elements for the Sunday service and the youth service began. A treasure of ritual verses comes into being. At the same time, a priest of the Old Catholic church, who was a member of the Anthroposophical Society, approached Rudolf Steiner concerning the difficulties he and two colleagues were experiencing in the practice of their religious ritual: they received a German version of the Latin Mass, which was not just a translation, but was the first indication of a transition to a religious ritual appropriate for the present. Then came former Protestant ministers who were often asked to christen children: Rudolf Steiner gave them a christening verse. When this Swiss Old Catholic had given up his parish, he was often asked to perform funerals for anthroposophical friends who had passed away: a funeral ritual arose.

This was the time in which the beginnings of a movement for religious renewal became evident, which led to the founding of the Christian Community, and which immediately found whole-hearted encouragement from Rudolf Steiner. Steiner's help in fashioning the words, to which is owed the whole rich treasure of sacramental rituals of the Christian Community, did not arise without this prelude. One rarely saw him radiate with such bright and enthusiastic creative joy as when he brought a number of pages containing such texts and put the recipients on the spot by asking: Isn't that beautiful?

As Rudolf Steiner gave the treasure of verses to equip the daughter movements, the mystery-verse revelation which had begun so carefully and prudently, now emerged as a broad current. At the same time, the specialization of this new wealth of verses brought with it that much of the material became hidden again, not because it was reserved for a particular esoteric framework; quite the contrary — it served a specific cultural impulse in the world and therefore was not intended directly for everyone. Through the turn to the outside, the Logos-sphere, which had formerly existed as a quiet source in the background, experienced a significant metamorphosis in the arena of general cultural life.

After the Goetheanum fire, the creation of verse culminates with dramatic greatness. The year 1923 is like a great new spiritual beginning. Verses for the seasons of the year arise, but now on a quite different, more energetic level. The mysteries of the year's course are now fully unveiled in rich abundance. Mystery-verses resound, mystery-wind blows, while the Anthroposophical Society goes through a severe crisis, and Rudolf Steiner presses with the most intense energy for consolidation of the Society. We mention only one example, the Ephesian mystery-verse, which is filled with the sense of unison between the conflagration of Ephesus and the one on the Dornach hill:

> Behold the Logos
> In scorching fire;
> Find the solution
> In Diana's house.

With the breakthrough of revelation at the Christmas Conference, the view of the goal opens up; the goal toward which, through all the tensions and trials up to now, the path has been leading. Now the verse, 'Soul of Man ...' with the Christmas verse, 'At the turning point of time ...' arise. This Foundation Stone mantra is like an entire book of verse in concentrated form. Rudolf Steiner indicated that in these verses everything was gathered together which could be brought from the spiritual world during the time of the destiny of war. And when, throughout the days of the Christmas Conference, these verses are spoken by him in ever-new combinations, he stands like a priest celebrating a sacrament. The verse-element becomes ritual.

In the meantime there had been two attempts to reestablish an esoteric circle; both times, the attempt had been given up soon afterwards. But now, after the Christmas Conference, Rudolf Steiner took the big step. On February 15, 1924, the first Class lesson was held for those who have been admitted into the First Class of the School of Spiritual Science. Through the months until the onset of Rudolf Steiner's illness at Michaelmas, the golden chain of Class verses continues. A book arises of world-encompassing mantras, which can last for centuries if put to proper use. In September, a part of these verses was repeated. The verses of the First Class filled the time between the Christmas Conference verses and the last verse, which Rudolf Steiner gave as a legacy and farewell on the eve of Michaelmas 1924.

Although an esoteric work was once again formed, representing in a certain way the rebirth of the Esoteric School on a new level, the element of the unveiling of the mysteries continued. For, within the context of the Class lessons, the earlier personal teacher-pupil relationship was superseded and everything within the School of Spiritual Science is based on each individual's taking upon themselves the guidance and responsibility for their own spiritual striving.

Rudolf Steiner has truly given an infinite wealth for the meditative life. The treasure of mantric verses that he gave is such that if it is worked with, and if it is accorded proper importance over everything else, the anthroposophical movement will not perish. Nor can it suffer any defeat in the cultural confrontations which are imminent.

The last verse that Rudolf Steiner gave was the Michael-verse with which he closed his Last Address on September 28, 1924:

> Springing from powers of the Sun,
> Radiant Spirit-powers, blessing all worlds!
> For Michael's garment of rays
> Ye are predestined by thought divine.

One of the participants described the event immediately afterwards in a letter:

> As powerful as was the content of this address of twenty minutes, the manner in which it was spoken and the atmosphere that filled the room were just as significant. Indeed, I have

never heard Rudolf Steiner speak like this. There was absolute silence before he came; then everyone rose; it was simply a matter of course; one had not known it before, but in a moment one knew it. It was likewise at the end. Rudolf Steiner's face looked as though chiselled in stone; every feature stood out sharply; I couldn't help but sense: in this face lies something of the soul of a man who is struggling with the forces of death. During the first sentence I was afraid: will he be able to carry through to the end? But then he spoke without strain and perhaps more easily than usual. Yet behind the words lay an infinitely bitter grief for the world, for the world's darkness, if one may be permitted to use such an image; there was something like a Gethsemane-mood behind what was spoken. The words themselves one experienced as a kind of legacy and a last warning-cry to human beings to awake, to be awake, to awaken from sleep finally... .
Particularly the last mantra — I cannot say otherwise — sounded like a great, soul-shaking cry, a call using all his last strength in the world, a proclamation of all that had been revealed to the world by Rudolf Steiner throughout a lifetime. It was not a peaceful proclamation out of the spiritual world, as on other occasions; instead, one suddenly saw how this Michael-address and this Michael-life has been wrested from all the demons and powers of darkness of the world.

Mantric Verse and Poetic Art

From notes in Emil Bock's diary

The mantras, as meditative material, are totally different from personal poetic art.

Poetry: thus speaks man.
Mantric verse: thus speaks the spiritual world ('God's Word').
The word from below — the word from above.

In both, there exist adaptability and intensification: making human the word of God; and making 'divine' the human word, i.e., the drawing near of the human word to the level of the mantric word. The latter is supra-personal art of the verse, is supra-poetic art of poetry. In Goethe we find a treasure of such verses, although Goethe *wishes* to stay within the realm of poetry. It is the same with Christian Morgenstern. There, on occasion, meta-poetry is consciously created. The Psalms and the Proverbs of Solomon in the Old Testament are perhaps most related and comparable to the mantras. Or old incantations. Also, the Song of Olaf Åsteson.

In mantric verse, the spiritual world speaks. The language of the Angels is nearer the Logos, nearer the Word that contains creator-power, the creator-Word that created the world. One senses that Exousiai dwell within it. It is active; it changes the world. It bears a magical will-intent. Mere reading aloud of what has been written down is not sufficient, but speaking it is at the same time a writing, an engraving. Repeated speaking 'impresses' it on the memory, yet this will not occur in a mechanical fashion, so that a mantric verse is easily recalled or even hovers about the memory, so to speak. It is necessary for him who makes use of it to impress it ever and again on his memory. In this sense, meditation is an enhanced self-engraving. Therefore it is already an achievement to speak regularly such verses to oneself, even if a full meditative act is not united with it each time.

The mantric texts exist in the spiritual world. The Angels hold them ready, and it is only a question of how they are discovered and read. For the Angels they are signposts given to them by higher powers for the inner guidance of man. When a human being meditates, he follows these signposts. He enters, as it were, into the functions of his Angel.

These signposts are always in advance of an age. The Psalms of David were once signposts for the epoch of the personal 'I' quality. 'As the stag cries for fresh water, so my soul cries for Thee, O Lord.' There, the longing for the 'I' speaks. Today, man must follow the sign-posts that lead him to the supra-personal. Poetry, in contrast, always follows behind, after what once had been the signpost of the angel-being has been passed over to man. This is why, beginning with a certain moment, the psalm became the seed of poetry embodying the personal element.

The Dispute about the Holy Spirit

The lack of confidence about what to do with the old Christmas customs, an uncertainty which becomes more noticeable every year, is connected at a deeper level with the fact that a new Christmas event from the future is taking the place of the backward-looking commemoration of the Christmas event two thousand years ago. The first deed of Christ which lies in the past is being followed by an approaching new deed of Christ which will increasingly define the nature of the Christmas festival in the future. Because we are aware of this, we are able to face the lack of confidence in the experience of Christmas and all the trivializing of the Christmas customs which we encounter around us with calm and patience. The first Christmas event took place on the level of *physical existence*. A healing deed was brought to humankind through grace from a higher world, irrespective of whether human beings were able to become conscious of this at that point or not. The new Christmas event which constitutes the real meaning of our century does not take place in an earthly sense on the level of physical existence, it calls upon *consciousness*, because the level where it exists has been lost to human consciousness. Human beings need to advance in consciousness in order to bridge the gulf between themselves and the level of the new Christ event.

*

As an introduction to the historical and karmic reflections which I wish to make, I should like to continue this Christological theme for a moment. The deed which took place two thousand years ago was first of all a deed of the Son. The being whom we call Christ and behind whom the being of the Son of the world appeared, prepared to enter the stream of earthly life. But soon after the event of Golgotha, the first seed of a new event followed. When we speak of the Holy Spirit, this is really a hieroglyphic mystery for many people. We will increasingly learn to understand why it was that the deed of Christ was followed by a deed of the Spirit. The events at Whitsun contained the beginning of a new fundamental deed of the Trinity which was experienced by the disciples fifty days after Christ's resurrection. But actually this was nothing other than a prophetic preview of the far future. It was not yet a fulfilment. There were other great seeds which also gradually prepared the ground for this great new event: Damascus was a further step in the Whitsun event, as was the hour of the Apocalypse on the Island of Patmos, when John in old age once again experienced a wonderful culmination of his Christian initiation. This was all of a prophetic nature. The real fulfilment of the deed of the Spirit at Whitsun when the power of the Holy Spirit filled humankind is the event of the etheric Christ which, as Rudolf Steiner never tired of stating, is what gives meaning to our age and the near future.

The appearance of anthroposophy itself is also one of humankind's Whitsun steps which is already approaching fulfilment. This is where the preparation begins to lead into fulfilment, as it were. Ten years before 1933 — which Steiner often referred to as the time when the new deed of Christ would unfold — destiny provided us with the remarkable inspirational event which we describe simply as the Christmas Conference. This was the point where we were especially aware of how the prophecy was fulfilled and how the new substance of Christmas entered the old Christmas festival. What took place there was one of the first gifts of the Second Coming, of the etheric Christ. After the deed of the Son the new deed, that of the Spirit, began to fully enter humankind, only humankind was not yet aware of it.

Both Christmas events — the first historical one and the second which is now taking place in a concealed manner and which we are only beginning to enter — were and are connected with a mystery of the Holy Spirit. There has always been an awareness of the Holy Spirit's participation in the old Christmas event: 'Born of the Virgin Mary, conceived by the Holy Spirit.' This is the Mary form of the Holy Spirit, the 'old' Holy Spirit which still worked through existence, not through consciousness. The Holy Spirit was involved in the development of the purely physical sheath into which the being of Christ was then able to be born.

Since Good Friday and Easter the principle of the Holy Spirit has worked in a totally different way. This is the working of the 'new' Holy Spirit which we mentioned before, that which calls humankind's consciousness to the heights.

But the Holy Spirit will again help to form the sheath which Christ needs once this process has progressed further. This will require human beings who enliven their thinking and their consciousness so that these living thoughts, these spiritual thoughts which are truly thought by human beings, will contribute to Christ's etheric sheath in which the new Christmas event will approach humankind. Then the Holy Spirit will not only work from the Father into the world of existence, but human beings will also carry responsibility and participate in what the Holy Spirit means for our time.

This is an important key to the riddle of historical development, in particular to understanding the historical problem under discussion here, the difference between the *old* Holy Spirit which was active up until the beginning of the Christian era and the *new* Holy Spirit which has been active since the Mystery of Golgotha. Before the coming of Christ, the Holy Spirit emanated from the Father, from the general earthly substance of the old creation. The Holy Spirit was holy to the degree that it had not become unholy and so appeared in the Mary form, the form of innocence, the purity of the paradisal condition which had not yet been lost. When the old purity finally threatened to be lost, the Father — who had first sent the Spirit — now sent the Son. Since the Mystery of Golgotha the Holy Spirit can only work when it does not arise from the Father in a general way only, but emanates from the fire which has been lit in the hearts of human beings through Christ's deed. From this point onwards the Son sends the Holy Spirit. This is why in our times, the Holy Spirit assumes a Michaelic character rather than the old character of Mary. Michael must tear back the curtain. The old Holy Spirit is the one who existed before the 'I,' the old spirituality which had not yet fallen into sin. The new Christian 'Holy Spirit' is the spiritual sphere to which the 'I' penetrates anew through the power of Christ.

What is the secret of the great chaos and conflict in our age? In the end it is the fight between the spirit and lack of spirit. The lack of spirit stems from the fact that the old kind of spirit came to an end long ago and changed into its opposite, and also because Christians have not yet brought the new kind of spirit into the world. So the terrible crisis approaches, which also threatens Christianity as such. Because the time has now come when the working of *existence* which arose from the Mystery of Golgotha can no longer support us if the working of *consciousness* coming from a new spiritual knowledge is not added to this. This has come about because Christians — including the churches — are no longer able to understand Christ the Son without new inspired thoughts entering from the Spirit. Dogma becomes blind, even blinder than it always was and is no longer in a position to impart knowledge about Christ.

*

Today I should like to set the scene in which I plan to give a more detailed picture of the ninth century in later chapters. This requires us to take a look at the entire span of human history and focus on two stages in the impending 'twilight of the gods' which is currently reaching its climax. The first stage which will be discussed briefly relates to the fourth century, the second stage is the ninth century and the third is our present time.

In the fourth century Christianity was suddenly released from the catacombs, from the era of persecution, owing to the change brought about by the Emperor Constantine the Great. The tables were immediately turned and thenceforward those who refused to join the established church were persecuted. On the surface, Christianity had been freed from all danger and oppression at a stroke and gained ground as no conqueror could ever have done by military means. But at the same moment as Christianity was given access to a great public vessel, a deep crisis appeared. The vessel naturally needed to contain something and this content became a problem exactly at the moment when it acquired not only great protection through the vessel, but also the possibility of exercising so much power. The first major crisis can be described by saying that *uncertainty about the Son* appeared.

One of Constantine's first acts after declaring Christianity as the state religion was to convene the Council of Nicaea in 325. This council was characterized by the discussions between the adherents of Arius and those of Athanasius. The problem was the relationship of the Son to the Father. How is Christ related to God? Is he of the same essence as him or not? We need not concern ourselves here with whether Arius was right or Athanasius was right, or to what degree one or the other was right or wrong. What is of interest is that suddenly the natural certainty about Christ and the relationship of the Son to the Father which was inherent in early Christian centuries ceased to exist and great uncertainty set in. The tragic avalanche of theological discussion began. It was a sign that no one knew anything with certainty any more, because when you know something, discussion is unnecessary. This was an unfortunate legacy of fate for Christianity which outwardly had now become so powerful. Christianity was able to expand to an unprecedented degree under the protection of the state, but it was characterized by a strange uncertainty about the being of Christ himself.

In addition, at this first critical point there appeared to be currents, as though issuing from a dark realm, which then began to triumph when a twilight of the gods set in. In 1921/22 Rudolf Steiner mentioned this very specifically and insistently on several occasions, for example in Oxford on August 22, 1922 in the lecture 'Adam Kadmon':

> It was the Roman world which eradicated initiation science so that only old dogmas should remain. In the fourth century after the mystery of Golgotha there was a particular association in Italy who made very effort to ensure that the old initiation methods were not transformed into new ones. People should only have knowledge of the outer physical world and nothing but old dogmas should be related of the spiritual worlds.

Steiner also mentioned the retarding school of dogma in the fourth century at the following points:

> Then, from about the fourth century onwards, came the time when, ... the sun was no longer regarded as anything but a physical orb in space ... In the fourth century there were schools which taught primarily for the further expansion of Christianity that the sun-mystery must remain untold, that a civilization knowing nothing of the sun-mystery must now arise ... Julian the Apostate ... fell by the hand of a murderer because he was intent upon passing on ... the threefold mystery of the sun. (November 6, 1921)

His murderer was one of those who counted it a sin to communicate the lofty teachings of initiation to the general run of humankind. (April 24, 1922)

So, at the beginning of the fourth century, we see a kind of school on Italian soil which took up the fight against the old initiation principle ... It sought to perpetuate the existence of Rome, to replace the direct individual endeavour of each human being by historical tradition ... Everything which was still to be found within the old initiations about the dwelling of Christ in the figure of Jesus was ... to be covered up by this school ... (July 16, 1922)

Now, it is a strange fact that, while on the one hand Roman existence succumbed to decay and the new peoples arrived from the North, a school developed on the Italian peninsula ... which actually set itself the task of using all available means to eradicate the old perceptions root and branch and only to allow those writings which this school found suitable to reach later generations.

History says nothing at all about this process, but it nevertheless took place. If a historical description of this were available, it would simply mention this school which had developed as a legacy of the Roman pontiff college in Italy, which did away thoroughly with everything which did not suit it and handed on the rest to future generations in a modified form ... It was in this school that the impulse arose to permit the spirit of Rome to be carried on as a mere inheritance, a collection of dogmas ... for many generations to come. Nothing new was to be allowed to be seen in the spiritual world for as long as possible, according to this school. The principle of initiation was to be eradicated root and branch ...

The old vision declined because the Roman conspiracy against the spirit in that organization ... eradicated everything of a direct human connection to the spirit. (July 23, 1922)

In Italy a society had even been founded to eradicate all spiritual paths of knowledge. (October 1, 1922)

17. THE DISPUTE ABOUT THE HOLY SPIRIT

In the shadow cast over the life of early Christianity by the great historical crisis, a black magic association was engaged in its own politics. A certain dark side turned the advancing twilight of the gods to its benefit. The first systematic campaign against the Holy Spirit was undertaken by the launching of the dogmatic principle itself. This took place at the moment when, at the Council of Nicaea, the deep uncertainty about the Son came to light.

But also in the fourth century, when exoteric ecclesiastical Christianity was becoming ever more outwardly imposing but was inwardly not only in the process of losing its knowledge about Christ, but also of being driven by the men of darkness in the background to strangle the spirit, something else occurred. A kind of opposing assembly to the council of 325 took place, and indeed completely unnoticed and essentially not even on the physical plane. This is revealed in the cycle *The East in the Light of the West* which was given from August 23–31, 1909 in Munich on the occasion of the performance of Schuré's mystery drama *The Children of Lucifer*.

In the ninth lecture of this cycle (August 31), Rudolf Steiner spoke of how, in the fourth century, when outwardly Christianity had turned away from the spirit as it were, provision was made for the future in an inner way. It had to be ensured that the old wisdom would one day be able to be revived in order to be placed at the service of an understanding of Christ in a new form. The churches had already lost all possibility of doing this: it had to take place outwith exoteric Christianity. Steiner described a spiritual council, called into being by Mani or Manes who had died as a martyr just under a century earlier in Gondishapur in the Persian Empire. He is one of the most important initiates of humankind and he in his turn gathered together important leaders of humankind for a discussion:

> It is said that a few centuries after Christ had lived on the earth, there was held one of the greatest assemblies of the spiritual world connected with the earth that ever took place, and that there Manes gathered round him three mighty personalities of the fourth century after Christ ... to consult with them as to the means of reintroducing the wisdom that had lived throughout the changing times of the post Atlantean age and of causing it to unfold more and more gloriously in the future. The three individuals who were the principal advisors to Manes in

this spiritual council, were named as Zarathustra, Buddha and Skythianos. Whilst on the outer plane exoteric ecclesiastical history got underway, here on the sidelines on a spiritual plane, a watch was kept for an esoteric stream which would bring about a transformation of the old wisdom for understanding the mystery of Christ. The ecclesiastical Christianity with its lack of wisdom would be opposed by a wisdom-filled Christianity, the exoteric Christianity by an esoteric one. It was as though a spiritual plan for the future was established. And this was *also* part of the fourth century.

I should like to mention in passing that it was no coincidence that the cycle at the end of which Rudolf Steiner made this disclosure followed the performance of Edouard Schuré's drama *The Children of Lucifer*. At the beginning of the introduction which Steiner wrote for Schuré's book, *The Great Initiates*, we find the following words:

> The plot and characters in this work are taken from the spiritual streams of the fourth century. Schuré wished to portray the two fundamental impulses of humankind's struggling soul at a particularly characteristic point in human development. The one impulse as it experienced the soul's divine roots and the other as it sensed the soul's divine future. It is as though Christ, the God become man, and Lucifer, the man struggling for divinity, are in the background of this drama.

The drama takes place in the fourth century and shows how, after the founding of ecclesiastical Christianity, an initiate from heathen circles, here in the form of Phosporus, prompted by his love for a Christian woman, attempts to introduce the wisdom of the mysteries into Christianity. In the introduction written by Steiner in 1905 it says: 'What is taking place here in the fourth century when Hellenism and Christianity fought the great fight ...' So, in 1909 in Munich a drama was performed in legendary mythical images which conjured up the circumstances of the fourth century. What Rudolf Steiner elaborated at the end of the lecture cycle therefore conveys the message: what do people really know of the events of the fourth century? They have no idea of what was really important. For in the spiritual world Manes' council to plan the future took place when he gathered the highest initiates around himself.

Three councils can be seen at the same time: the bishops and theologians who were called together by Constantine the Great at the

17. THE DISPUTE ABOUT THE HOLY SPIRIT 173

Council of Nicaea; the association of the men of darkness who set about turning the previously living knowledge of Christ into the form of dogmas; and above the heads of humankind Manes' council which took place in the spiritual realm.

*

We know what arose from the Council of Nicaea in AD 325. But what came of carrying out the lofty decisions which were taken by the circle Manes?

Let us first look more closely at the fourth century. What was going on there? Perhaps something will be revealed which could be the bearer into the future of the decisions taken by the spiritual council.

What is immediately noticeable is how Providence came to the aid of the church with such generosity and tolerance, for at this point all those individuals were born — as though coming to a great gathering of geniuses — who are known as the church fathers. They were contemporaries, the three great men in the West: Ambrose, Jerome and Augustine; the three great men in the East: Basil the Great, Gregory of Nazianzus and Gregory of Nyssa and, standing between the two groups, John Chrysostom. They were all born after 325 and some lived on into the beginning of the fifth century. Heaven did what it could to fill the vessel of a Christianity which had become the state religion. But the ecclesiastical stream was unable to free itself from the inheritance of uncertainty. It named itself after Christ, but the uncertainty about the being of Christ increased even further and this was to the benefit of the circles acting in the shadows who aimed to preserve dogma.

However, there was one contemporary of the church fathers in whom it was possible to see what was called for spiritually. This was Julian the Apostate, the youth who came to the throne as one of the successors of Constantine the Great. He only lived to be 32 and was Emperor for only two years. Immediately after ascending the throne he attempted to carry out a great programme of reforms. Although he did not wish to persecute Christianity as the emperors before Constantine had done, nevertheless he attached more importance to the last remaining mystery centres of the old world than he did to the circles of the Christian church. He himself had undergone initiation in Eleusis and so strove for a revival of the old mystery wisdom against which the dry and tedious elements of Christianity would not be able to prevail. But when he then set off to conquer the East, perhaps with the intention of coming to a place where Manes had worked and where traces of the ancient mysteries of Asia Minor might still be encountered, he died at the hands of a murderer. So for a moment an impulse had arisen to counter the spiritual paralysis, but a dagger flashed out from the shadows to nip this impulse in the bud.

The karma lectures reveal important perspectives at this point. How did the individuality who lived as Julian the Apostate but was wrenched away from life at such an early age nevertheless achieve the aim that lived in him? This individual entered a new incarnation in the ninth century but this time as a woman. From the fifth lecture of the fourth karma volume we know that this was Herzeloyde, Parsifal's mother. We therefore need to make a connection from the fourth century into the ninth century and focus on a new nodal point in historical development. Added to this is something which I mentioned in my book *The Three Years*, how in an old esoteric lecture Rudolf Steiner describes how Manes himself went through further incarnations and how he, as an individuality of greater stature, became the personality behind the mythical figure of Parsifal in the ninth century. Herzeloyde /Julian the Apostate became Parsifal's mother and the one who, in the fourth century, called together the spiritual council for the benefit of an esoteric Christian future, himself entered history again and concealed himself behind the figure of Parsifal. We are thus led from the fourth to the ninth century in a surprisingly clear manner. Behind the veil of the mythological images of the legend of the Grail — which should not be taken directly as they appear as a description of historical facts — we become aware of great individualities who do not appear in the foreground of the story but consciously remain unnoticed in the background. As we can see, just as the exoteric stream continued in the church fathers in the fourth century, here over an interval of five centuries the plans of the spiritual council from the fourth century became reality and we can recognize the Grail kings. The subject of church fathers and Grail kings could well be the key to unlocking the full Christian history of the first millennium, of which we otherwise only get to know the outer side.

*

Let us now turn to the outer situation in the ninth century. Between the fourth and ninth centuries a great deal of dramatic history had taken place. The Germanic migrations had swept across central and southern Europe and had there made an end of the old ways and founded new ones. The decline of the old Roman regime was not due solely to the influx of Germanic migrants, but also to its own inner lack of substance. Rudolf Steiner described how even movement of money to the eastern frontiers to pay the huge army of mercenaries contributed to the decline of the Roman Empire. By the first half of the ninth century a new empire had emerged. The development of the Carolingian Empire which culminated under Charlemagne took place under a Germanic tribe which was least characteristic of the Nordic element. This was the Franks whose intellectual capacity had to a great degree outgrown the mythological attitude of the other Germanic tribes.

This impressive empire collapsed within a very short time, splitting into fragments. But there was also something positive in this, because the peoples who had migrated possessed so great an urge for freedom and innovation that the political system which had been taken over from the Romans broke down.

In the eighth and ninth centuries the inexorable advance of the Arabs came up against a largely chaotic Europe. They had a highly developed intricate civilization and attacked Europe in the south from Asia Minor via Crete, North Africa and Sicily to Spain, advancing as far as the gates of Rome.

In its chaotic condition, the whole of Europe trembled before the Arabs. In the East where, after Constantine's move from Rome to Byzantium, the real spiritual centre of the Roman empire now lay, the old eastern spirituality remained but was now becoming decadent. The emperors changed in quick succession: most of the time it was not the ruler's son but his murderer who succeeded him. The Caesarean madness of Rome eight hundred years earlier, now reappeared frequently in Byzantium. However, what remained of a spiritual mood there appears to me of greater importance.

In the West amongst the migrated peoples the urge for freedom was the energy which both destroyed and kept things alive. The remnants of old mythopoeic European consciousness provided the spiritual nourishment for this urge for freedom. In Byzantium it was not people's longing for freedom but the last flickering of the insanity of the Caesars which destroyed the forms of the old world. But there the old wisdom which streamed across from Asia to Europe was still to be found, even though in a fading and often decadent form. The old eastern wisdom was given a certain intensity due to the contact with Islam, acquiring an intellectual slant especially from the Persian scholars at universities such as Gondishapur. Up to this point the Slavic peoples had not been involved with eastern Christianity at all. They gradually approached Christianity only in the ninth century. So eastern Christianity was without the moderation and transparency of soul which the Slavic culture would one day bring to it.

This was the cultural situation in Europe in the ninth century. What is important is that it now grew more acute, though this was not visible outwardly. For now in the course of history a second uncertainty made itself felt: to the fourth century's uncertainty about the Son was added the uncertainty about the Holy Spirit. The ninth century is full of discussions about the being of the Holy Spirit which is a sign that this mystery was about to be lost for good.

In the East and West very different attitudes and ideas about the Holy Spirit were formed. In the East there was a tendency towards a certain deification of the Spirit. In the East the being of the Holy Spirit always awakened the most fervent feelings in the soul. The principal church of eastern Christianity in Constantinople, founded by Constantine the Great and massively extended in the sixth century by Justinian, was the Hagia Sophia. The Hagia Sophia was dedicated to Mary as the personification of Sophia, that is, the Holy Spirit. The principal church was not dedicated to St Peter as in Rome, but to the Holy Spirit, to the Holy Spirit of Mary, I might almost say, the pre-Christian Holy Spirit.

In 1453 the crescent was placed on the Hagia Sophia in Constantinople by the conquering Muslims. The principal church of eastern Christianity was turned into a mosque.

The deification of the Spirit in the East was expressed in the fact that people held the view that God the Father sends the Holy Spirit. People wanted to hold onto the way in which the Spirit had worked since ancient times before the Mystery of Golgotha, to retain the universal spiritual which existed before the awakening of individuality in humankind, because then you could say: the Father has sent the Spirit, as he has sent the Son. In this way Christ and Sophia stood next to one another. The Holy Spirit was worshipped in the figure of Mary, thus making it Christ's equal. It was only much later, in Gothic times, that worship of Mary was adopted in the West. For eastern religious practice it has been the living element from the beginning.

In contrast to this, western Christianity in the ninth century had a different character and, it must be said, rightly so. If the Holy Spirit is to be understood from a Christian basis, this can only be done in the spirit of what happened at Pentecost. And that resulted from what had taken place on Good Friday and at Easter. The Holy Spirit took on a new form from Christ's deed, working in the individual 'I' of human beings. Centuries ago this led to the western church stating in its creed, that the Holy Spirit proceeds from the Father *and from the Son,* or as the Latin Athanasian creed states, *Filioque.*

The East did not go along with this step. The East resisted the idea that the Holy Spirit proceeds from the Son, wishing to hold on to an eternal holy spirituality which had always been active from the very beginning. The West dogmatized the centuries old theology that the Son sends the Holy Spirit. But what did the western church understand by this? It did not even understand the Son himself. So it could only be a dogmatic statement which is expressed by the word *Filioque.* Despite this, the dispute over the word *Filioque* in the ninth century finally led to the division of the eastern and western parts of Christianity. The split in the church, the schism between East and West in the Christian realm appeared and could never be reconciled again.

In itself, if we look back at our starting point, the word *Filioque* is a wonderful key to the great change in spiritual working which resulted from the Mystery of Golgotha. But what use has the West made of this key? This finally appeared in another council which Rudolf Steiner mentioned countless times: in the great council which took place in Constantinople in 869, in the Hagia Sophia itself. The location is like a magnificent symbol of the spirit of history.

The crucial passage in the council records concerns the problem of the Spirit. Steiner repeatedly made use of the abbreviated expression that the Spirit had been abolished at the council of 869. This was the harsh and unambiguous wording which he used for the matter. It is true of the inner attitude and intention which defined the council, even if a pedantic, literal reading of the records might claim that there is no evidence. What an irony: in the church of the Holy Spirit, the Holy Spirit is abolished! Looking back at the raising of the crescent over the Hagia Sophia in 1453, we might do well to recall that Christianity itself had done away with the Christian Spirit before this, in 869. How did this come about?

The West prevailed at the council. Although in its confession of the Spirit the West had had the word *Filioque* accepted, in contrast to the deification of the Spirit which was cultivated in the East, it had a tendency to trivialize the spiritual. The passage at the end of the council report did not deal with the divine Trinity — the relationship of Father, Son and Spirit — but with the human being, in other words with the question of whether the human being is made up of body, soul and spirit, or only of body and soul? How people view the Holy Spirit is not irrelevant for how they view the human being. The fact that the human being consists of body, soul *and spirit*, that it does not just consist of its vessels but that the spirit of the human 'I' inherently lives within the vessels, was not understood either in the East or the West. The dispute resulted from certain eastern theories which were defended by the most brilliant thinker of the day, by Photius, of whom more later. Human beings have a body and a soul, but here a distinction must be made — as was stated in the East — between the lower soul which humans share with the animals and the higher, thinking soul. So it was not claimed that the human being consisted of body, soul and spirit, but of body, soul and soul. The West disagreed violently with this, saying that it was nonsense, the human being has *one* soul and not two. From its condemnation of the view of the double soul nature of the human being without intending it directly, the West let the Spirit slip out of its hands entirely. The human being consists of body and soul and then there were certain spiritual attributes, but this has nothing to do with the fact that something spiritual lives in the human being itself.

This leaves us with two principle symptoms of the uncertainty which appeared in relation to the Holy Spirit, or to the Spirit in general: first, the *Filioque* dispute and second, the resolutions of the council of 869. Knowing this can explain why humankind really does not wish to know anything about the spiritual nowadays. This process first started in the Christian church. All the antipathy of modern scientifically-minded people against spiritual connections, against the spirit

17. THE DISPUTE ABOUT THE HOLY SPIRIT

as a reality in itself, does not stem from the present technical age, but came about on ecclesiastical ground. We can now draw the following conclusion.

Nowadays,* apart from the fact that evil is rife, the East-West problem has even taken physical shape, a hopeless demarcation and gulf between the East and the West. This tragic world conflict cannot be explained on political or economic grounds. The split between East and West began without doubt on the soil of the Christian churches in the ninth century. When the eastern and western churches, when Byzantium and Rome fell out with one another, the foundation was laid for the Bolshevik eastern bloc and the American western bloc being enemies today. Thus the connections of our present to the ninth century have deep roots. What started in the religious field has now entered the stony ground of political and economic realities. From this uncertainty about the spirit, East and West have gone their separate ways and confront each other across an unbridgeable gulf.

*

In just what a specific way the destinies of the ninth century continue and intensify in the present day only becomes clear if we venture to cautiously approach deep karmic indications that Steiner gave. This requires us to become familiar with important leading figures of the ninth century, both in the foreground and in the quiet veiled mythical background. This will form the subject of the following two chapters. But in order to round off what I have said so far and, with the help of the perspectives opened up here, some of the material will be outlined here.

Both in the East and the West two figures appeared as exponents of the drama of the times, as far as the outer authority and power structure were concerned. In the East it was two patriarchs: Ignatius, a pious early Christian figure and his opponent, Photius, a more political figure, a man with apparently dazzling learning and sharpness of intellect who, without any ecclesiastical training, succeeded in passing through all the levels of the church hierarchy in a few days and forcing Ignatius from the patriarch's chair. The old wisdom of the East which had been intellectualized in the Islamic schools reached up once

---

* These words were written in the 1950s at the beginning of the Cold War.

again in him to a Luciferic flame. It was his activity in particular which made the leading men of the western church, Pope Nicholas I and his close adviser, Cardinal Anastasius Bibliothecarius, realize that the eastern church formed a dangerous temptation for the emerging European spirit. Pope Nicholas supported Ignatius and on several occasions succeeded in forcing Photius temporarily return the patriarchal honour which he had snatched from him.

Nicholas and Anastasius feared for the unity of the church, but they had to defend themselves against the extreme and feverish one-sidedness of the spirit which threatened from the East. They realized with increasing certainty that the West would have to go its own way. Perhaps the time was over when it was rightly said, *ex oriente lux,* from the East, the light; perhaps one day it might be said, *ex occidente lux,* from the West the new light must come. But which path should the West take? It appeared as though only the path of dogma was left and this must have aroused dejection and anguish in the soul of Pope Nicholas.

But the state of hopelessness was not due to the circumstances alone. Things were helped along by the dark side, thus making the tragedy complete. The demonic circle which had set itself the task of opposing the living flowing spirit through the principle of dogma back in the fourth century was still in existence. Its centre was now Capua and it made use of the Carolingian imperial court which at the time usually resided close by in Benevento. It sent one of the darkest figures of the day to influence Nicholas and Anastasius. This was Arsenius who was a high dignitary, but who was soon seen and described by ecclesiastical circles — for example the Benedictine order from Monte Cassino — as a devil incarnate. Nicholas was not able to fully see through the machinations of Arsenius and those behind him, and so in the end all the efforts for a separate European Christian spiritual life tragically remained stuck in a dogmatic blind alley. A consequence was that this opened the door for the lust for power and money within the church hierarchies.

It was this destiny of the ninth century which played directly into the European tragedy which broke out openly with the First World War. In the play, *The Head of the General Staff,* Albert Steffen first showed the European public in an artistic form the karmic indications made by Steiner, that Pope Nicholas I was reincarnated in General von

Moltke who was the German Chief of General Staff at the outbreak of the First World War. Moltke encountered Arsenius and the people from Capua again in certain characters around him. He was crushed by their machinations which he rejected, being morally superior, but could still not see with total clarity. Act upon act, the drama of disaster of the great East-West conflict passed across the stage of history.

The uncertainty about the spirit in the ninth century and the resulting split in the churches of the West and East, and in particular the suppression of the real European spiritual impulse, throw their shadows across our time. Huge metamorphoses and intensification of the tragedy which arose in the ninth century in the realm of the spiritual life now fill the arena of outer life.

*

But as we mentioned previously, the ninth century was also the time when Herzeloyde and Parsifal lived. In the hidden background of all the worldly power structures we must picture the quiet esoteric circles which on the one hand formed the Arthurian round table, an impulse which reached from Britain to France and Germany, and which on the other were gathered around the Holy Grail. The Arthurian Knights may have been active in the field of knightly poetry, the troubadour culture and other cultural endeavours. When they fought with sword and shield in the legends, this should be taken symbolically as a portrayal of spiritual or poetic contests.

As regards the circle around the Holy Grail, the question of where the castle of the Grail might have stood must not be asked in a fixed manner. It would have involved various stages. It was not a matter of a specific building, but one of inner building principles and so the centre of this quiet circle was not always to be found in the same place. When it is said that the Castle of the Grail was built on Montserrat in Spain, this refers back to earlier centuries when, though not manifest historically, a centre of this movement really did exist in Spain. Later, in the thirteenth century, an important centre was on the northeast slopes of the Pyrenees, in the south of France, at Montségur, the castle of the last defence of the Cathars and Albigensians. In the ninth century the centre must have been further to the north. It is perhaps not going too far to suggest that it was located in an area around that most important of European pivotal points formed by the bend in the Rhine at Basle, where the Vosges, the Black Forest and the Swiss Jura meet. Here we may well be looking at the landscape where, in the ninth century, the destinies of those who can be recognized behind the veil of the Grail legend took place.

Now a certain reciprocation took place between the Arthurian circle and the Grail circle. Some of those who were mentioned in the Grail legend belonged to the Arthurian circle, such as Gahmuret, Parsifal's father, but also Gahmuret's squire Schionatulander who twice accompanied him to Baghdad into Arab lands and then brought the news of his death to his widow Herzeloyde. Between Herzeloyde and Gahmuret we can see how the Arthurian and Grail circles move towards one another. The interrelationships of the Grail are represented in the legend primarily by the five brothers and sisters: the brothers Amfortas and Trevrizent and the three sisters Schoisane, Herzeloyde and Repanse de Schoie. Schoisane died young and her role was taken over by her daughter Sigune who grew up with Herzeloyde. Repanse de Schoie was the guardian of the holy chalice in the castle of the Grail.

Now, according to the legend, it is easy to imagine that Herzeloyde guarded her boy anxiously in the lonely forest. Finally she was no longer able to keep him away from the world because he had met the knights in the forest and she had to let him go. Nothing indicates that Herzeloyde played an active role in this. Rudolf Steiner, however, who did not quote the legend, but had the historical happenings before him, described it differently in the karma lectures mentioned previously.

> This was Herzeloyde, Parsifal's mother, who was a historical figure but about whom history says nothing, who through Gahmuret ..., who perished through betrayal on a Crusade to the Middle East, was made aware of her own destiny in an earlier life as Julian the Apostate ...

Julian the Apostate fell victim to a dastardly murderer on a Crusade to the Middle East. The same fate befell Parsifal's father. When Herzeloyde discovered this her own earlier life appeared before her. Steiner says:

> ... through this information which went deep into her heart, Herzeloyde accomplished what is now recounted in the legend but is absolutely true to history, about Parsifal's upbringing by Herzeloyde.

17. THE DISPUTE ABOUT THE HOLY SPIRIT

Herzeloyde brought up Parsifal quite intentionally to fulfil what Julian the Apostate was unable to fulfil. But the legend does not make this clear. Keeping Parsifal away from the world was not a negative but a positive active course of action. This was made quite clear by Rudolf Steiner in the following passage:

> The soul of Julian the Apostate which had remained in the lower realms so that you might think that it had actually been called to show Christianity the right way, this soul then appeared in the Middle Ages in a female body, a female personality who sent Parsifal out into the world to seek the esoteric path and show it to Christianity.

Every word is important in the way that Steiner expresses things, including the fact that Herzeloyde 'sent out' Parsifal. At a certain point the veil in the legend suddenly starts to reveal unexpected historical connections. Parsifal was intentionally sent out by his mother, but she then died because of this. At first Parsifal was an Arthurian knight until, after repeated wanderings, he finally found his way to the Grail.

In the London karma lectures we find the following important statement on this subject: it was in 869 that the Arthurian stream and the Grail stream joined. This was also the time when Parsifal fully found his way to the Grail. Parsifal became the Grail king in the forests in the centre of Europe at the same time as it was decided to do away with the Holy Spirit in the Hagia Sophia in Constantinople. A magnificent picture is revealed: on the one hand is *uncertainty* about the Holy Spirit as a basic historical symptom of the day; and on the other hand is *certainty* about the Holy Spirit amongst the people around the Holy Grail. This is their element: the dove of the spirit above the chalice of the Grail. This is the source of their life, not a school of thought but their actual being.

This was the nature of history in the ninth century: exoteric Christianity at a loss and falling apart; esoteric Christianity quietly in reserve, but filled with the knowledge that it was cultivating the Christianity of the Holy Spirit, carrying esoteric Christianity into the future. For them the Holy Spirit was not an article of faith but the air that they breathed.

The development of exoteric Christianity in the ninth century is the root of the misfortune of our age which lies in the East-West problem, in humankind's whole present confusion in the struggle between the spirits of good and evil. The seed of the tragedy of exoteric Christianity in the ninth century is coming to life. But at the same time something was done in the ninth century to lead out of the chaos. In the company of the Grail which arose from the planning in Manes' assembly in the fourth century, a seed was sown which has quickened in the work of Rudolf Steiner and should continue to grow through us. It is possible not only to know about the Holy Spirit, but to live with the Holy Spirit and work from the Holy Spirit. It is not only the exponents of the outer history of the ninth century who appeared again — the Grail stream is also present again in a different form. Or, it *should* be there. Nowadays the Grail spear — which previously led to sickness in a form of thinking which had become sick — must be transformed into a Michaelic spear in that form of thinking which Anthroposophy opens up to us.

18

Figures in Rome and Byzantium

In the following I wish to fill in the individual figures and their destinies within the framework of what has been outlined before. In the process, some material will of necessity be repeated so that our subject can be presented in full clarity.

An outwardly energetic but inwardly lethargic humanity has formed the notion that human beings and therefore the culture produced by them is a product of economic and political circumstances, almost as an apology for its own inner lethargy. But it is a fundamental truth which we must take as our starting point for everything that, on the contrary, the economic and political circumstances always arise from what is done or left undone, from achievements and failings, in cultural life. There is no more striking example of this than the emergence of the tragic and seemingly insoluble East-West conflict of our time from the theological discussions on the Holy Spirit in the ninth century and the resulting schism between the eastern and western Christian churches. Something began in the realm of the cultural life which today darkens the political stage like a terrifying many-headed spectre and destroys relationships between different peoples as never before. Even if historical development is considered only superficially, without taking the deeper karmic levels into account, it is little wonder that the loss of Spirit in exoteric Christianity caused humanity to sink into materialism which renders souls blind to ideas and living without hope, despite all our technical ability. If the churches themselves no longer provide the source of enlightenment, where then should the awakening world of ideas and science find anything other than materialistic ideology?

In the West everything ended up in an increasingly effective dogmatic tendency, in the mummification of doctrine and ritual and so to a progressive impoverishment of the true living spirit, although in the *Filioque* clause people confessed to a *new* spirit proceeding from Christ. In the East people clung to the increasingly Luciferic *old* spirit and thus laid the foundation for a fanatical utopian one-sided spirituality, up to the present-day socialist ideology in the East.

Nowadays the seeds of disaster from the loss or one-sidedness of the spirit in the ninth century are sprouting. But back then a healing spiritual seed was also entrusted to the soil of human souls. In seclusion, far away from the highroad, was the silent circle of an esoteric Christianity which had no uncertainty about the Holy Spirit, whose inner belief stemmed more from a lively certainty about the Spirit. Those assembled round the symbol of the Holy Grail knew from their own ongoing experience what it is like when the dove of the Spirit comes down to rest on the holy chalice. This was their one and all. A seedbed was created for humankind's reascent. Through Rudolf Steiner's life's work — which aimed to bring the spirit back to humanity as an ordering and healing power for a cultural condition that had descended into chaos — the opportunity is presented out of a new sense of responsibility for esoteric Christianity for planting a spiritually ascending culture in the burgeoning disaster.

*

Years before Rudolf Steiner delivered the wealth of the karma lectures — something he did not do for the sake of informing us of interesting historical facts, but to show us how to read our own destiny in the magic mirror — he entrusted some people with deep insights which clarify important personal karmic relationships between the ninth century and the present day.

Helmuth von Moltke was Chief of the German General Staff when war broke out. But after only a few weeks he was unable to continue carrying out the task assigned to him as the responsibility was taken away again. Previously his relationship to Rudolf Steiner had been a casual one and they had only conversed on rare occasions. Now in the deep suffering which shook his soul he sought out and found advice and support which Steiner gave with great willingness and devotion. For Moltke it was not only a comfort but a real support and source of new courage to discover with what an assured gaze the spirit of the German people looked down upon him in his pain and suffering. Even though he could only form vague notions of it, on Steiner's instructions he studied the ninth century, particularly the figure of Pope Nicholas I. This karmic connection with the ninth century was publicly revealed a long time ago in Albert Steffen's play, *The Chief of the General Staff*, in the form of an artistic work which describes but at the same time protects what is described.

I should like to give rough portraits of three different groups of figures: those around Helmuth von Moltke in Berlin, then in Byzantium and finally in Rome.

General von Moltke was the soldier on whom everything depended at the decisive moment, because all those around him had failed. But he was basically not a solider in the way that is normally imagined, he was first and foremost a *human being* and he took his responsibilities seriously, whilst those around him — up to the crowned heads — very often did not take things too seriously because rank and glory were their first priority. Moltke was the embodiment of the deepest solemnity which the personality has to offer. The course of events must have affected him all the more as he was not simply a tough hardened soldier by nature. He had a tender heart and his incorruptible conscience and acute sense of justice always gave priority to the human being in him.

He stood at the centre of the circle of those figures who held power in Central Europe. He might have realized sooner and more clearly how different he was from almost all the military figures around him and therefore how lonely in his professional circumstances, had he not considered himself first and foremost a loyal servant of his master.

There was also a figure whom he could hold onto inwardly when, from deeper layers of his consciousness, feelings of alienation arose in this circle. This was his uncle, the Field Marshal Helmuth von Moltke, often called the Elder to distinguish him from his nephew, the Younger. The uncle was fifty years his elder and his nephew supported him as a companion and carer at his great age. The uncle was also far more than just a soldier: he was one of the last great characters in a soldier's uniform, a man of few words who could have said so much had he wished to. What was embodied in him was more like a wise man from ancient times than someone who had previously been in such an outward-oriented profession. The Elder confronted Wilhelm II very openly and critically, for his career was already over when this 'young master' came to the throne. So Moltke the Younger also occasionally opposed the Emperor's unbearable theatrical high-handedness, even though it took a great deal of will power. But because Wilhelm II actually always saw Moltke the Elder through him and never withdrew his trust, Moltke the Younger was always prepared to display every reverence. His attitude towards the Emperor was the reason why he did not at first suffer to the extent which he might have amongst the other pompous uniformed pawns in the Emperor's entourage who, as it later turned out, were Moltke's deadly enemies.

Moltke was not only part of the military milieu through his uncle's link to this world, but through his wife he was also in contact with the world of Rudolf Steiner. He was totally immersed in the first of these two contrasting worlds — Steiner's work was something which he could at first only follow from a certain distance. Eliza von Moltke was amongst the very first who embraced the work of Rudolf Steiner in the Theosophical Society and then in the Anthroposophical Society with the greatest enthusiasm. It was through her that Helmuth von Moltke also got to know Steiner. But a closer link only became possible once the lightning from the stormy skies of the time had struck him. The hours in which the German mobilization was being decided crushed him even to the point of his physical health. In a memorandum which was only published after his death, he described the events during the very first stage of the war, which caused him such devastating suffering and made him an exponent of the destiny of his time. Now he was completely open for Steiner's spiritual message.

*

To elaborate on what was outlined in the last chapter, let us now place representative figures from the ninth century before us.

Both in Byzantium and in Rome, the eastern and western centres of ecclesiastical Christian life, there was a pair of figures who stood out above all the others. In the East this was Ignatius and Photius who alternately filled the office of the Patriarch. First Ignatius held the office, then Photius, then Ignatius again and, after his death, Photius

18. FIGURES IN ROME AND BYZANTIUM

once more. In the West in Rome it was two figures who worked together, Pope Nicholas I and his loyal and close confidante, Cardinal Anastasius Bibliothecarius.

Ignatius was a quiet pious character as though from the age of the apostles themselves. His greatness did not lie in the field of theology, but in that of piety. But a great deal came from him of a kind which can often still be experienced in our time, when so much pious goodness and heart-felt wisdom radiates from simple old priests of the eastern church. He was a son of the Byzantine Emperor Michael I who only reigned for two years before entering a monastery where he lived for another thirty years. The son Niketos, who then called himself Ignatius, also grew up in the monastery. Just as his father had relinquished the throne, so Ignatius did not regret the opportunity to have succeeded his father as Emperor. In 846 Ignatius was made Patriarch. As the spiritual head of eastern Christianity he formed a true centre of faith and blessing. Such people leave no writings behind. There is also nothing much to be found in works of reference about them because imponderables so easily remain unnoticed by written history. He was Patriarch for ten years until the Luciferic vibrations of the East drove him from the Patriarch's seat. One of the successors of Michael I to the throne who was not a relative was Michael III, but he was still a three-year-old child when he came to the throne, and his mother was regent. This enabled certain dark figures who were the real bearers of power to remain hidden in the background. When the mother died, her brother, a man by the name of Bardas, emerged. He was one of the typical dark sinister figures from the East, in a similar mould to those we shall have to deal with later in Rome, a glittering Luciferic character with a thirst for power.

The first thing he did after getting his hands on the regency was to depose the pious Patriarch Ignatius and put another man by the name of Photius in his place. But Photius was no man of the church. As head of the bodyguard for the child-emperor he had been advisor to his mother while she reigned. Within six days he took all the holy orders, one after the other, and became Patriarch of Constantinople at Christmas 857. Ignatius was locked up in a monastery. Photius was an intellectually brilliant figure, perhaps the most universally educated man alive at the time. There was no one anywhere in the world who could equal his intelligence. He was a person of almost dazzling all-round talent, a Lucifer in person. All kinds of legends had grown up around his birth.

It was said that he found his teacher in mysterious circumstances and his teachers had even included Jewish cabbalists. He studied astrological and other magical writings. He undertook long journeys even as a youth, always as an envoy in the service of some group or other, for example to Assyria and Persia. He spent a long time at the court of the Caliph of Baghdad where he learned from Arab teachers. It is probable that he also stayed in Gondishapur which was not far from Baghdad. He assimilated the Arabian sharpness of intellect completely. He was also a famous mathematician and wrote a Greek dictionary, as well as medical and comprehensive works on ecclesiastical law. One book was called *Bibliotheka*. In this he had compiled extracts from 280 Greek writers and disseminated this in book form, so that it is through him that we know something about a large number of writers of the late Greek period. Amongst his books there is also one about the Manichaeans. He was always particularly interested in the esoteric background to things. We are also in possession of a work by him called *De Spiritus Sancti mystagogia* (On the mystical guidance of the soul by the Holy Spirit). Like a Faust of ancient times he was knowledgeable in all the esoteric sciences. This character was propelled onto the patriarchal seat in Constantinople. It was exactly a year before Nicholas I became Pope in Rome.

What was actually meant by the 'East' at that time? What did eastern Christianity comprise? What was the eastern church and how was it viewed from Rome, for example? This was the first difficulty with which Nicholas I was presented as Pope. Should he recognize Photius who had been put on the patriarchal throne by the glittering courtier Bardas or should he exercise his authority and assist the deposed Ignatius to reclaim his rights? It must be remembered that the area covered by the eastern church was not of any great significance in quantitative terms at the time, as the Slavic peoples, the Bulgarians, Russians, Czechs, etc. had not yet converted to Christianity. Later of course the religious fervour which the Slavs brought gave the eastern church its character, but at the time in question the eastern church was still limited in extent. But this pre-Slavic East concealed immense imponderables involving a great mystery. Europeans only got the opportunity to look behind the scenes here during the Crusades. In the ninth century it was all still hidden and unknown.

The idea in Europe was that large areas had become Christian, even if not in the sense of ecclesiastical Christianity. It was believed that, in the wake of the three holy kings, whole peoples had become Christian through the Oriental schools of wisdom, in other words from the great wave of Gnosis which passed through the Middle East. People were under the impression that extended kingdoms existed under the leadership of Prester John. The Manichean and Nestorian movements did exist in the East although far less widely than people in Europe imagined. The existence of a kind of Gnostic Christianity extending far into the Orient was something which people supposed rather than knew for certain. Even in Constantinople there were no contacts further into Asia than the cities which had become the seat of Arab culture. Islam had even penetrated the mystery-enshrouded realms of Oriental Gnostic Christianity and from there begun its assault on Europe. This was the picture which people in Rome conjured up when they imagined the eastern church and its background. This gave a feeling of uncertainty, a sinister mystery associated with the Christianity of the East.

When the warlike Islamic conquests advanced, spreading its culture as far as Spain, it followed in the tracks of earlier migrations from East to West. In fact, parts of that Gnostic world had already been on the move before Islam and had travelled across North Africa as far as Spain. A first stage of Manichaean Grail Christianity had arisen in Spain as a result, to which the legend of Titurel's building of the temple on Montserrat can be traced. After the Arab advance, people must have looked with a fearful fascination from Rome towards the East whence both Gnosis and Islam had come. Even in the days of Charlemagne people were able to see that what was cultivated as a kind of academy in Aachen was extremely primitive in comparison with the flourishing cultural life in Baghdad. When Harun al-Rashid sent gifts to Charlemagne, the Europeans' awe was tempered by a fear of the people of the East who possessed such unimaginable riches. When Nicholas I became Pope, the Arabs were not only in Spain, but also in Sicily and the southern part of Italy and were in the process of advancing North.

The East had both: it had Ignatius — quiet, pious early Christian figures — and it had those dazzling characters whose level of education was unimaginable without the influence of the Arab world. Even just looking at a figure like Photius must have aroused an uncanny feeling in the West. It evoked fascination, but one could never be certain what to expect next.

*

The two main figures in Rome were also extremely different, but they were close allies rather than being in opposition to one another. Nicholas I can be more easily compared with Ignatius than with Photius. He was well educated, but was no scholar. He was first and foremost a man who was experienced as a light which cast its radiance afar in the chaos of his time. When his successor to the papacy said that he had been a new Elijah, a new Phinehas, this was not merely a pious eulogy, but expressed how the world had viewed Nicholas.

At that time the Archangel Raphael had begun his leadership in the series of Archangel periods. The age of Raphael was characterized by figures who had outstanding and illuminating influence on their time, characters who were larger than life, such as Frederick Barbarossa. In Nicholas I, people really saw a son of the Raphaelic age and at the same time an incorporation of the spirit of the time. A man like him was needed in the moment when Islam was advancing causing a continual tension as the great Carolingian Empire was falling into ruins.

Nicholas decided against recognizing Photius. This flickering light could never be to the good of humankind, even though it went with a learning which was worthy of the greatest admiration. His accession had not come about in the right way. Ignatius' fall had occurred unjustly and Nicholas was a man of justice. For the first time the conflict between the East and the West became acute.

But Nicholas had to make a firm stand not only towards the East but also within a crumbling Europe threatened by the Arabs. This became a problem, in that his authority was no longer accepted as a matter of course. People in Europe had reached a point when the urge for freedom assumed every possible form. Various national attempts to gain independence emerged. Should the national churches, the dioceses of France, in Tours, Rheims, Strasbourg and Metz be subject without question to the authority of the Roman Pope or should they make their own decisions? The urge for autonomy erupted, both at a national level and in individual figures. The collapse of the Carolingian Empire was actually a consequence of this urge for autonomy that began to work beneath the surface. How could a unifying power be founded in this threatening chaos?

Something belongs in this connection which the history books omit in connection with Nicholas I. Mention is made of the *Pseudoisidorian Decretals,* which are believed to be a forgery but which Nicholas adopted. They mainly consist of statements and decrees by Roman bishops going back to Peter which claim to prove the authority of the Roman bishops over all other ecclesiastical authorities, in other words, the primacy of the papal authority. Nicholas I clutched at these decrees, because he found himself in a position which obliged him to be the calming influence in the tide of events.

What were the *Pseudoisidorian Decretals*? The Vatican in Rome was named for a very good reason. Vatican means the 'place of the oracle.' In pre-Christian times there had always been an oracle on this spot in Rome. After state recognition — in other words beginning with Sylvester I who received the office of Pontifex Maximus from Constantine the Great — the popes made use of the mediumistic traditions of the oracles which had been practised there since time immemorial. This had been done by the Caesars in earlier times and the popes continued it in their own manner. These kind of texts which were received through mediums and then reworked formed the core of many decrees which the popes issued to the world. So the claim by the Roman Catholic Pope to be able to speak from inspiration, not just from human opinion but from a higher source, was based on something quite straightforward in terms of religious history. It might well have been documents of this kind which were involved when Nicholas I was handed a bundle of papers which purported to show that the Pope had a claim to be the leading authority in the Christian world. Someone like Nicholas still pictured this authority as something which issued from a real connection to the spiritual world. Politics had no part in this. The essence of the figure of this Pope was that he was fully human, and with a humanity filled by the Holy Spirit.

At his side was his close advisor Anastasius Bibliothecarius. Many mysteries surround this individual. We know that in 847 he was ordained and was made cardinal at the same time. So an ordination intended for certain high offices was performed on him. But what happened? He disappeared from the picture and could not be traced for seven years. Pope Leo IV, a predecessor of Nicholas, ordered him to attend to his duties, but he did not appear. After waiting for three years in vane, the Pope excommunicated Anastasius. After a further three years he was anathematized, cursed. But still he did not appear. Where had he vanished to? In 855 he suddenly reappeared, but not alone. He was accompanied by the highest ranking person of the time besides the Pope, Emperor Louis II who had just ascended the Carolingian throne. Louis II and a very influential man by the name of Arsenius brought along the banished and excommunicated Anastasius and wanted to appoint him Pope. A new Pope, Benedict III, had just been elected but as the Emperor's legates had not been involved in the elections in the right way the Emperor's followers asserted that Benedict was invalid and presented their own man. But Anastasius was only Pope for three days before he disappeared again. So Benedict III was reinstated and was Pope until his death in 858. A new pope was to be elected, and the Emperor suggested a man — and it is clear that Arsenius' influence played a role in this once more — who was then elected; this was Nicholas I. From the moment they appeared on the stage, both Nicholas and his advisor Anastasius maintained connections to the imperial court.

What kind of mysteries surrounded the figure of Anastasius? The annals make no mention of him for several years but it may be assumed that, after Nicholas became Pope, he became the papal advisor directly or very soon afterwards. From 862 onwards the annals name him as the first advisor to the Pope and also as abbot of the monastery of Santa Maria in Trastevere. The question has never been resolved regarding the degree to which a man who is excommunicated and anathematized by the church can fill such a role. Nicholas had the generosity to be close to this man granting him a great deal of influence. After Photius, Anastasius was the most highly educated man of his age. He was one of the few in the West who had such a grasp of Greek that he could read the writings of the Greek church fathers and also write in Greek. Apart from Photius and Anastasius, only Scotus Erigena was able to do this. At any rate, Anastasius had used the time when he had disappeared from the scene to widen his education enormously. While Nicholas was more of a man of the heart, of moral *piety,*

Anastasius was the one who represented *consciousness*, who contributed the right thoughts and instincts.

In the East the two representative characters, Ignatius and Photius, were joined by the deceptive figure of Bardas as the exponent of a group operating in the shadows. In Rome, it was Arsenius who joined Nicholas and Anastasius in this way. Arsenius occupied a very high office which was established in the time of Emperor Constantine. He was the *apokrisiarius sedis apostolicae,* the nuncio, the representative of the Pope at the court of the Holy Roman Emperor, so that the entire clergy around the Emperor, those responsible for policy-making, were subject to him. He occupied the position which provided the best opportunity for having a hand in everything which went on between the Emperor and the Pope. Arsenius made every imaginable use of this opportunity with the greatest skill and without scruples. History books often state that Anastasius was Arsenius' son, because there are letters with the salutation, 'My Dear Son.' But this is certainly not meant as an indication of family ties. There is also a letter where Anastasius addresses Arsenius with the words 'My Dear Uncle.' But Anastasius was not Arsenius' nephew either. According to the detailed descriptions which Rudolf Steiner provided, Anastasius came from the north of Europe, from Scandinavia. He may well have been almost as old as Arsenius. He brought something of the unspent energy of the North to Rome. Arsenius, in contrast, was a typical Roman. He now also placed himself beside the Pope, so that it appeared as though Nicholas had faithful advisors to his left and right, Anastasius on one side and Arsenius on the other. But Arsenius' duplicity soon came to light.

One incident after another occurred which required Nicholas to intervene in order to provide moral stability in the chaotic confusion of events. This landed him in a dispute with the Emperor. The Emperor's brother, Lothar II, had an affair. He had accorded all those rights which properly belong to his wife to his mistress, Waltrada. This business caused quite a stir. Although Louis II rushed to his brother's aid with arms, Nicholas stood firm. He did not yield, finally withdrawing to a room inside St Peters which no one was allowed to enter. After three days his opponents gave up. Nicholas had achieved a moral victory. He then demanded a settlement of the contentious matter with Waltrada and the appropriate sentences were passed.

Naturally, Arsenius always appeared to be on Nicholas' side and kept quiet about whatever else he did. Nicholas entrusted Waltrada to Arsenius, to be taken to a distant town as a kind of banishment, but Arsenius let her escape.

Similar things happened in various conflicts which were disputed between Nicholas and a number of bishops who represented the egotism of their particular churches. Nicholas sent out legates who were meant to carry out the negotiations, but whenever these appeared anywhere to carry out the Pope's bidding, they argued for the other side. Arsenius was instructed to call them to account, but he let them go free, which showed that he had had a prior hand in the business. He showed himself to be a thoroughly duplicitous character. It was even said that he took bribes. But this in itself cannot be the solution to the mystery. A dark group which strove for power by magical means made its appearance through him, a group which also wished to use the Pope as a pawn. Nicholas was not suspicious in the slightest, because with his upright nature he never expected anything false from others. There are strange stories about this. It is said, for example, that Arsenius once appeared dressed as a Jewish astrologer, demanding that this Cabbalist uniform be introduced at court. This was finally more than Nicholas could take and he gave free rein to his anger with Arsenius. But such frivolous will-o-the-wisp conceits really served as a mask to conceal more sinister things.

Nicholas was only Pope for nine years. He died in 867 after being seriously ill for some months. After his death a number of tragic events followed. The two Slav apostles Methodius and Cyrill, whom Nicholas had asked to come to Rome, arrived too late. These two brothers who were born in Salonika had begun converting the Slavic peoples and were responsible for the first large influx of Slavs to Christianity. Where were the Christian Slavs going to turn, towards Rome or towards Byzantium? This question was an important one, so it is understandable that Nicholas invited the two to Rome. The brothers were very different. Methodius had a quiet nature while Cyrill — who had originally been called Constantine — was educated and was a student of Photius. It was through him that the Slavic people who were without writing at the time had come by their letters, the Cyrillic alphabet, and so become literate. Cyrill and Methodius still bore good will to all. They did not want the East split off from the West, but

18. FIGURES IN ROME AND BYZANTIUM   197

wished to join a unified church with Rome as the centre. So they answered Nicholas' call. But then, instead of being received by him, they were met by Anastasius and Arsenius. It is not clear how the talks went, but a tragic sense of failure hung over the whole business. Cyrill died very shortly afterwards. No lucky star shone upon the moment when the Slavs wished to attach themselves to Rome. They became allied to the East which then split off from Rome.

Soon after another tragedy befell, the victim this time being Arsenius himself. This involved a very sinister business. Arsenius' son, Eleutherius, abducted the daughter of Pope Hadrian. It was not uncommon for the pope to have a wife and children, because celibacy was not obligatory for priests at that time. The sensational abduction had already led to a major trial when Eleutherius went a stage further and killed the pope's daughter along with her mother. When news of this became known, Arsenius fled, which showed that Arsenius must have been involved in evil machinations in the background. It is said he fled to Benevento, the seat of the imperial court, and gave his entire wealth into the safekeeping of Engelberga, the Emperor's wife. He himself fell sick with a mysterious fever which was accompanied by unsightly swellings and boils, dying a similar death to Herod and so entering the legends. Throughout the Middle Ages the story of the death of Arsenius was told as an example of how a villain perishes from sores and leprosy. This story is recorded as a warning in the archives of the Benedictine monastery on Monte Cassino. Thus ended the demonic figure beside Nicholas I and Anastasius.

After a new Pope had been elected, we find Anastasius at the imperial court, in fact as a teacher of Irmingard, the daughter of Louis II. In 869 he was sent to Constantinople, not because the great council was taking place there, but to arrange the wedding of the German Emperor's daughter to the son of the Byzantine Emperor. The marriage did not take place, but Anastasius had the opportunity to take part in the last part of the famous council in the Hagia Sophia. He participated as a scholar in the final sessions at the start of 870, wrote up the records and also obtained the records of the previous sessions. As the original council records were lost when a ship went down, the copies made by Anastasius are the only documents through which we know what was discussed at the council. Anastasius lived on for several years and then died in isolation.

Arsenius was connected to a group of dark figures who influenced the history of their age from the shadows. Their headquarters was in Capua which is not far from Benevento. Capua had long been the centre of a kind of anti-Grail community who basically made plans and passed resolutions against the spiritual world. They knew how to influence politics. Since times of old, Capua had been a place where anyone who lingered fell into a sweet slumber and was alienated from humankind. Even Grillparzer called the Vienna of his day the 'Capua of ghosts.' The citizens of Vienna seemed to him like people who were lost in a dream, who had fallen asleep under hypnosis.

The figure of Arsenius can only be understood if you assume that he did more than merely mediate between the Emperor and the Pope. He had a clique behind him who influenced the imperial court and employed all possible means of exercising influence on the Pope and his entourage as well. The Capua clique in the ninth century was a continuation of the black magic school which, as discussed in the previous chapter, in the fourth century strove to entomb all living spiritual knowledge in dogma. In the lecture which Steiner gave on Nicholas I he states, 'In Italy a society was even founded to eradicate all spiritual paths of knowledge.' This is the sentence which refers to the demonic succession which led from the fourth to the ninth centuries. The aim of this dark group was to use the spiritual as a means of power for the few and to prevent other people from having access to it. The esoteric potential of the soul was exploited for the benefit of the group themselves who made sure that it was suppressed outside in the world.

Nicholas and Anastasius struggled to come to terms with the idea of Europe out of a purely human connection to the spirit of their time. They believed that the Luciferic atmosphere of the East should not be allowed to affect the future of Europe and so decided on a western path which ultimately caused the schism of the church. They felt the necessity of a separate European spiritual life.

Living sources of spiritual life existed in the West in those days, though in seclusion. There was first and foremost the community of the Grail. The biographical facts which form the background to the legend of Parsifal belong to this period and it can be seen by following the indications given by Rudolf Steiner, that Nicholas actually had certain connections to those circles which were part of the community of the Grail, in other words, to circles around Mont Sainte-Odile which practised an intensive spiritual life a hundred years after St Odile. There are old writings according to which two counts of Andlau lived in the ninth century. One held a position in Rome, the other lived opposite Mont Sainte-Odile in Andlau Castle. The Count of Andlau in Rome might very well have been a mediator for Nicholas. It might well have been that Nicholas and his close advisor were brought to the decision to send an energetic refusal to what had become a Luciferic spirituality in the East on account of the view of esoteric spirituality cultivated in these kind of quiet circles, even though this made the tragic schism between the eastern and western churches final. Perhaps the thought passed through their souls as a presentiment and hope that one day the old words *ex oriente lux*, 'from the East, the light,' would have to be replaced by *ex occidente lux*, 'from the West the new light must come.'

But had Europe come to the point of being able to accept the new spirituality which was coming to life in the West, or was this not really a matter for the future? Would it not be courting danger if an undertaking was made to awaken something for which humankind in general was not yet ready? These doubts must have lived in Nicholas and Anastasius. They were the exponents of the tragedy in which the middle found itself: Europe lay between the eastern spirit which ought *no longer* to exert its influence and what was beginning to emerge in the West which could *not yet* act on a broad scale. To bring Europe to its own Christian spirituality was a great risk. This experience was the destiny of Nicholas and his part in the 'uncertainty about the Spirit' of that time.

This situation was misused in the worst possible way by Arsenius and the Capua circle and exploited for their own ends. Following on from the dark machinations carried out by that organization in Italy in the fourth century to bind the still living early Christian knowledge in ecclesiastical fixed dogmas, they now arranged for the last remnant of Christian truth to be rigidified into dogma, in fact mummified. Similarly the Christian rituals, which kept their vitality for a while in the East, were subject to a mummification process; but even in the East this process was inevitable. The aim was to make dogma and ritual into instruments of power for the clergy and the church. Mummified knowledge and mummified ritual evoke only apparent individual development in people's soul, but give the few who reserve knowledge of the mysteries for their own circle the possibility of ruling the people and using them to their own purposes. The power of the clergy over human souls and the church's trend towards political power were thus developed consciously. It is no surprise that Rome, which was in the process of separating from the East, now also separated from the living spirit, something which took place at the eighth ecumenical council soon after the death of Nicholas I in 869.

Nicholas and his cardinal who had really wanted to found a new spiritual Roman church were unable to prevent the tragedy of this development. Morally they were obviously superior to the people in Capua. But destiny had brought them into such close contact with the latter — perhaps Anastasius had even spent some of the time when he disappeared not far from this circle — that they were not actually able to see through what was going on there. They themselves radiated a stream of real humanity, a true European Christian impulse down through the centuries. But the Klingsorian shadow of this light was also present through the group around Arsenius and this shadow gained ground quickly because it made use of the instrument of power. It would one day lead Europe into the greatest crisis of its destiny.

In the lecture of October 1, 1922 about Nicholas I, Steiner described how in the West the Grail community still cultivated a knowledge which reached the etheric of the cosmos and how the East had ritual practices, crowned by the idea of pilgrimage and Jerusalem, which kept the etheric bodies of human beings alive. Through the fact that the Christian stream split in Europe, so that both the cosmic etheric and the human etheric aspects began to evaporate, what then became called the Roman Catholic Church arose. Steiner summarized the spiritual results of what happened in the ninth century in the following words:

> Whilst the realities of the ritual vanished into the vast emptiness of Asia, ... on account of the discovery of America — if I may express myself pictorially — the esoteric secrets of the western stream fell into the Atlantic Ocean.

Spirituality vanished towards the East and the West, leaving a dried out centre.

*

18. FIGURES IN ROME AND BYZANTIUM

Let us now move on to our own time. Nicholas stood at the culmination of a tragedy, in a way. He died shortly before the moment when the fateful dogma which did away with the spirit was decided at the Hagia Sophia in Constantinople. Helmuth von Moltke stood at the moment when the great avalanche of disaster which was set off in the first days of August 1914 was triggered. Just as Nicholas died shortly before the decisive moment, so Moltke died shortly after the decisive moment. Actually, the death blow had been delivered at the point when he was left alone by all those in charge. Moltke stood in world history even more as a human being than as a soldier and strategist. On whom should the German folk spirit rely at that moment? Should it rely on the official dignitaries? It had perforce to rely on the figure who truly embodied what was entering the great test of destiny at that point. It is an objective historical truth to state that this man stood there amidst the storm, already struck by lightning, but it was on him that the spiritual power which held the leadership over the destiny of Central European humanity relied. Although he was bowed with suffering, this entity still shone in him. The fact that he was at first unable to see through Wilhelm II and the figures around him was not something negative, but arose from his positive attitude, from the trusting disposition of his whole nature. So this was tragic in the sense of classical tragedy. Because amongst those whom Moltke was unable to see through, the Capua people were present again, those cold dazzling characters who, though they were in charge did not take this seriously, as their ambition was satisfied by being promoted and reaching high office. Moltke's sworn enemies could soon be clearly discerned, men who were definitely soldiers and nothing more but who could not even take their soldiering really seriously, because being only a soldier without putting your heart into it is meaningless.

Moltke died on June 18, 1916. In the afterlife the curtain which in life had prevented him from seeing through what was really going on around him was drawn back. He was able to look back into his earlier life on earth and understand the real sources of these obstacles. He began to see who it was who had interfered in the fate of Europe at that earlier date. And at the same time a preview opened up showing him future tasks on the earth. These are connected to the East from which he and Europe had to separate in the ninth century.

*

I wish to take a rather indirect route in order to round off this discussion. We shall turn our attention to someone who was a friend of Moltke's and who, like him, pursued a military career. So there were actually two figures who, as exponents of humanity, rose above being merely officers. The second figure was Field Marshal von der Goltz, who appears in Steffen's play as the field marshal of the East. He was six years older than Moltke. Von der Goltz died of typhus in the eastern theatre of war in Baghdad on April 19, 1916. He was then taken to Constantinople where he was buried on June 23. On June 18, a few days before the burial in Constantinople, a remembrance ceremony was held in the Reichstag in Berlin. It was a Sunday. Moltke, though seriously ill, held a commemorative speech at this ceremony for the Field Marshal with whom he had been close. Immediately after holding the speech he collapsed and breathed his last. Thus the two destinies were joined in death.

Whilst in Moltke's case the karmic reflections which look towards the East only appear at certain points, above all when he travelled to St Petersburg on behalf of the Emperor, in Field Marshal von Goltz's life such reflections stand in the foreground.

We need to sketch the course of this life with a few strokes. Baron von der Goltz was a sickly child but nevertheless became a cadet and took up a career as an officer. Right from the beginning he was unable to be totally absorbed by being a soldier and was therefore often sorely misjudged by the stalwart types. He was an author and even wrote novels, such as the three-volume novel, *Pius the Infallible and His Black Riders*, when he was 28. This was when Pius IX had announced the infallibility of the Pope during the Vatican council of 1870. A three-volume novel on this subject was written by a German officer of the General Staff! When he was forty he was sent to Turkey as general inspector of the educational system. His task was to help raise the Turkish people from their uncultured state to a more educated level. But an odd military idea was behind this.

The German politicians expected an unavoidable clash between Germany and Britain at some point and anticipated the benefit of taking on the British Empire where it was most vulnerable, in India. This preventative strategic concept led to efforts as far back as the 1880s to establish an alliance with Turkey, in other words, a permanent mobilization of the Turkish army in the interests of Germany's future prospects.

Von der Goltz treated the Turks with humanity and tried to understand them, but was immediately reproached for this, being told to treat the lazy fellows more strictly. This he did not do, but continued to try to reach his objective through empathy and in a human way. It was not his fault that a rather warped idea had provided the impetus for the whole undertaking. He went about his task with love for his country and loyalty to his Emperor. He remained in Turkey for twelve years until he was recalled. Then he did his best for the moral education of the German officer corps. He wrote a book, *Moral Homesickness*, in which one sentence reads: 'No effort should be spared to fill the officers once again with the pride of poverty which the knight once experienced when he ... swore eternal fidelity to this god.' However, this was not well received. The ideal that he laid down no longer accorded with the attitude in his circles. He was given a severe dressing down by the chief of personnel in the military cabinet, General von Hülsen. Von Hülsen died in a strange manner. Once when the Emperor and his entourage were making merry together in Donaueschingen, Hülsen appeared as a prima donna and started dancing, suffered a stroke and fell down dead.

Now I shall relate something which throws light on what Moltke had to suffer. In 1912 when von der Goltz was long back in Germany, the Balkan war broke out and Germany abandoned Turkey whose federal cooperation it had taken such pains over. Von der Goltz had to be the scapegoat — when he had been in Turkey he had not dealt with the people firmly enough — and was dismissed. Let us be clear about this. The idea had originally been to attack Britain in India by going through Turkey, but nothing was done to put this into practice. It remained an illusion floating in the air and those who had really done their best for this idea were punished, although at this point they had nothing whatever to do with the matter. Von der Goltz was plunged into mental anguish especially because, at the outbreak of the First World War, he now had no task.

Let us compare Moltke and von der Goltz. Moltke was burdened with an almost unbearable excess of responsibility which was then abruptly removed from him and Goltz had no job at all. Both men were totally crushed by this.

In the end Von der Goltz was sent to Belgium. A rapid advance had been made there and the territory behind the front had to be secured.

Goltz did this in a humane way which immediately earned him a reprimand from Falkenhayn who became Moltke's successor in addition to being minister of war. Falkenhayn was in favour of driving the Belgians like animals instead of treating them like human beings. The turmoil in the days when the battle of the Marne took place was also noticeable in Belgium. Cosmic darkening filled people's souls, deceptions of an Ahrimanic nature. At the end of November 1914, the 72-year-old Von der Goltz was sent to Turkey again. Something needed to be done down there. The efforts of others had ended in failure and now it came to mind that Goltz knew the country. He was charged with intervening, which he then did, fighting in Mesopotamia and Persia. At his advanced age he was on the front line. Then followed another striking scene. In December 1915 Falkenhayn talked to Wilhelm II and led an infamous sideswipe against von der Goltz by saying: 'Those enthusiasts for an Alexandrian campaign to India are quite mad! We need the troops to attack Verdun.'

So people take their own ideas seriously and let others who have fought for these ideas — although they were not their own — fall without mercy. Von der Goltz died in Baghdad on April 19. We can see how Goltz's destiny led over to the East: twelve years in Turkey and the First World War spent in Mesopotamia, Arabia and Persia. The East-West relationships from the ninth century flit across the earth like mirages.

Now destiny continues its symbolism. When Moltke was dismissed, Falkenhayn became his successor. When Goltz died Falkenhayn also became his successor after an intervening period. The Alexandrian campaign which had been the butt of his joke was now to be led by him because he had failed in the West. But Jerusalem, Damascus and Baghdad fell one after the other and Germany's entire position in the East collapsed. Falkenhayn wore his elegant uniform with exaggerated care until the last moment. The smooth elegance of such men always contrasts with the destinies which surround them because they never take anything really seriously.

It is no surprise that the catastrophe finally had to spread further, entering into our time. Nowadays the anti-Grail leaning of the Capua people of the ninth century who appeared on the scene once again has led to a total anonymous loss of spirit. Cultural conditions are becoming ever more fully dominated by Ahriman. But in this great twilight of the gods, humanity has been led to the threshold of the spiritual world. What began in the confluence of the Grail stream and the Arthurian stream in the secret background of the ninth century must now find its metamorphosis. This has been provided through Steiner's life work in the seeds of a renewal of cultural life through the spirit, from the foundations upwards. As chaos has arisen through spiritual error, the future must be born from spiritually creative deeds which lead beyond the threshold to which humankind has been brought.

Nowadays blocks have formed in the East, the West and the South. Instead of Christianity providing a living centre, it has also become a mummified block and a political power. It is basically of no importance whether it currently makes deals with America or with other sides. It is still only a static centre instead of a living creative centre in the sense of the principle of the Son, of the impulse of Christ. Today the way has opened through anthroposophy, if only people grasp it and endeavour to develop their way of thinking, and thence cultural life in an appropriate way.

19

Ephesus and the Castle of the Grail

Rudolf Steiner's great historic mission for our age which stands under the inspiration of Michael, was to raise the human power of intelligence once more into spiritual heights. Anthroposophy is, as he himself often pointed out, a new and decisive stage in the spiritual development which led from Aristotle and Thomas Aquinas. Human intelligence had once to be brought out from the hidden realm of the mysteries into the open light of everyday life. This happened through Aristotle's shaping of philosophy which set Europe on its particular western path. Now Aristotelianism has to be resurrected in the sense that the realm of the mysteries can be entered with fully awakened intelligence. Through Thomas Aquinas human intelligence connected with Christianity was raised to a new level Christian Europe. The task of anthroposophy is now a further development and enhancement of Thomism through raising the spiritualized intelligence to a new knowledge of the supersensory world and in particular of the mysteries of Christ.

It was of great significance for the pioneering achievements of Aristotle and Thomas Aquinas that they were not drawn from the practices and traditions of initiation in the mysteries, which still continued in the background of history. They were achieved through the conscious 'I,' the free personality, in the clear light of public life. And this applies even more to the achievements of Rudolf Steiner. Nevertheless all that has matured in secret, cultivated by the mysteries and in quiet esoteric circles, has had its effects on these steps in human development, which are marked by Aristotelianism, Thomism and anthroposophy. An indirect help came about in a karmic way, as the great creative individuality which incarnated in Aristotle and

Thomas, passed each time previously through a short incarnation in which there was a direct participation in the mysteries. Both these lives in the quiet background of history had their particular character. The one which helped prepare the life of Aristotle was set in the Artemis mystery at Ephesus; the one which preceded the incarnation as Thomas Aquinas fell in the ninth century, a time related to the present which will be considered here. At the same time in which Christendom was in conflict about the Holy Spirit, and the Eighth Ecumenical Council 'abolished' the spirit of man, the quiet groups of people concerned with the Round Table of Arthur and of the Grail offered to that individuality with which we are concerned, insight into the esoteric Christianity which was secure in its knowledge of the Holy Spirit.

*

It will be understandable that the events in the ninth century concerned with the Grail, which provide the karmic foundations for the spiritual progress of the present time, cannot be described as directly as the external history of that period in which the seeds of the dangers and disasters of present-day Europe lay. We can only feel our way through the veil of the legend towards the figures whose destiny formed the history of the Grail. We have to attempt an indirect approach.

Let us look back at the young Rudolf Steiner in Vienna, approaching his twenty-eighth birthday. He was particularly connected to two circles of people. One, consisting only of very few people, surrounded his respected teacher, Karl Julius Schröer. Here everything was concerned with Goethe, without regard to the problems of Christianity. At the same time he shares the life of another circle which is particularly concerned with Christianity, consisting largely of Cistercian professors of theology. Here there is no favourable reaction to Goethe, so that Professor Schröer was there only once when he introduced his pupil, Rudolf Steiner. Schröer felt so repelled by their aversion to Goethe and, connected with this, their pessimistic conception of the world, that he never came again. In this circle another name stood at the centre: that of Thomas Aquinas. The respected doyen was Professor Karl Werner, author of the great work about Thomas Aquinas.

This was the time in which Rudolf Steiner was struggling to take hold of the conception of reincarnation in a comprehensive way. The theoretical formulations which he encountered in Theosophical circles were of no use to him. Destiny now brought it about that two moments struck him like lightning flashes in conversations that arose in each of the two groups. On November 9, 1888, a few months before his twenty-eighth birthday, at Schröer's suggestion Rudolf Steiner held a lecture about Goethe in the Vienna Goethe Society. Afterwards, the most active of the Cistercian professors, Neumann, approached him saying, 'Thomas Aquinas.' Doubtless he only wished to say: What you have just described is in accordance with the thought of Thomas Aquinas. But his words tore apart like a flash of lightning the clouds of the centuries, releasing in the soul of the young Rudolf Steiner a vision of earlier times. The turning point in the thirteenth century became visible, when Thomas Aquinas and other Dominican teachers brought about the marriage between European thinking and Christian thinking.

Soon afterwards, about February 1, 1889, he visited his teacher Schröer. Two days earlier the tragedy of Meyerling had happened, Crown Prince Rudolf of Austria had taken his life under dramatic circumstances. Naturally everyone in Vienna was deeply moved by this event. When Rudolf Steiner came to Schröer, the latter said enigmatically, 'Nero.' Once more a curtain is torn apart and a far-seeing vision becomes possible.

These two moments brought to Rudolf Steiner much more clarity about reincarnation than theoretical, philosophic considerations. But the two occasions were very different. In the first conversation a name was mentioned, which was the object of a vision into the past. This vision reached back into the thirteenth century, when the great Dominican gave European thinking its Christian stamp. In the conversation with Schröer it was not the word spoken, not the object of the sentence, which enkindled the vision into the past, but it was the subject, the one who spoke who brought about the vision into the past. It was not so much a matter of Nero and his destiny, but that the one who said 'Nero' was none other than the reincarnated Plato, as was then described thirty-five years later in the last of the karma lectures. The vision into the past revealed the scene in Athens when Plato had some pupils about him, among them Aristotle and that personality who was later reborn as Goethe.

At such moments a clear view became possible of the two significant turning-points: the world of Aristotle and the world of Thomas Aquinas.

The qualities of two environments become evident. That mood of the Middle Ages which was expressed when Professor Neumann uttered the name of Thomas Aquinas, remained for a time in the background, as if behind a mist. Rudolf Steiner had first to develop with all his power the stream from ancient Greece which had revealed itself to him then, and became ever clearer. He first had to give Goetheanism and Aristotelianism a form appropriate for the present. This he did in the early works written in the 1880s and 1890s. Only after the turn of the century could he turn fully to Christianity. One can perhaps read out of the karmic connections of destiny the reason why Rudolf Steiner was unable to take up the task of Christianity before the turn of the century, but how he then took it up of necessity.

When Rudolf Steiner was twenty-eight he was about to leave his native soil. In summer 1889 he first visited Weimar. A few days before his journey, on July 15, 1889, he was standing in Graz beside Peter Rosegger at the grave of Robert Hamerling. There a man was laid to rest of whom we know from the karma lectures that he too once belonged to the outstanding pupils of Plato in Athens. Here Rudolf Steiner reached a kind of completion of what was possible on his native Austria. Two or three days later he travelled to Weimar. The way was free. During seven years at Weimar he began the foundation of his life's work in connection with Goethe, one of the great pupils of Plato. Here Steiner brought his contribution to the development of thought.

*

Leet us now make a great leap to the end of the year 1910, when Rudolf Steiner held what can be called the first Christmas cycle, *Occult History,* in Stuttgart. The unprecedented thing was that he now began to describe concrete karmic connections on a great scale. He began to describe the figures of Aristotle and his pupil Alexander the Great, as if as paradigm of the studies in karma on which he was now setting out. He showed how figures of ancient Babylon, reaching back into the mythical period of the mysteries, were reincarnated in these two individualities. In the third millennium before Christ, Alexander the Great has been Gilgamesh, and Aristotle has been Eabani the teacher and friend of Gilgamesh, a figure less conspicuous in external life, but all the more significant spiritually. Rudolf Steiner began to reveal the karmic background which influenced the first great turning-point, the foundation of European thinking. Later he spoke in such a way that light fell upon the other turning-point, the foundation of a Christian development of intelligence by Thomas Aquinas.

It is important to see what events preceded this revelation of karma in 1910, which was like a herald of what was to come. It can never be sufficiently emphasized that an unprecedented event took place at the beginning of 1910, that Rudolf Steiner spoke of the new Christ event in city after city. Beginning in Stockholm, after January he spoke in many places of the appearance of the new etheric revelation of Christ. From this followed the beginning of his artistic creative activities, for in this year the first of the four Mystery Plays, *The Portal of Initiation*, was written. The first scene contained the event from which developed all the dramatic soul-processes of the four Mystery Plays: the Theodora scene in which the seeress beholds the ethereal Christ. What is important for an understanding of the purpose of the Mystery Plays as Rudolf Steiner also said in lectures about the drama was that through the announcement of the etheric Christ a prophetic view to the future opened up. For some millennia humankind will have time to grow into the experience of the etheric Christ; and a reacquiring of clairvoyant capacity will be connected with this. A beacon for the future is raised which also shines back into the past, as far as it does into the future. Beholding the etheric Christ is at the same time a source of new knowledge about karma. In the Mystery Plays the prophetic element is closely connected with such visions into the past; for after the way is opened through Theodora, several people are able to look back into their own earlier lives on earth.

What happened between the first lectures about the etheric Christ and the performance of the first Mystery Play at Munich in August?

In the course of that spring and summer Steiner's journeys were particularly wide and frequent. There was hardly a year in his life in which his journeys made a more striking pattern. In January 1910 he was in Stockholm, where in the course of a lecture cycle about St John's Gospel he spoke for the first time about the coming of the etheric Christ. He continued this theme in many cities, until in March he travelled eastwards: in Vienna he held the lectures, 'Microcosm and Macrocosm.' In April there followed an important journey to Italy. First he visited Ravenna. Then Steiner stayed for some time in Rome; this had been prepared by a short visit to Rome in the previous year. Between Rome and Naples he went to Monte Cassino, and was drawn deeply to this district where Thomas Aquinas had spent his boyhood. He was particularly interested in finding any traces of this life. It is no accident that, in the region in which Benedict of Nursia founded the first Benedictine monastery, Rudolf Steiner prepared himself for writing the first Mystery Play in which a central figure bears the name Benedictus. Finally the journey reached Palermo; from far in the north he has reached the southern tip of Europe. And from Sicily he went straight back to Scandinavia. In Oslo the great lecture cycle, *The Mission of Folk Souls*, is given. It seems that something demanded simultaneous contact with the furthest regions of the north and to the south of Europe.

It was not unconnected with this pattern that the first Mystery Play came into being in that summer, and at the end of the year the first lecture cycle about karma was given. The karma cycle at Christmas was prepared at Whitsun by the lectures, 'Revelations of Karma,' in Hamburg, held on the way from the furthest south to the furthest north. The theme of karma had taken on an urgency once it became possible to proclaim the mystery of the etheric Christ.

What is to be found about karmic relationships in the cycle *Occult History*? Through the figures of Aristotle and Alexander the Great we are led far into the past. The old Babylonian civilization is spread out before us, in which man has not yet really come to the human measure. They are larger than life, vessels of higher beings rather than of men; thus it is said of Gilgamesh that he was two thirds man, one third God. Greatness did not yet lie in the human individuality itself, but in the capacity to be vessels for a being of the Hierarchies.

It is significant for our theme that in this cycle, given at Christmas in Stuttgart, a motif appeared which is later developed; it is indicated that between the period of the life of Gilgamesh and Eabani in the third millennium before Christ and the time of the appearance of Aristotle and Alexander at the height of Greek civilization, these two individualities were incarnated in a quiet environment. We are to be shown that it was necessary for Aristotle, before grasping the classical mission for Europe which he had to fulfil, had to pass through the intimate atmosphere of secluded mysteries. An intermediate incarnation comes to light, without anything being said about the place or the time, and much less about names and the like. Only in a quite general way is it said that a mission like that of Aristotle cannot be fulfilled without the mysteries, with their spiritual substance and intimacy, working on the karmic paths of the individual. There was no initiation in the life of Aristotle. His achievement was to make exoteric, what had previously been guarded esoterically. But the intimate element is in the background.

> We can here bring as an example, how Eabani in his incarnation between the personality of Eabani and that of Aristotle, could receive under the influence of the old mystery teachings with the powers that they bring from supersensible worlds the qualities through which the human soul was developed in certain mystery schools ... The soul of the pupil of the mysteries had to pass through an education leading to a comprehensive, universal feeling of compassion and a universal feeling of fearlessness. Every soul passed through this, in those ancient mysteries in which Eabani participated, in the incarnation that stands between Eabani and Aristotle. He too passed through this. And it appeared again in Aristotle like a memory of earlier incarnations. Thus he could give the theory of tragedy, because from such memories he realized as he contemplated Greek tragedy that an echo is present in this ... of that education in the mysteries in which the soul is purified by compassion and fear.

Thus Aristotle's theory of the nature of tragedy, that it educates human beings through compassion and fear, depended upon an immediate memory; the individuality of Aristotle himself had passed in an earlier time through a training in the mysteries of compassion and fear. We realize that behind Aristotle's tremendous work of bringing knowledge into the exoteric realm, there lies a quiet place of the mysteries. This is the womb in which European thinking had to develop before its birth. At the end of 1910 the beacon of knowledge about karma could shine back into the past as far as this.

*

Let us take another leap in time. On New Year's Eve 1922/23 flames shot across the sky, destroying the first Goetheanum. They not only caused deep pain; they too were a mighty beacon shining into the past. Through the flames of the burning Goetheanum another destruction by fire becomes visible. On the night of Alexander the Great's birth in 356 BC the famous Temple of Artemis at Ephesus was set on fire and destroyed by Herostratus. History became transparent: through the flames at Dornach could be seen the flames at Ephesus. What did this reveal?

When the temple at Ephesus burned, Aristotle was twenty-eight and lived at Athens. He was following his own path; he had been Plato's pupil for years, and had gradually separated from him. It was plain that he had a task that reached far beyond Plato's. The fire at Ephesus shook him profoundly. Why was this? What led to such an intimate relationship? Through the insights into karma given after the burning of the Goetheanum we find that the view into the past not only led to the burning of Ephesus, but reached further. We see Ephesus around 500 BC. There, in the quiet, intimate realm of the mysteries were the two individualities who, not so very long afterwards, would play their part in the course of history as Aristotle and Alexander. What had been shown only in outlines at Christmas 1910 was now shown in detail.

A decisive change took place at Ephesus in the year 555 BC. Until then the Temple of Artemis on the Ionian coast was a quiet and remote sanctuary, whose holy tradition reached back for many centuries. Only with the greatest reverence was this temple thought of or spoken about in the ancient world. We can imagine the times when Homer passed that way, around 1000 BC. Then in the year 555, in the confusion of war, the place of Ephesian mysteries was seized by the Lydian ruler, Croesus; a town was founded in the immediate neighbourhood of the temple. Nothing could have destroyed the intimate peace of the place more effectively. Just before this catastrophe Pythagoras had been one of the last pupils of Ephesus while it was still unspoilt. As a young man he could receive everything which Ephesus was able to give out of its ancient, holy traditions.

Soon afterwards Heraclitus was on of the first in the new Ephesus who suffered bitterly from the changed conditions. He was born in the new town, the child of a noble family. A fire raged within him growing into a hatred of a humanity capable of profaning the sacred into superficiality. In his mature years Heraclitus left behind him all his tasks among men, in profound bitterness, and lived as a hermit close to the temple. Since he was recognized and honoured in his spiritual greatness by the leaders of the temple, he was given a special position there. He was not a priest of Ephesus, but the priests of Ephesus were his pupils and listened to his teachings. He had pupils too, who came there for his sake, but also took part in the life of the mysteries. In the lecture cycle given during the Christmas Foundation Conference in 1923 Rudolf Steiner said that the two individualities who later incarnated as Aristotle and Alexander were pupils of Heraclitus in his last years. It is not impossible that one was a man and the other a woman at this time. The old Heraclitus was full of contempt for the profane world spread out in the new town, although it was his own birthplace. Through his temperament he was a peculiar representative of Ephesian wisdom.

Rudolf Steiner described him vividly in his *Riddles of Philosophy,* where he shows that the conceptions of the early Greek philosophers had a significant connection with their individual temperaments. Thus the philosophy of Heraclitus originates in a choleric temperament. Concerned with the future, he always spoke about the importance of *becoming,* never about the importance of *being.* He spoke of fire as the original principle of all things, because fire does not leave things as they are, but compels continual change. This is connected to the often quoted saying, *panta rhei,* 'all things are in flux.' To have had such a teacher who directed all his thoughts exclusively towards *becoming* must have had a deep effect on the experience of freedom. Philo, the Jewish philosopher, writing in Greek, said that Heraclitus experienced the Logos in Fire just as Moses experienced Yahweh in the burning bush. This is a particularly characteristic and illuminating comparison; for what was passed on to his pupils by the embittered hermit of Ephesus had something of the power and dynamic quality of the great prophets like Moses. We can picture the deep impression made upon both pupils by the death of their teacher around 470 BC. Heraclitus must have been about sixty-five or seventy years old; there are no exact dates for his life.

A few sentences from the description of Heraclitus in *Riddles of Philosophy* may be quoted here:

> An unprejudiced consideration is compelled to regard Heraclitus's conception of the world as an immediate expression of his choleric inner life. ... A soul that expresses itself in such a choleric way finds itself akin to the destructive effect of fire; it does not live in easy, quiet being; it feels itself as at one with 'eternal becoming.' A soul of this kind feels immobility to be nonsense; the famous sentence of Heraclitus is thus 'All things are in a flux.' It is only apparent, if enduring being is to be seen anywhere. ... Heraclitus's way to thought is usually described by means of the saying: one cannot step twice into the same stream — for the second time the water has changed. One of the pupils of Heraclitus, Cratylus, developed this saying further, by saying that one cannot even step once into the same stream. It is thus with everything; while we gaze at what appears to endure, it has already changed into something else in the general stream of existence.

One of the pupils of Heraclitus is named here; so that we have an indication for forming a conception of those two pupils of Heraclitus, whose names are not mentioned, in whom the two individualities with whom we are concerned prepared for their great European mission.

As a little aside, just as at a significant point in history we find Pythagoras and Heraclitus at Ephesus, so we can picture St Paul and St John worked in the same place just after the time of Christ? Figures of a similar greatness were then working as messengers of Christ, just as once Pythagoras and Heraclitus lived there.

*

In the course given during the Christmas Foundation Conference, *World History and the Mysteries,* Rudolf Steiner said many intimate things about the experience of Heraclitus' two pupils when they absorbed the quintessence of Ephesus:

> Destiny led the two personalities of whom I spoke ... to be reincarnated as adherents of the mystery of Ephesus ...
> Thereby their soul-configuration was inwardly consolidated.

That is to say, the preponderance of the cosmic in which the two personalities had been involved, in particular Gilgamesh, during the Babylonian period, was now balanced out. The mighty content of the spiritual world was received in such a way that it is related with the clarity of thought to earthly life.

> And so these two personalities were able on the one hand to judge the spiritual of the higher world that came to them as a result of life experience and that lived in them as an echo from their earlier incarnations. And now, as the origin of the kingdoms of nature was communicated to them in the mystery of Ephesus under the influence of the goddess Artemis, they were able to judge how the things on the earth external to man came into being. ... And the life of these two personalities — which partly coincided with the last years of Heraclitus living in Ephesus, and partly with the period that followed — became particularly rich inwardly, imbued with the light of great cosmic secrets.
>
> ... The time in Ephesus was relatively peaceful; a time of digestion and assimilation of all that had passed through their souls in earlier, more agitated times.

In Ephesus the two individualities could still feel echoes of the old order of the world, in which for example Asia Minor was not yet felt as part of the earth, but still as the lowest rung of heaven. This worked strongly in their souls, and later arose in Aristotle and Alexander.

> The whole of Asia — in the form that it had assumed in Greece, and in Ephesus in particular — was living in these two. ... If we form an idea of this, we can grasp the fact that on the day on which Alexander was born, Herostratus threw the flaming torch into the sanctuary of Ephesus; on the very day on which Alexander was born, the Temple of Diana of Ephesus was treacherously burnt to the ground. It was gone, and with it the sanctuary's monumental documents and all that belonged to it. All this was no longer there, the only thing surviving was the historical mission in the soul of Alexander and in his teacher Aristotle. ... You will now be in a position to appreciate the resolve that Alexander made in his soul: to restore to the East what she had lost; to restore it at least in the form in which it was preserved in Greece, as a shadowy picture. Hence his idea of going to Asia, going as far east as it was possible to go, in order to bring to the Orient once more — albeit in the

shadow form in which it still existed in the Grecian culture — what she had lost.

Thus when Aristotle and Alexander were living this stream reached an end — but continued through these two personalities. On the one hand it led to the impulse for Alexander's conquests, and on the other, the great teaching activity of Aristotle. The one went eastwards seeking to fertilize Asia with the spirit of Europe. The teaching of Aristotle sought to translate what came from the East into western thoughts.

But what concerns us particularly in relation to Ephesus is the description given by Rudolf Steiner to bring us with our feelings into the special environment of the temple of Ephesus. He brings before us in living colours the cosmic, poetic quality of this environment. In the lectures held at Torquay in 1924 he says:

> Strong and powerful influences of initiation formed themselves into that temple, where on the eastern side there stood the statue of the goddess Diana that has become known to the world — the goddess of fertility, who expresses the abundant fertility which is everywhere in nature. The greatest secrets of existence, profound spiritual mysteries, were expressed in words, when conversations were held, for instance immediately after those taking part in the mysteries had received mighty influences through the rituals and through all their detail, in the temple of Ephesus. The profound conversations continued this. When those who had taken part in the ritual left the temple, and perhaps at the time of day when the outer world is most fruitful for such things, in the twilight of evening, they would walk along the path leading from the gate of the temple into a wood through which there were many wonderful paths — a wood where the trees were deep black green, and the paths vanished into beautiful distances in different directions from Ephesus.

Those who took part in the mysteries came out in the evening, deeply moved by the ceremonies in which they have taken part and walk along the carefully laid out paths through the dark grove surrounding the temple; and they held conversations, in which a teacher may say to his pupil, 'See — we are walking through the twilight. Sleep, which reveals the divine world, which makes it visible, will soon come to us. Regard yourself in your whole human form. Below, from the earth, the plants are growing; around us is the wonderful wood, casting its shadows in the twilight, in its green, darkening twilight; and above us the first stars are already beginning to sparkle. Look upon all this. Behold its majesty and sublimity, and behold too the ever-springing, quickening life both above and below. Then, behold yourself. Think how within you there lives and weaves a whole universe.

We feel the magic of such conversations, held in the evenings in the wonderful environment of the holy groves about Ephesus. In such conversations the teacher brought the pupil into connection with Persephone, the goddess Natura — with the spiritual powers in the kingdoms of nature. Through this mood we see how the cosmic poetry of such an environment formed the necessary maternal womb for the task of Aristotle, which turned entirely towards the outer world, a century later.

*

In the lectures given after the burning of the Goetheanum, in particular during the Christmas Foundation Conference, there is a clear description too of the great turning-point which followed in the thirteenth century. The two figures, who again and again form the paradigm of these karma studies, now work within the Dominican Order. Aristotle has returned in the personality of Thomas Aquinas. The name of the other individuality is not mentioned; he does not stand in the foreground of history. Earlier it was a question of Europe, now it is a question of Christianity. Now the question is, how is the development of the human intelligence to proceed after the Mystery of Golgotha?

To go into detail here about Thomas Aquinas would lead too far. We shall consider the intimate preparation for the incarnation as St Thomas. Just as Rudolf Steiner showed how the peaceful haven of Ephesus prepared the incarnation of Aristotle, he pointed to an intermediate incarnation before the incarnation of Thomas Aquinas in the environs of the quiet, poetic mysteries.

We come here to two passages in lectures of 1924, and observe their tentative, guarded way of expression. These things were never said bluntly. The intimate character of these incarnations which lie between is reflected in the way they are described. In the karma lectures given at Torquay in August 1924, it was shown how Aristotle and Alexander, while in the spiritual worlds, not only observed what had become of their activity on earth; they saw too how an entirely new impulse had entered human evolution through the Mystery of Golgotha. They experience how Christ became man. For the earth this was his coming; but experienced from the sun it was a departure. Christ left the sun, and the souls who were in that realm experienced the pain of a Good Friday, at the Christmas event on earth. The two individualities realized that everything through which they had passed, everything that they had achieved, in their destiny up to now, had to change utterly; a great turning point was necessary. Steiner described that in AD 869 the individualities of Aristotle and Alexander, in their life after death, had a spiritual encounter with the individualities who were incarnated in the Arab civilization as Harun al-Rashid and his adviser.

> Since their karma brought them down into earthly life before this meeting with Harun al-Rashid had happened, they lived as unregarded, unknown personalities who died early in a corner of Europe that is indeed important for anthroposophy; looking as though through a window into western civilization, receiving impressions but not imparting significant impulses themselves. This they reserved for later.

A second passage is contained in the fourth volume of the Dornach karma lectures.

> Thus Alexander and Aristotle lived on. Their real individualities entered only once briefly into earthly life during the first Christian centuries — in a region interesting from anthroposophical points of view — and returned into the spiritual world, where they were at a time when Harun al-Rashid and his adviser had already left the physical plane for some time. Aristotle and Alexander followed other paths; their real incarnations went with the development of Christianity, westwards.

This quiet intermediate incarnation has its significance in the fact that the two individualities are now able to find a change of direction, from the mood of Greece into that of Christianity. What is the corner of Europe which is important for anthroposophy? It is the area where three countries touch, France, Switzerland and Germany, and three mountain ranges meet, the Black Forest, the Vosges and the Swiss Jura. It is the region near the bend in the Rhine where Basle stands, and in the hinterland the hill on which the Goetheanum was built. On the day

19. EPHESUS AND THE CASTLE OF THE GRAIL

before the Foundation Stone of the first Goetheanum was laid, in September 1913, Rudolf Steiner wrote to Alexander von Bernus who had offered a site near Heidelberg for the building:

> Karma has pointed so clearly to this point that I would no longer give the *Johannesbau-Verein* any other advice but to build [here] ... And I have to say that each day more spiritual reasons arise in my soul which make the situation which to a certain extent was forced on us appear to be the right one. So I no longer have anything against laying the foundation stone here tomorrow after sunset.

Thus he indicates the complex karmic background which led to the building of the Goetheanum on the Dornach hill and not somewhere else. When the foundation stone was laid next day Rudolf Steiner said in his address:

> We stand at this moment, led by karma, at the place through which have passed important spiritual streams: let us feel this evening the earnestness of the situation.

The were led by karma to the hill, over which important spiritual streams had passed. The environment of the Goetheanum is in fact the region of this intermediate incarnation, just as Ephesus was the place of the earlier intermediate incarnation. The landscape of the Goetheanum is like another Ephesus. A deep karmic connection unites the temple of Ephesus and the first Goetheanum; this is also shown in the fact that they were both destroyed by fire at night.

What led Rudolf Steiner first to this place behind Basle, which according to the legend goes back to a foundation by Gilgamesh? In May and June 1906, an important congress took place in Paris. Rudolf Steiner met Edouard Schuré for the first time. In Chapter 11 on the Fifth Gospel I have written in detail about the significance of this Alsace poet and writer in Rudolf Steiner's destiny; Schuré's poetic dramas about the mysteries were performed in Munich before Rudolf Steiner's Mystery Plays. In Schuré Rudolf Steiner encountered a man who brought with him a particular karmic substance. This was expressed in his enthusiastic support for Richard Wagner's work. He gave this because Wagner had developed and realized the idea of mystery drama in a festival theatre, and because he developed the Grail myths in artistic form. After Rudolf Steiner and Edouard Schuré had met in Paris, Steiner visited Bayreuth for the first time and attended

Parzival. Whether that had been arranged earlier, or came about through the encounter with Schuré, can be left open; but the two events belong together. At the beginning of September Steiner was Schuré's guest for more than a week at Barr at the foot of Mont Sainte-Odile. The two had much to discuss. It was a significant moment when they climbed Mont Sainte-Odile. They talked particularly about the figure of St Odile in the eighth century. Rudolf Steiner said, that he had not found her here, but could follow her better in Arlesheim.

St Odile took refuge in a cell near the hermitage in Arlesheim, when she had to flee from her father. Arlesheim was at this time a great estate belonging to the lord of Mont Sainte-Odile. The monastery was founded later. Thus in 1906 Rudolf Steiner already knew the landscape where the Goetheanum was later to be built. He had been in Basle several times to give lectures. Immediately after his stay with Schuré at Mont Sainte-Odile the Theosophical branch in Basle was founded on September 19 and 20, and on November 19 a public lecture was given on St John's Gospel.

Basle soon became an important centre for Rudolf Steiner's work; from the start his predominant theme there was esoteric Christianity. A whole series of important cycles on the Gospels were held in Basle: a cycle of eight lectures on St John's Gospel (not identical to the published lectures of Hamburg or Kassel) in 1907, the cycle on St Luke's Gospel in ten lectures in 1909 and the cycle on St Mark's Gospel in 1912. Between these, in 1911 there was the lecture on the etherization of the blood, the heart of all the lectures dealing with the etheric Christ. During the course on St Mark's Gospel in September 1912 Dr Steiner was offered the site on the Dornach hill, after planning permission for a building for the Mystery Plays in Munich had been turned down. He went to look at the site, and the decision was made that the building should be erected there. Thus destiny led to this point in Europe, which is so significant for anthroposophy and for human history in general.

Can these events, which shine into the present from the depths of the past, with their intimate karmic relationships, be described more concretely? We can think once more of the journey through Italy taken by Rudolf Steiner in 1910, during which he contemplated the region around Monte Cassino, and went as far as Palermo, where he held a lecture about Empedocles. He was only in Rome for a few days; but he

19. EPHESUS AND THE CASTLE OF THE GRAIL

spoke later in the lectures, *Christ and the Spiritual World*, about a significant moment during these days in Rome. He describes how for a long time he had not really found what it meant that the name of Parsifal appeared in connection with the Grail. Several indications brought to him by destiny had remained unclear.

> Once more, I did not know what to do with the impression which I received, coming out of St Peter's at Rome, from Michelangelo's sculpture [the *Pietà*], which is there on the right side; the mother with Jesus, the mother who still looks so young, with the body of Jesus upon her knees. Under the influence of seeing this work — not like a vision, but as a true Imagination from the spiritual world — there appeared the picture inscribed in the Akashic record which shows Parsifal, after he left the Grail Castle for the first time. He had not asked about the mysteries ruling there. In the wood he meets a young woman, who holds the body of her betrothed upon her knees, and mourns for him. I knew that this picture had a meaning — whether it is the mother or the bride who has lost her bridegroom (for Christ is often called the Bridegroom). The connection, which had come about in truth without my action, I knew to be significant.

Thus there arises before Rudolf Steiner's soul, as he leaves St Peter's with the impression that follows from looking at Michelangelo's *Pietà*, a picture which is a scene from the story of the Grail: Sigune with the body of Schionatulander, her bridegroom, upon her knees. Parsifal is passing upon his way, and sees this picture, and is deeply moved. Rudolf Steiner said in conversation that this scene of the Grail story happened historically in the neighbourhood of the Goetheanum, once more near the hermitage at Arlesheim, where St Odile had taken refuge a hundred years before from her father. Further, he indicated that behind these two figures of the Grail story are hidden historic personalities, in whom the two individualities whom we are considering passed through a quiet intermediate incarnation.

In the Grail story history is disguised. It does not quote places and times in a historical sense but wraps them in the protecting veil of imaginative pictures. But we may be certain that historical facts are behind the mythical scenes. Behind the mythical figures there are human beings who actually lived. They are personalities of the ninth century. Once more there is spread before us a wonderful, cosmically poetic environment, balancing that of Ephesus: the woodland landscape of the Grail, the forest of Soltane, into which Herzeloyde withdrew and bore her son Parsifal, hoping to protect him from the temptations of the world. This woodland region, with the particular quality which it acquired at this turning point of European history, extending into Alsace and into the Jura, provides us with a background against which the quiet events of the ninth century can be pictured. I do not say that one could fix a particular point as that of the Grail Castle. One should not picture the Grail Castle as an externally visible building at all. But if we speak of the landscape in the wider surroundings of the Goetheanum we are tentatively in the footsteps of the region of the Grail.

What does this mean?

Ordinarily the figure of Parsifal is regarded as the centre of the Grail story. But one can think too that Schionatulander and Sigune are no less central to the events of that time. The scene in which Parsifal encounters the Pietà group, Sigune with the body of Schionatulander upon her knees, is told by Wolfram von Eschenbach in his great Parsifal epic. But there is a fragment of another poem by Wolfram von Eschenbach, called *Titurel*. If this had been written down and preserved in its entirety, the hero would have been Schionatulander. The extant parts are concerned entirely with this figure. In the old French form of the Grail story written by Chrétien de Troyes Schionatulander also appears, though his name is not mentioned. But there is also a more recent form of the Grail story, which is more comprehensive: the Titurel epic by Albrecht von Scharffenberg. This includes, with great detail, the content of both epics by Wolfram, *Parsifal* and *Titurel*. It is striking that here not Parsifal but Schionatulander is the hero. His destiny is described at great length; thus a figure stands clearly before us, which must interest us particularly in the great historic connections which we are considering.

Who are Sigune and Schionatulander?

Sigune belongs to the Grail family. Titurel was succeeded as King of the Grail by his son Frimutel. The children of Frimutel are the brothers, Amfortas and Trevrizent, and the three sisters, Schoisane, Herzeloyde and Repanse de Schoie. Schoisane dies when her daughter Sigune is born. Sigune is brought up by Herzeloyde, before she becomes the wife of Gahmuret. Long before she became the mother of Parsifal she was Sigune's foster-mother. She is part of the close circle guarding the Grail.

And who is Schionatulander? He is the grandson of Gurnemanz. But Gurnemanz in the old stories is not a knight of the Grail, as in Wagner (who called Trevrizent Gurnemanz); he is a characteristic figure among the knights of King Arthur. Schionatulander was as a boy a page of the French queen Anflise. She gives him to Gahmuret, and he grows up as his page. According to certain statements of Rudolf Steiner he received instruction in the art of the troubadours, so that he could stimulate those around him through the power of music and poetry. When Gahmuret went on his first journey to Arabia, soon after the death of Harun al-Rashid, he took Schionatulander with him as page, so that he too became acquainted with the Arab world, with the civilization of Islam. Then he returned with Gahmuret to Europe. Gahmuret married Herzeloyde; and there Schionatulander found Sigune. Now a wonderful romance began between these two young people which is comparable to the archetypal epic of love of Flor and Blancheflore. The romance of Schionatulander and Sigune is described in full. But then Schionatulander had to depart, accompanying Gahmuret once more to Baghdad to the court of the Caliph. He was now a mature and active man. Gahmuret was then killed by treachery and Schionatulander had the sad task of bringing home this news. Herzeloyde received the tragic tidings of her husband's death just as Parsifal was born to her.

Schionatulander became regent Herzeloyde's realm. He went on adventures and fought knightly battles, fulfilling the ideal of a knight of the Round Table in all countries. One day he was sent precious gifts from the Caliph in Baghdad. For the third time Schionatulander travelled into the world of Arabism.

After his return something happened which has a legendary character; the story of the Hound's Leash. Sigune and Schionatulander were in a wood when a hound, which was on one side cinnabar red and on the other black, with a white breast and white legs, broke out of the undergrowth following game. They caught the hound, which had a long and precious leash wound round its neck on which there was an inscription formed in jewels. When they caught it and were beginning to read the writing on the leash, the hound pulled itself free and dashed away. Sigune then had the deepest longing to read the hound's inscription to its end. This quest became more important for her than anything else. For her sake Schionatulander had to set out on adventure, until he could bring back to her the hound's leash. In these images we can recognize that Schionatulander and Sigune are on a quest for esoteric knowledge. Then Orilus came and killed Schionatulander in anger. In this way the Pietà image of the bride by the wayside mourning her dead bridegroom came about. Then Parsifal came, and was deeply moved by this sight.

This is told differently in different versions. In Wolfram von Eschenbach, Parsifal is still at the beginning of his pilgrimage. He had just forced his way as a young fool into the tent of Jeschute, the wife of Orilus, and taken her ring and bracelet. Orilus pursued him furiously in order to avenge this deed. But he met Schionatulander instead of Parsifal. When Parsifal came along this way immediately afterwards he saw the dead man, who had been killed instead, upon the knees of his bride who was stunned by grief. In Chrétien de Troyes the course of events is different. Parsifal had already been in the Castle of the Grail. But he had failed; he did not ask the question. On the next morning, driven from the realm of the sanctuary, he was in a lonely region. He saw then the Pietà image: Sigune with the dead Schionatulander. Through the deep shock that he experienced a dim sense of his own failure began to arise in his consciousness. And Sigune gave to him, although she herself was sunk in deep sorrow, the first instruction into the meaning of the Grail. She reproached him, for not having asked the question. In Wolfram von Eschenbach's account she tells Parsifal his own name. When he said what his mother called him — *cher fils, beau fils* — she recognized in the intonation that he was the son of Herzeloyde, with whom she was so closely connected.

We can see what follows from the different versions. In Wolfram von Eschenbach the scene in which Parsifal met the Pietà group is near the hermit's cell of Trevrizent. This is to be pictured in the valley behind Arlesheim where the slope up into the hills begins. In Chrétien de Troyes the same scene is in the immediate neighbourhood of the Castle of the Grail, in the place where Parsifal on the morning after his failure passed again, driven out from the sacred halls into the lonely, deserted region. Then he saw the mourning woman and the dead man and Sigune began to explain to him how he had failed. In one description the place is near Trevrizent's hermitage, in the other it is near the Castle of the Grail. Does it not follow that these places are near to one another? We leave the question open. In any case we are in the region of the Grail, and the hill at Dornach upon which the Goetheanum was built in our time touches in some way the possibly extensive region where those guardians of the Holy Grail lived. We need not pursue the question of exactly what stood at this place in the ninth century. The hermitage of Trevrizent must also have been the place where Sigune afterwards guarded the grave of Schionatulander and to which Kundrie the sorceress fetched some meagre food and drink every Saturday from the Castle of the Grail. It is the same hermitage to which Parsifal later came and received instruction in the Grail from Trevrizent. The location of the Grail Castle itself we have to leave open, for its characteristic is to defy a precise place and time in history.

So Schionatulander, coming from the circle of King Arthur's knights, had come this way; if Orilus had not killed him he would have been one of those in whom the Arthur stream and the Grail stream intermingled. In Parsifal this then really happened. Schionatulander died before the pre-Christian mystery stream — Rudolf Steiner spoke indeed of a 'pre-Christian Christianity' — and the Christian mystery stream could unite. What did Schionatulander take with him through the gate of death? Above all the impulse arose for his coming life to complete what had been broken off, to help bring about the encounter between the pre-Christian wisdom and Christian wisdom. Thus in the thirteenth century the great Dominicans, led by Thomas Aquinas, made the first step towards this achievement, leading human thought towards its permeation by Christ. The complete fulfilment of this task begins to arise for us above the horizon of history, when we see how a great arch reaches from the ninth century, the century of the Holy Grail, into the present time.

We should be quite clear that it is not a question in this connection of simply regarding the steps of an individuality through repeated lives on earth as equivalent to one another. With such outstanding personalities as Rudolf Steiner quite different standards apply. Nevertheless, with all necessary reserve, we can make clear to ourselves the following steps in the spiritual evolution of humanity. The great steps lead from Eabani to Aristotle, from Aristotle to Thomas

Aquinas, from Thomas Aquinas to anthroposophy and the man who brought it into being. But the intermediate steps are not without significance. Through these, the quiet mysteries made their contribution to the wide, exoteric history of human thought, with its increasing importance in culture. The contemplation of a quiet environment, filled with cosmic poetry, where an esoteric mood permeated what had to be developed exoterically — the contemplation both of the groves of Ephesus and the forest of the Grail region with its spiritual atmosphere — can help us follow the steps which must be taken by the spirit.

In our present time, the Rudolf Steiner's life work has accomplished a synthesis of all those significant steps taken in the past by the outstanding individuality here described. In Greece, Europe was born as bearer of thought; in the Middle Ages a Christian life was born which was permeated by thought. In the present time the seeds have been sown of a spiritual civilization for all humanity, derived from a thinking that becomes capable of seeing. This includes the gift from the time of Heraclitus, an inner Ephesus, and the gift from the ninth century, an inner realm of the Grail.

Sources

9. Rudolf Steiner and the Theosophical Society
An essay written in September 1952.

10. The Christmas Festivals
Based on a lecture given in Stuttgart, December 15, 1949. Translated by Maria St Goar, first published in English in *Newsletter, Anthroposophical Society in America,* Winter 1979–80.

11. The Fifth Gospel
Based on a lecture given in Stuttgart, October 1, 1950.

12. The Structure of the Karma Lectures
Based on a lecture given in Stuttgart, September 14, 1950. Translated by Maria St Goar, first published in English in *Newsletter, Anthroposophical Society in America,* Autumn 1980 & Winter 1980–81.

13. Resurrection of the Word — Logos and the Word of Man
Based on a lecture given in Stuttgart, April 5, 1950. Translated by Maria St Goar, first published in English in *Newsletter, Anthroposophical Society in America,* Autumn 1982 & Winter 1982–83.

14. From Theosophy to Anthroposophy
Based on a lecture given in Stuttgart, May 21, 1952.

15. The Preparation for Esoteric Circles 1904–6
Based on a lecture given in Stuttgart, March 31, 1957.

16. The Creation of Mantric Verse
Based on a lecture given in Stuttgart, February 27, 1949. Translated by Maria St Goar, first published in English in *Newsletter, Anthroposophical Society in America,* Winter 1981–82, Spring 1982.

17. The Dispute about the Holy Spirit
Based on a lecture given in Stuttgart, December 26, 1952.

18. Figures in Rome and Byzantium
Based on a lecture given in Stuttgart, March, 14, 1955.

19. Ephesus and the Castle of the Grail
Based on a lecture given in Stuttgart, February 27, 1952.

Index

Abel 138, 143
Alexander the Great 66, 69, 73, 210, 212, 214, 217–20
Ambrose, St 173
Anastasius Bibliothecarius 180, 189, 193–95, 197, 199
Andlau, Count of 199
Aquinas, Thomas *see* Thomas Aquinas
Arabism 73, 175
Aristotle 69, 73, 207f, 210, 212–14, 217–20
Arius 168f
Arlesheim 58, 61, 222f
Arsenius 180, 194–200
Athanasius 168f
Augustine, St 173

Bacon, Sir Francis 73
Bardas 189f
Basil the Great 173
Bauer, Michael 128
Benedict III, Pope 194
Benedict of Nursia 212
Bernus, Alexander von 51n, 221
Besant, Annie 9–13, 11, 16f, 126, 129, 147–49
Blavatsky, H.P. 12, 20, 136, 143, 147
Brockdorff, Count 15, 55
Buddha 172
Byzantium *see* Constantinople

Cain 138, 143
Capua 180, 198–200
Charlemagne 175
Chartres, School of 76f

Christ in the etheric 25, 27–29, 36f, 46, 108f, 121, 166, 211, 222
Christian Community, The 82, 159
Christmas Conference 1923 40f, 65f, 68, 166
Collins, Mabel 127, 133
Constantine the Great 168, 172f, 193
Constantinople, Council of (in 869) 177f
Copernicus, Nicholas 20
Cratylus 216
Croesus 214
Cyrill 196f

Dominicans 77

Eabani 69, 211–13
Eastern School for Theosophy (EST) 126
Eckstein, Friedrich 59
Eleutherius (Arsenius' son) 197
Elijah 41, 54
Empedocles 222
Engelberga, Emperor's wife 197
Ephesus 66, 160, 208, 214, 216–18, 224
Eschenbach, Wolfram von 224, 226
Esoteric School (ES) 12, 126–36, 142, 147–50, 152

Fifth Gospel 36f, 44, 46f, 49–53
Filioque 177f
First Class 72, 161
Foundation Stone mantra 160
Franz Joseph, Emperor 120
Frederick Barbarossa 192

Freemasonry 126, 133–43
Freie Hochschule 14
French Course *(Philosophy, Cosmology and Religion)* 67f
Friedrichshagener 14

Gahmuret 182, 225
Gilgamesh 69, 211f, 216
Giordano Bruno League 14
Goethe, Johann Wolfgang von 77, 93, 163, 208, 210
Goetheanum 60, 220f
—, burning of 65–67, 85f, 97, 160, 214
—, laying of foundation stone 34, 221
Golz, Field Marshal, Baron von 202–4
Gondishapur 171, 190
Gregory of Nazianzus 173
Gregory of Nyssa 173
Gurnemanz 225

Hagia Sophia 176f
Hamerling, Robert 210
Harun al-Rashid 73, 220, 225
Heraclitus 214–16
Herostratus 66, 214, 217
Herzeloyde 174, 181–83, 225f
Holten, Frau von 10
Hülsen, General von 203

Ignatius 179, 188f
Irmingard (Louis II's daughter) 197

Jacobowski, Ludwig 14
Jerome, St 173
Jeshu ben Pandira 129, 154
Jesus, two children 25f, 47
Johannes building 49
Johannesbau-Verein (Johannes Building Association) 155
John Chrysostom 173
John the Baptist 41
John, Prester 191
John, St 216
Julian the Apostate 169, 173f, 182f

Kommenden 14, 18
Krishnamurti 154

Leadbeater, Charles 136
Leo IV, Pope 194
Liebknecht, Wilhelm 14
life processes, seven 110, 119f
Lord's Prayer 52, 55
Lothar II 195
Louis II, Emperor 194f
Ludwig II, Emperor *see* Louis II
Ludwig II, King of Bavaria 59

Macrologos 66
Manes (or Mani) 171–74, 184
Manicheans 138, 190f
Methodius 196f
Michael I, Emperor 189
Michael III, Emperor 189
Michael, Archangel 78–80, 118f
—, School of 78f
Michelangelo 223
Micrologos 66
Moltke, Eliza von 188
Moltke, Helmuth von (the Elder) 187f
Moltke, Helmuth von (the Younger) 115–17, 119f, 181, 186–88, 201–4
Montségur 181
Montserrat 181, 191
Morgenstern, Christian 37, 130, 163
Moses 215
Mystica Aeterna (MAe) 126

Nero 209
Nestorians 191
Neudörfl 137
Neumann, (Professor) Father Wilhelm 209f
Nicaea, Council of (in 325) 168
Nicholas I, Pope 180, 186, 189f, 192–97, 199f
Nicholas of Cusa 20
Nietzsche, Friedrich 15
Niketos *see* Ignatius

INDEX 235

Odile, St 58, 61, 222f
Olaf Åsteson, Song of 156f
Olcott, Henry S 10
Ordo Templi Orientis 133

Parsifal 61f, 174, 181, 182f, 198, 223–27
Paul, St 216
Philo 215
Photius 179, 188–90, 192, 196
Pietà (Michelangelo's) 61, 223
Pius IX, Pope 202
Plato 209f, 214
Pseudoisidorian Decretals 193
Pythagoras 214, 216

Raphael, Archangel 192
Raphael (painter) 35
Rashid *see* Harun al-Rashid
Reuss, Theodor 133f, 151
Rittelmeyer, Friedrich 49, 122f
Rosegger, Peter 210
Rosenkreutz, Christian 29, 154
Rudolf, Crown Prince 209

Sainte Germaine, Count of 138
Sainte-Odile, Mont 58, 61, 199, 222
Sauerwein, Jules 67
Scharffenberg, Albrecht von 224
Schiller, Friedrich 77
Schionatulander 61, 182, 223–27
Scholl, Mathilde 127, 129, 148
Schröer, Karl Julius 81, 208f
Schubert, Franz 73
Schuré, Edouard 55–61, 57, 63, 67, 172, 221
—, *Children of Lucifer, The* 55f, 172
—, *Drama of Eleusis* 56, 58
—, *Great Initiates, The* 56, 172
Scotus Erigena 194
senses, twelve 109f, 115, 117–20
Sigune 61, 223–27
Sivers, Marie von 10, 12, 16, 55, 126, 129, 134, 147, 151
Skythianos 172
Steffen, Albert 115, 180, 187

Stein, Walter Johannes 106
Steiner, Marie *see* Sivers, Marie von
Steiner, Rudolf:
—, *Anthroposophy (a Fragment)* 105–7, 113f
—, *Arts and their Mission, The* 88
—, *At Home in the Universe* 68, 101
—, *Christ and the Spiritual World and the Search for the Holy Grail* 34, 50, 61, 223
—, *Christianity as Mystical Fact* 15, 56
—, *Cosmic New Year, The* 39
—, *Drama Course* 81
—, *East in the Light of the West, The* 171
—, *Esoteric Science* 105, 113
—, *Evolution of Consciousness* 68
—, *From Jesus to Christ* 29, 154
—, *Genius of Language, The* 38
—, *Guardian of the Threshold, The* 111
—, *Harmony of the Creative World, The* 68, 88
—, *Knowledge of the Higher Worlds* 113f, 127
—, *Last Adddress* 161
—, *Manifestations of Karma* 110
—, *Man's Being his Destiny and World Evolution* 68
—, *Mission of Folk Souls, The* 212
—, *Mystery Dramas* 152, 157
—, *Mystery Knowledge and Mystery Centres* 68
—, *Mysticism at the Dawn of the Modern Age*
—, *Occult History* 210, 212
—, *Occult Science see Esoteric Science*
—, *Pastoral Medical Course* 82
—, *Philosophy of Freedom* 114
—, *Philosophy, Cosmology and Religion* (French Course) 67f
—, *Portal of Initiation, The* 45, 110, 153, 211
—, *Riddle of Man, The* 114, 118
—, *Riddles of Philosophy, The* 113f
—, *Riddles of the Soul* 114, 121

—, *Road to Self-Knowledge* 113
—, *Secrets of Creation, The* 45
—, *Soul Calendar* 29, 153, 156f
—, *Soul Economy; Body, soul, and Spirit in Waldorf Education* 39
—, *Soul's Probation, The* 56–58, 153
—, *Spiritual Guidance of the Individual and Humanity* 92
—, *Theosophy* 127
—, *Threshold of the Spiritual World, The* 113
—, *World History and the Mysteries in the Light of Anthroposophy* 40, 68, 216
—, *World of the Senses and the World of the Spirit, The* 28, 156
Stryczek, Paula 133
Sylvester I 193

Thomas Aquinas 77, 207–12, 219
Troyes, Chrétien de 224, 226

Vischer, Friedrich Theodor 73
Wagner, Amalie 133
Wagner, Amanda 133
Wagner, Anna 128, 133
Wagner, Günther 128, 133
Wagner, Richard 58–60, 221
Waldorf School 159
Waltrada, Lothar's mistress 195f
Werner, Professor Karl 208
Wilhelm II, German Emperor 201, 204
Wilson, Woodrow 120
Workers' School in Berlin 14

Zarathustra 172

The Life and Times of Rudolf Steiner

Volume 1

People and Places

Introduction

1. *The Search for Felix the Herb-Gatherer*
2. *The Groupings of Destiny in Rudolf Steiner's Vienna Decade (1879–89)*
3. *Figures Close to Rudolf Steiner in his Viennese Time*
4. *The Transition from Vienna to Weimar (1890–97)*
5. *Rudolf Steiner and Nietzsche's Destiny: Clarity about Christianity*
6. *Rudolf Steiner in Berlin Before the Turn of the Century*
7. *Rudolf Steiner in Berlin at the Turn of the Century*
8. *The Occult Movement in Germany at the End of the Nineteenth Century*